THE
Underground
Church

Praise for The Underground Church

"Is there a way to cut through the tiresome and antiquated divisions between the so-called 'conservative' and 'liberal' wings of American Christianity? Robin Meyers's book not only argues that there is, but demonstrates it with sparkling examples from contemporary church life. Readable and engaging, this book will also keep the healing process going and open new possibilities."—Harvey Cox, author, *The Future of Faith*

"Do not read this book alone; read it in the company of a group able to have a conversation. This is to say, in a group with enough in common to be able to talk but with enough differences to need to talk. Then, if everyone is not changed, read it again, this time from end to beginning. Dr. Meyers won't mind."—Fred B. Craddock, Bandy Distinguished Professor of Preaching and New Testament, Emeritus, Candler School of Theology at Emory University; author, *As One Without Authority*

"DANGER: The contents of this book are explosive and could turn the world upside down. About time!"—Bill Moyers

"When was the last time you thought of going to church as dangerous? Once we challenged the status quo; now we mostly defend it. *The Underground Church* tells the story of how we forgot where we came from and why we must recover our subversive roots. Read it if you dare. Become part of the movement if you are daring."—Archbishop Desmond Tutu

"Read this book. Written by a wordsmith, it is a passionate and challenging call to churches to be liberated from the cultural captivity of convention and into the 'underground church.'"—Marcus Borg, canon theologian, Trinity Episcopal Cathedral; author, *Speaking Christian*

"*The Underground Church* invites Christians to encounter a radical Jesus, to practice a subversive way of life, and to move beyond belief to love. This is no longer merely church—rather it is a movement that many are aching to join!"—Diana Butler Bass, author, *Christianity After Religion: The End of Church and the Birth of a New Spiritual Awakening*

"As I read Robin Meyers's new book, I felt afresh how subversive the Christian way of life should be in relation to today's partisan ideologies and consumerist assumptions. He depicts a subversive, transformative, and hopeful identity for followers of Christ—one that I hope will be increasingly contagious."—Brian McLaren, author, speaker, activist (www.brianmclaren.net)

"This beautifully written manifesto, grounded in the author's deep faith and faithful ministry, is manna for those of us who love what the church is called to be—but who have a lover's quarrel with the way it too often distorts the good news about love, justice, mercy, and care for 'the least of these.' May *The Underground Church* rise up and flower everywhere!"—Parker J. Palmer, author, *The Courage to Teach* and *Healing the Heart of Democracy*

Other books by Robin Meyers

With Ears to Hear: Preaching as Self-Persuasion

Morning Sun on a White Piano: Simple Pleasures and the Sacramental Life

The Virtue in the Vice: Finding Seven Lively Virtues in the Seven Deadly Sins

Why the Christian Right Is Wrong: A Minister's Manifesto for Taking Back Your Faith, Your Flag, and Your Future

Saving Jesus from the Church: How to Stop Worshiping Christ and Start Following Jesus

Spiritual Defiance: Building a Beloved Community of Resistance

Saving God from Religion: A Minister's Search for Faith in a Skeptical Age
(forthcoming)

THE
Underground
Church

RECLAIMING THE SUBVERSIVE
WAY OF JESUS

Robin Meyers

Fortress Press

Minneapolis

CONTENTS

This is how the conservative and liberal forms of religion will meet, when desire and hope for the kingdom of God and fellowship with the spirit of Jesus again govern them as an elementary and mighty force, and bring their world-views and their religion so close that the differences in fundamental presuppositions, though still existing, sink, just as the boulders of the river bed are covered by the rising flood and at last are barely visible, gleaming through the depths of waters.

—ALBERT SCHWEITZER

In memory of my father, Robert Rex Meyers

ACKNOWLEDGMENTS

The true inspiration for this book comes not from the heavens, but from the remarkable and radical people who call Mayflower Congregational UCC Church of Oklahoma City their spiritual home. To have been their pastor for thirty-five years is a blessing beyond words. Together we have created a beloved community that truly marches to the beat of a different drummer. Every time I am about to give up, or give in, they remind me that being subversive for the cause of love is powerful beyond words. For all the good that Mayflower has done, in the community, in the world, and even for their pastor, I am humbled and inspired.

I am also mindful that to bring a book like this one to market is an act of courage, facilitated at every turn in the road by people whose job it is to bring ideas to print and power to the people. It is all an act of faith. Thanks to my beloved wife, Shawn, who keeps me grounded, and to Fortress Press for acquiring the rights to republish *The Underground Church* and editor Scott Tunseth. I want to say a special word of thanks to my original editor at Wiley, Sheryl Fullerton, who was a joy to work with, and who always believed that this book had a powerful message more relevant today than yesterday. What a joy and privilege it is to be an author as well as a pastor.

Empty Sermons,
Empty Pews

First the bad news: the church of Jesus Christ in the Western world is in terrible shape. Mainline churches are dying on the vine. Cathedrals in Europe have become museums. A whole generation has written off the church as hypocritical and obsolete. The Catholic Church has been shaken to the core by widespread sexual abuse of children by priests and wounded itself even more deeply by covering up the crimes. Organized religion in our time is reeling from a lack of credibility.

For centuries, the church provided all the answers to all the questions that anyone might dare to ask. It claimed to hold the keys to heaven and wielded absolute power over the forces of darkness. The church built humanity's cosmological house, and most people were either content to live there or afraid not to. In the Dark Ages when life was short and brutish, it was the church that had a monopoly on hope—if not in this world, then at least in the next. It existed to have the last word on all things and the power to hide its mistakes and cover its scandals.

The Renaissance and the rise of science put an end to all this. In trying to silence Galileo, the church gravely wounded itself. If it knew less than a man with a telescope about the heavens, then what did it really know about heaven? In its fear and loathing of women, it proved itself to be a boys' club, cut off from and deeply distrustful of Sophia. In its persecution of saints, its rejection of mystics, its incestuous marriage to the Empire, its hypocrisy and paranoia about sex, its fear of allowing the common man or woman to read and interpret the Bible, the church has become for many a cartoon of self-preservation, institutional hypocrisy, and cosmic cluelessness.

Yet humanity's spiritual impulse remains. It is hard-wired into our brains as we seek transcendence in the midst of impermanence. Millions now call themselves "spiritual" but not "religious"— because they no longer trust the church as an institution. In fact, the very definition of the word *faith* itself is in crisis. The "faithful" are not so faithful anymore. They suffer from what the French philosophers called *la douleur de voir trop clair*—the pain of seeing too clearly.

Every Sunday morning, countless people wake up with both a desire to go to church and a gnawing sense that it won't be worth it. They know that they "ought" to go, but that if they do so it will be mostly out of habit or guilt rooted in childhood. Few wake with a sense of real longing or anticipation for what might happen in the sanctuary. Many have accepted boredom as the cross one must bear for church attendance. They expect little more from worship than social respectability, often wrapped in the dull air of familiarity. The last thing anyone thinks about church is that it might be dangerous.

North American Christians, for example, don't stop to think about which route they should take to the sanctuary, or look over their shoulder to see if they are being followed. They do not pass sermons to one another in plain brown wrappers, meet in secret locations, or sit in public places facing the door. There are no secret passwords or handshakes. To the contrary, they advertise their identity, usually by covering their cars with bumper stickers. NO JESUS, NO PEACE: KNOW JESUS, KNOW PEACE. Going to church is safe, not subversive. It builds character perhaps, but it does not threaten the status quo.

More passion is generated by a service that runs too long than by the destruction of the planet. Churches split over how to serve communion. An unfamiliar hymn can sour the whole morning. In the kitchen, the gossip mill cranks out the latest chatter: someone is rumored to be mad at someone for saying something about someone else who was mad at the first someone to begin with about something—or was it about someone? Spread the word.

They say there is no fight like a church fight, and that's often because the intensity of such a battle is inversely proportionate to the significance of the subject matter. Should the youth group be allowed to eat pizza in the parlor? Why don't the "younger women" want to be part of the guild anymore? Who is that sitting in my pew? And then, of course, there is the minister—imperfection without end and certainly not like the imperfection we had before!

Gone is the sign of the fish scratched on the doorpost to mark another secret meeting of the Jesus People. Gone is the common meal that was intended to feed the poor. Gone is the idea that to be baptized is to become a pacifist. Gone is the idea that a Christian should ever hang on to more than he needs in a world where so many have less than they need. Gone is the radical hospitality that made the first Christians a smelly, chaotic, unruly ship of fools. Gone, most of all, is the joy.

To be honest, however, we should admit that our world offers up some very compelling reasons to stay home on Sunday morning. The paper and a cup of coffee for starters, the chance to catch up on sleep, the golf course, the morning talk shows, a favorite fishing hole, or even NPR's *Wait Wait . . . Don't Tell Me!* They can all seem more "real" than the hour one might spend in church listening to too many announcements, a volunteer choir struggling to stay on key, and a tepid sermon. The drive to church is often made in silence, with kids grumbling and parents making promises about better options in the afternoon. It all seems more like a duty than like a field trip to a "thin place."

In fact, the church is in such disarray, so tempted to save itself by redecorating, changing ministers, or hiring the right band, that a dirty little secret must now be told. To ignore it any longer is akin to pretending that the bad odor hanging over the sanctuary is best treated by spraying, rather than by confessing, "Something stinks!" Of all the reasons given for the decline of the church in our time, the number one reason is often left unsaid: *no one really expects anything important to happen.*

This makes church, for the most part, dull and dishonest. One gets the feeling that there are vital truths that must be told from the pulpit. There are painful confessions that need to come from the hearts of those at worship. There are deep and destructive illusions by which we are living unsustainable lives. But alas, we are too busy pretending that they do not exist. Or we think that church should be lovely and "nice," and if anything truly prophetic or indicting were said, people might gasp—as if a wild animal had suddenly wandered into the sanctuary and was stalking the pulpit with wild eyes, putrid breath, and mangy fur. It's one thing to praise prophets for being visionaries after their time, but it would be quite another to actually encounter Isaiah, Amos, Micah, or Hosea in the vestibule not properly dressed for the occasion and speaking in what kindergarten teachers call an "outside voice."

Most of our churches are friendly, comfortable, and well appointed. But who goes there expecting to be "undone"? Who expects to weep at recognizing the world as it really is, or to shudder at the certain knowledge that until we start taking risks it is likely to stay that way? Who demands that worship should peel back the stupefying crust of a frantic, franchised culture? Who suggests that perhaps we should plan an attack on the mall that rivals the ferocity with which Jesus attacked the temple? Who dares to be a *fanatic* these days for something other than a football team?

Try this. Ask most people to tell you the subject matter of any particular sermon (even right after they have listened to it), and you are likely to draw blank stares. "Well, I was impressed that he doesn't use any notes." Or "She is so engaging and sincere." Or "He has such a good sense of humor." *But what did he say?* "Well, generally speaking, I'd say he is for God and against sin. Amen."

Generally speaking? That may be precisely the problem, as there is nothing "generally wrong" with any of us. We don't live our lives in general, love in general, or betray those closest to us in any general sort of way. We are very *specific* about it. Yet most sermons are like airplanes that circle over the congregation in a perpetual holding pattern. They neither take off nor land on a street we recognize or in the neighborhood where we live. Then before you know it, the fasten seat belt sign comes on to announce the final hymn, even though no one has experienced a single moment of turbulence.

As a member of the Academy of Homiletics (a group of academics who teach preaching), I attended a national meeting once whose theme was "prophetic preaching." In workshop after workshop, we listened to noted preachers and teachers explain what constitutes prophetic preaching, how it can be done with support from scripture, and what rhetorical strategies are most effective. In other words, we covered the *idea* of the prophetic from A to Z. But at no time did anyone actually *say* or *do* anything prophetic.

Just before this meeting was convened, the infamous torture photos from the prison at Abu Ghraib had come to light, documenting a world of physical, psychological, and sexual abuse of Iraqi prisoners under U.S. control. The painful truth about so-called evildoers is that this capacity is not limited to our enemies. It was on full display for all to see, but the preachers seemed to live suspended above their own subject matter. One participant, sensing the irony, moved that we adjourn, read the morning paper, study the photos, and then reconvene in the town square for a demonstration. We are not apologists. We are preachers.

Sometimes I wonder if the clergy really understand how desperately the world needs them to be independent contractors for the gospel. Considering that we are just about the only people left on earth who don't work for the Empire, you would expect us to have something of an advantage when it comes to speaking truth to power. But sadly, of the many good qualities that pastors possess (they are often described as "nice"), real courage is not their strongest attribute.

Most pastors keep most of what they learned in seminary a secret for fear of offending a big contributor. They avoid controversy, especially on matters of economic justice, because they are looking directly into the eyes of the parishioners who pay their salary. Besides, in all probability, most people sitting in the pews see Jesus as an apologist for democracy and free-market capitalism, a kind of chaplain for the Jerusalem branch of the chamber of commerce. Since the Great Recession, money is tight, so the preacher gets even tighter. The clergy begin to see their work as the protection of assets at all cost.

So it is that on most Sunday mornings, the expectations are low and the rewards even lower. We are all on our best behavior but bored out of our minds. The good reverend comforts the afflicted, but seldom afflicts the comfortable. Indeed, the unstated message of church often bears a striking resemblance to the essential delusion of "The Emperor's New Clothes." Nakedness is completely apparent but adamantly denied. The great preacher Fred Craddock may have been spot-on when he said that the greatest sin of the church is *silliness*.

Now for the good news: *the church of Jesus Christ in the Western world is in terrible shape.* That's right—the good news is the bad news—and that's good news. Why? Because, according to the distinguished scholar of religion Phyllis Tickle, apparently about every five hundred years the church holds a sort of giant rummage sale. It must decide what goes and what stays, what is dispensable and what is irreplaceable. Five centuries after the Protestant Reformation, we find ourselves passing through precisely such a time. Think of it as a kind of spring cleaning. We are sorting through our theological stuff and asking painful and disorienting questions about where it came from, what it's worth, and why the once lucrative market for creeds and doctrines seems both depressed and depressing.

Oh, we feel guilty about the prices in our rummage sale. Surely someone will pay more than a nickel for justification by faith? You can't just give away the Virgin Mary. How about the Trinity? Shouldn't we at least have an auction for each of the three persons? (And should it be three for the price of one or one for the price of three?) Whatever, but don't break up the set.

Meanwhile, our kids have already moved on. They want deeds, not creeds. They want mission, not musings. They think we talk too much. They think not all our music should sound like monks in mourning. They have nothing against the Middle Ages, but they don't live there. We say "text," and they think about something they should not be doing while driving. We say "lowdown," and they hear "download." They watch a lot of crime lab and hospital dramas, perhaps because these are the only places they hear serious conversations about life and death. But they are not dumb. They are wonderful, and they are watching us.

So to the reader I make this promise. If you have read this far (and plan to read further), I will not pretend to be an unbiased voice. I have given my life to the church in the hope that precisely such a moment as this would come. Granted, there is widespread weariness about organized religion, and some very spunky and ambitious atheists out there (God bless them) who think we are all idiots. Well, are we?

Perhaps the time has come to practice a little of the faith we are so fond of talking about? Perhaps the Jesus People can think of something to do in this broken world besides argue over abortion and gay marriage? Surely we can admit that if religion just makes

us meaner and more judgmental then we ought to bulldoze it—
better yet, turn all the churches into low-cost housing or free
medical clinics. Maybe God doesn't want us to be rich? Maybe the
browning of America is not a crisis, but a blessing? Maybe the hour
has come, and now is, when people will stop yelling at one another
long enough to sigh and say, We have lost our way. Whatever
happened to the common good?

Empty sermons make for empty pews. If we are the Beloved
Community, then why do we continue to act as if our real gospel
is every man or woman for himself or herself? Human beings are not
commodities, so why do we continue to live by the myth that the
marketplace can solve all the problems of life? In the face of
desperate need, abandoned children, and violence as a way of life,
why are we still spending so much time and energy debating
theological ideas? Which of the beatitudes in the Sermon on the
Mount says, "Blessed are the theologically sound, for they shall be
smug"? Are we Easter people or just the latest version of the Good
Friday crowd? As the poet Yeats put it,

Turning and turning in the widening gyre
The falcon cannot hear the falconer;
Things fall apart; the centre cannot hold;
Mere anarchy is loosed upon the world,
The blood-dimmed tide is loosed, and everywhere
The ceremony of innocence is drowned;
The best lack all conviction, while the worst
Are full of passionate intensity.[1]

Those haunting final lines describe both politics and religion
in our time. Alas, the American church is joined at the hip to a
declining Empire. Because confession is good for the soul, honesty
demands that we admit how irrelevant we seem to most of
the world, how quaint but clueless. After all, who really looks to

the church these days for social change? Who fears its collective power to be leaven in the loaf of the Empire? Who suggests that Jesus Followers should be put on the no-fly list—not because we are violent, but precisely because we are not?

Once, when a patient in crisis came to see his therapist, he began the session by saying, "Doc, I feel miserable." "Good," the therapist replied. "Can you stay with the feeling?" A crisis really is a terrible thing to waste.

"After great pain, a formal feeling comes," wrote the incomparable Emily Dickinson. The pain of the church in decline has given way in many quarters to a "formal" willingness to talk about things we never thought we would discuss before—with people we never thought we would be talking to. It's time to bring everyone into the same room. It's time to start auditing one another's classes.

You're a Methodist? Good for you. Did you know that Wesley said you should give away all your money to charity before you die? You're a Pentecostal? Let the spirit move you. But don't forget how often the Holy Spirit has been confused with glands. You're a Unitarian? Fine; we could use a little critical thinking in church. But don't forget that knowledge alone is not redemptive. Lots of smart people are positively insufferable.

Here's the problem: *most of what people argue about in church doesn't matter.* That might be just sad except that we live in a perishing world. It might seem quaint that we are still addicted to the myth of redemptive violence, but this is terminal in the nuclear age. We might get a little help dealing with our guilt if we think God loves us more by giving us more stuff, but we certainly didn't get that idea from the Bible. We might love our tribe best and believe that God does too, but nobody in the early church believed that. They died for *not* believing it.

To my way of thinking, if the church cannot return to its radical roots—driven by a truly subversive anti-imperial message and mission again—then it deserves to die. It has nothing to offer the world except something to dull the pain, circle the wagons, or lie about the number of lifeboats. For millions the church is dead already—the victim of its own intellectual, spiritual, and moral dishonesty.

"God, we feel miserable." *Good* [replies I AM]. *Can you stay with the feeling?*

Like the determined friends of the paralytic who is brought to Jesus for healing, the church needs to do something now as drastic as tearing open a hole in our doctrinal roof. Or, given that people of faith are by definition metaphorical thinkers, imagine this: Richard Dawkins has been given a spear and permission to thrust it into the side of the church and put us all out of our misery. He complies, believing the world would be better off without tax-exempt meeting places for imbeciles. He announces a research project that will create grace in a test tube. In no time, he publishes a paper that dispenses with evil by announcing the creation of a software patch that can be downloaded day or night—triggered (ironically) by the search word "banality." A committee at Oxford volunteers to give last rites to the church.

Then, say about three days after the deed is done and the *New York Times* announces that the CHURCH IS DEAD, what's left of us lunatics could meet and take a walk to Emmaus. We could discuss all the "things that have taken place in these days" that our "eyes were kept from recognizing." After all, it doesn't take a theologian to know that the world is full of lonely, frightened people. It doesn't take a mystic to know that all of us are hungry and need bread. It doesn't take a celebrity to remind us that fame and fortune are nothing compared to a community. We need one another. Because let's face it, the age of the self-made man, the rugged individual, the rolling stone, has given us the most unhappy, the most addicted, the most broken, and the most fearful society on earth.

Maybe that's why everyone at least owes it to himself or herself to remember that before the gospel got turned into just another marketing strategy, it contained the two most powerful words ever to address the sickness of the age: *fear not.*

OK, so you don't consider yourself a "religious" person, but that doesn't mean you don't wake up in the middle of the night and wonder what it's all about. It doesn't mean you haven't wondered how on earth any two people can stay married for a whole lifetime and be happy. What's walking on water compared to this? It doesn't mean that your soul hasn't ached to know what true love is, hasn't gone looking for it, longing for it in the jungle of pretenders and hustlers. The object of life is to love and be loved.

What is missing is trust, and without trust the whole human enterprise collapses. Without trust there is no covenant, and without covenant there are no relationships. Without relationships there is no happiness.

Who could blame anyone these days for not trusting the church? Yet what we no longer trust is not the idea of a Beloved Community but the reality of a quarreling collection of petty, frightened people who have forgotten where they came from, where they are going, and to whom they belong. Most of all, we have forgotten that we signed up to be crazy, like Jesus was crazy.

Remember Jesus? The one with the world's most recognized name disguising the world's best-kept secret? The one they said was out of his mind? That's right, as in loco, flip city, deranged, mad as a hatter, crazy like a loon, not wrapped too tight. Strange as it may sound, the renewal of the church must begin here, with an honest discussion about the Galilean sage whom everyone admires but nobody seems willing to follow—not really.

Never thought of Jesus as crazy? Turn the page and think again.

CHAPTER ONE

Sweet Jesus
Talking His Melancholy Madness

When his family heard it, they went out to restrain him, for people were
saying, "He has gone out of his mind."
—MARK 3:21

O f all the words we associate with Jesus, surely the word *insane*
is nowhere to be found on the list. Son of God, Precious Savior,
Good Shepherd, King of Kings, Lamb of God, Lord of Lords,
Messiah, Prince of Peace, and Redeemer—they all fall from the lips
of adoring believers. When was the last time that anyone dared to
use words like *schizophrenic, delusional,* or *fanatic* in the same sentence
with *Jesus?*

In Paul's letter to the Philippians, we find the remnants of an
ancient hymn whose lyrics praise the name given by God "that is
above every name, so that at the name of Jesus every knee should
bend, in heaven and on earth and under the earth, and every tongue
should confess" *that he has lost his mind?* Well, that's not quite how it
goes. But the writer of Mark's gospel, the earliest in the New
Testament, makes it clear that even his family is worried about his
mental health. Yet nowhere in the liturgies of the church does a
Christian promise to "be crazy like Jesus was crazy."

That's why we owe so much to poets like Mary Oliver. Without
her, I would never have heard the phrase "melancholy madness" to
describe the holy fool of God. Without her, and others like her, the
world could get away with adoring Jesus instead of actually trying

to follow him and risk looking crazy too. He was a homeless single man, after all. He was a wandering teacher, healer, and teller of strange and subversive parables about the reign of God. If his contemporaries thought he was possessed by a demon, what would we think about him today? Only the poets can tell us. Thank God for poets.

Without them, we sink so deeply into the quicksand of sentimentality that Jesus remains frozen in stained glass or stuck in the sticky syrup of personal devotion. He hovers weightless above the ground in medieval art like the blue man in the Chagall painting—radiant, antiseptic, hairless, and perfumed. Without the poets, we begin to sleepwalk through the life of faith. We forget that being a prophet cannot be divorced from the pain of being prophetic. That is the path of *most* resistance. Prophets do not tell us what we want to hear, but what we *need* to hear. When they walk among us, unkempt and fiery-eyed, they are pitied by their peers. They are despised and mocked for calling so rudely for the end to the unjust status quo. Good and decent people avoid them on the street. Parents tell their children to look away. They are the last people we invite to a dinner party.

Indeed, prophets and poets have a lot in common. They are related through the blood of metaphor. For some reason, both find it impossible not to describe one thing as if it were another, instead of just calling something what it is. This habit of *seeing as* is deep in their DNA. Both see with the eyes of the heart, to save our souls from drying up. Both know that all our arguments about "taking the Bible literally" are literally foolish, considering that Jesus is often called the Lamb of God when in fact Mary did not have a little lamb!

Unfortunately, in this age of never-ending polemics, both conservatives and liberals miss the power of metaphor. Conservatives, on the one hand, are nervous about nonliteral meaning, insisting that the Bible says what it says and means what it means. Liberals, on the other hand, are so busy apologizing for metaphors as nonverifiable or superstitious that metaphors become harmless appendages to accessorize the unvarnished "facts."

Since the Enlightenment we have believed, as esteemed scholar John Dominic Crossan tells us, "that the ancients took their religious stories literally, but that we are now sophisticated enough to recognize their delusions. What, however, if those ancients intended and accepted their stories as metaphors or parables, and we are the mistaken ones? . . . It is only poets who know that metaphor is destiny and that literalism has sapped our metaphorical imagination."[1]

That is why I thank God for poets. Without them the world becomes a benign parade of disconnected and meaningless objects and events that we process but do not reflect on. We calculate but we do not conjure. We know *how*, but we do not know *why*. Without poets, language becomes a bag of Snap-on tools. Everything reads like a recipe or an owner's manual. Life is lived entirely in prose, which is, after all, the root of the word *prosaic*.

Consider this rather strange metaphor as it relates to what poets can do for us. A child attends a Mexican birthday party and enjoys the familiar sport of swatting open a piñata and scooping up the candy that falls to the floor. It is a familiar and harmless game, played by blindfolded children who delight in the violent disemboweling of this papier-mâché figure hanging by a rope from the ceiling. On the surface, it would appear to be nothing more than just another way to get candy and then get sick.

But the poet knows the history and symbolism of the piñata. How it was once used before Christmas as an allegory to evangelize the native people of the region. The original piñata was shaped like a star with seven points, each representing the seven deadly sins. The bright colors symbolized temptation, the blindfold represented faith, and the stick was meant to stand as a weapon for overcoming sin. The candy that fell out represented the riches of the kingdom of heaven that one would receive who did battle with temptation and prevailed.

The poet knows that once the context is lost, the meaning is lost. So the poet walks back into the empty room and stares in silence at the papier-mâché carcass still dangling from the ceiling. What was once a spiritual metaphor is now just a curious container for what the children covet. What was once a parable of spiritual struggle is now just a party favor. What was once a simple scene in a one-act spiritual drama is now just a mindless, selfish game.

Only the poet can see the sadness in that limp, empty foil. Only the poet can make the connection between those frenzied children, the piñata, and the church. In other words, only the poets can tell us about Jesus.

> Sweet Jesus, talking
>   His melancholy madness,
>   stood up in the boat
>   and the sea lay down,
>
> silky and sorry.
>   So everybody was saved
>   that night.
>   But you know how it is
>
> when something
>   different crosses
>   the threshold—the uncles
>   mutter together,
>
> the women walk away,
>   the younger brother begins
>   to sharpen his knife.
>   Nobody knows what the soul is.

So begins Mary Oliver's remarkable poem "Maybe." My wife read it to me one morning over coffee, and I couldn't get the phrase "melancholy madness" out of my mind. We'll get to the rest of the poem in a moment. But first we need to begin this book with confession, because confession is good for the soul. You, dear reader, need to confess it. So must I, your audacious author, confess it. We should probably do it on our knees, as this ancient posture of humility might make us think twice about lying. This is the gospel truth: *when it comes to Jesus, we know practically nothing.*

That's right—no matter how sanctified our particular community, how grounded in scriptural proof-texting and doctrinal purity, how clever in finding all the missing pieces to the Jesus puzzle, we are all in the same boat, perpetually adrift in the dead calm of what can't be found. Even though we are divided into a thousand ecclesiastical camps of certain self-righteousness (right and left, foursquare and new age, anti-intellectual and hyperintellectual, people who raise their hands in worship and people who sit on them), we all share this vast *ignorance.* When it comes to the life of a man who is arguably the central figure in human history, we know so little that can be verified, so little that resembles history, so little that would be admitted as evidence in a courtroom that the best thing we can do is listen to the poets. They hold the trump card of metaphor.

Poet laureate W. S. Merwin explained why we need poetry to understand the things in life that really matter:

> Prose is about something, but poetry is about what can't be said. Why do people turn to poetry when all of a sudden the Twin Towers get hit, or when their marriage breaks up, or when the person they love most in the world drops dead in the same room? Because they can't say it. They can't say it at all, and they want something that addresses what can't be said.[2]

Speaking of what can't be said, consider the task that faced those four gospel poets who wrote under more famous pen names in order to be taken seriously: Mark, Matthew, Luke, and John (in chronological order of composition here). These were the unnamed poets, the scribal elites, who took apostolic names and wrote decades after the life, death, and resurrection of Jesus of Nazareth. They wrote so that we would not forget the divine insanity of this man. They wrote as an act of faith. Their gospels are acts of devotion, not attempts at biography.

Yet these gospel poets still tell us more than mere journalists could ever tell us about Jesus' melancholy madness. These four portraits, these "sketches," were written by believers to encourage fellow believers and convert nonbelievers. These are love songs. It always helps to remember that no one who wrote a single word of the Bible thought at the time that they were writing a single word of the Bible, because it didn't exist yet.

Ultimately it all got chosen as part of what we now refer to as sacred writ. Thereafter it was read and interpreted by the somber and the serious, with mortal souls hanging in the balance. The gospel poets remember when Jesus stopped to talk to a wayside beggar, and now that spontaneous moment is the subject of exhaustive exegesis and countless books. He draws in the sand while pondering what to do with a woman caught in adultery. Ever since, we have debated over what he may have written, whether he merely doodled because he could not write, or whether he was just stalling for time until he figured out what to say. In the meantime, we lose the story, especially the sound of rocks falling to the ground. We squeeze exegetical blood out of the text until the story no longer has a pulse.

Something similar has happened in our search for the "historical Jesus." We have been looking for the "real" Jesus, the human Jesus. This is important and valuable work. But what the gospel poets seem to be telling us is that our concern for history was not their concern. The difference between the pre-Easter Jesus and the post-Easter Christ is helpful, but all we have is the post-Easter community's response to the risen Christ. We can glimpse the human

Jesus using the tools of higher criticism, but everything is seen through the prism of a body of believers who are writing (and please excuse the usual negative connotation here) *propaganda*. They are writing to "propagate" the faith.

Likewise the process by which the four gospels were chosen and sanctified by their inclusion in the canon doesn't mean that other known gospels are fictitious or inferior. But just like every book that must finally go to press, the canon had to be closed. In the language of the art world, someone had to jury and then hang the show. Whether it is opening night or the end of the age, there is a due date.

This has not kept us from having endless arguments over the historical Jesus, of course. Liberals search for the sake of veracity and a clearer picture of Jesus as radical teacher. Conservatives push back against what they see as a scholarly masquerade for debunking the divinity of Christ. This has been going on for two hundred years, and scholars have expended enormous academic and intellectual energy in a search that Albert Schweitzer concluded is futile. "He comes to us as one unknown," he wrote, "without a name, as of old, by the lakeside, He came to those men who knew Him not."[3]

Perhaps we should call for a truce in our search for the historical Jesus and turn our attention instead to something at least as important but often neglected: the search for the historical community. Asking, What would Jesus do? (WWJD) has become very popular these days. (Although the question seems mostly rhetorical, the answer might be truly frightening.) But there is another question that we need to be asking, one that is at least as important as questions about the historical Jesus: What did the historical community do?

After all, one of the ways that historians uncover the authentic message of a teacher is to study the behavior of his or her first students. Their questions were not our questions, of course, because they were not engaged in a search for true identity. Rather they were engaged in the politics of true discipleship. Their *actions* were their answers. What we have forgotten, much to the detriment of the church, is how strange and radical they really were—how truly subversive.

A New Search for a New Church

Schweitzer did not mean to diminish the importance of Jesus by his exhaustive critical work. To the contrary, he wanted to remind us of his essential finding: that we can only know who Jesus is by *following* him. He will never be met on the road and identified. The curtain will never rise to reveal a solitary figure on stage, his face bathed in a spotlight. Indeed, he will never be a figure of history because he was never the subject of biography. His face is the composite work of his followers, sketched by the hands of believers. His voice is a remembered voice, not a recorded one.

The gospels are part memorial, part testimonial. They are breathless tales copied and woven together from the storied scraps of his life, shaped and reshaped by changing circumstances. As each Jesus community faced new challenges (not the least of which was his failure to return as soon as expected), these four gospel portraits were needed to preserve and spread the message. In the midst of a painful divorce from Judaism and increasing skepticism about the second coming, the Jesus People needed their own text, their own Torah.

Of course, this makes Christianity considerably more complicated. Why? Because his voice *changes* with each representation. Do we follow Mark's Jesus (the first portrait), who is reported to have said with self-effacing humility, "Why do you call me good? No one is good but God alone" (10:18)? Or do we follow the self-proclaimed exclusive messiah of John's Jesus (the last portrait), where Jesus seems to be a kind of self-illuminated figure in a world where nobody seemed to notice that he glows in the dark. Now instead of a man who is humble and nervous about too much adoration, he has become a self-identifying messiah: "I am the way, and the truth, and the life. No one comes to the Father except through me" (14:6). How could the same man have said both these things?

Even the nature of faith changes, from the radical first-century ethic of the Sermon on the Mount, in which there is not a single word about what to believe, only words about what to do—to the fourth-century Nicene Creed, in which there's not a single word about what to do, only words about what to believe.

What then is a modern Christian to think? Are we "doers" after the example of Jesus, or are we "believers" in the mission of Jesus, as interpreted and packaged by Christendom? If the voice of Jesus changes, as well as the very essence of what it means to "believe" in him, are we not left to pick and choose our favorite passage, or recite with certain fervor our favorite creeds?

Liberals prefer the human Jesus, of course, the voice of the teacher of wisdom. They gravitate to the parables while turning up their noses at John's vision of the "I am" Jesus. They know that preaching from John is how conservatives support the idea that no one can be saved except through Jesus. My experience in listening to the sermons of evangelicals and fundamentalists is that they choose a text from John far more often than from the synoptic gospels (Matthew, Mark, and Luke). Here is a "real" messiah, a more muscular, impatient savior—one who is more interested in being recognized and understood than he is in telling a baffling parable. This fits the fundamentalist view that the world is hopeless and must be escaped. John's theology confirms the notion that Christianity is a kind of rope let down from heaven, even though most people don't recognize the exit sign when they see it.

In his book *The Great Awakening*, Jim Wallis describes how as a young man growing up in an evangelical church, he never heard

a sermon on the Sermon on the Mount. All that the preacher ever
talked about were the salvation passages from John and Paul. Think
how very different the gospel sounds when one sings Mary's radical
song, the *Magnificat*? It's no wonder that the body of Christ is splin-
tered into a thousand pieces. Like those blindfolded children and
the piñata, *everyone claims a different piece of Jesus, and then, in separate rooms,
they gorge themselves on it.*

To understand why, and to begin to imagine a different future,
we need only read the rest of Mary Oliver's poem.

It comes and goes
Like the wind over the water—
Sometimes, for days,
You don't think of it

Maybe, after the sermon,
After the multitude was fed,
One or two of them felt
The soul slip forth

like a tremor of pure sunlight
before exhaustion,
that wants to swallow everything,
gripped their bones and left them

miserable and sleepy,
as they are now, forgetting
how the wind tore at the sails
before he rose and talked to it—

tender and luminous and demanding
as he always was—
a thousand times more frightening
than the killer sea.[4]

Let's be honest. When it comes to Jesus, "tender and luminous" we like. But "demanding"? Not so much. Most of all, however, we run from Oliver's last line: *a thousand times more frightening than the killer sea*. Frightening? Is that how anyone thinks of Jesus? Do we not seek him out for comfort? Is he not the good shepherd wandering in search of one lost lamb? Did he not promise rest for the weary and food for the hungry? Isn't our whole approach to faith based on a simple transaction: *what we lack and need he has in abundance and can provide?*

This is, at one level, a poem about a well-known story in the gospels—the story of Jesus and his disciples crossing the Sea of Galilee when a sudden storm arises. It threatens to swamp their little boat and take them all to the bottom. But Jesus, who is fast asleep while his men are terrified, is awakened just in time to talk down the storm. In the church, we refer to what he did as "calming." Oliver almost suggests that the water has been reprimanded: "the sea lay down, silky and sorry."

Preachers in search of their pulpit lesson have never agreed on exactly what this story means. We so often read the Bible as if it were a collection of arguments that we fail to simply listen to the story. After all, we have an argument to make, so we sprinkle lines from the text over our closing statements to persuade the jury (the congregation) that we are biblical preachers. But there are no "proofs" in scripture. Just ordinary people, like us, reporting on what they have seen that both amazed and frightened them.

Liberals are very uncomfortable with miracles, so they carefully explain how these sudden storms blow up and then just as suddenly dissipate, creating the illusion of a miracle in the minds of adoring but sadly prescientific disciples. Once our enlightened minds have defended natural law, genuflected to reason, and apologized for foolish superstitions, liberals conclude that the text is really about the psychology of fear in a general sort of way, followed by the response of faith in a general sort of way. Any questions?

Conservatives, in contrast, find exactly the miraculous proof they go looking for. This is Jesus, after all, and he can do anything. In this text, he is "doing weather." He is not asleep in the boat because he is indifferent, but because nothing worries God. The disciples are frightened only because they don't get it. He probably ordered up the storm to begin with, as a test. Relax, says the preacher, the storms of life blow up suddenly—but when you've "got Jesus" you've got the ultimate lifeboat. In other words, here is the great divide in the church: *conservatives confuse certainty with faith, whereas liberals insist that knowledge alone is redemptive.*

If only the church had more preachers who were poets. They read between the lines, where the marrow of the meaning lies. In this story, for example, Jesus invites his disciples to "go across to the other side," which is Bible-speak for where the Gentiles live. This boat is headed to enemy territory. What's more, according to the writer of Mark's gospel, they "took him with them in the boat, just as he was"—meaning perhaps that he is still in the same boat where he began teaching that morning (as the first line of the fourth chapter indicates). The crowd was huge, and he tells parable after parable. By the end of the day, he is undoubtedly exhausted.

There is also a line in this story that is often overlooked: "Other boats were with him." To hear the preachers tell it, the disciples are out there all by themselves with nobody to rescue them. Also, how odd that we are told that Jesus is fast asleep "on the cushion"—this English translation is so misleading. It was no soft pillow. We're not talking goose down or memory foam here. Rather it was a hard mat for the steersman, part of a low bench at the back of the boat. The gospel poets may be trying to tell us something here about just how "dead to the world" Jesus was. Out like a light.

To test the waters in my own church, I once asked my congregation in a sermon to consider something—just for fun. "Do you think that Jesus might have been snoring?" The room fell silent. "Well, men do snore," I continued awkwardly, "especially when they fall asleep quickly. Come on now, we can do it," I implored my listeners. "Imagine this scene. The disciples are in a sorry, leaky, barely seaworthy little dinghy as darkness falls at the end of a long day. They have been doing crowd control all day while Jesus talked until he was hoarse.

"Now they are headed to the Land of the Unclean. Surely the disciples thought to themselves, *Who added this trip to the itinerary?* A storm blows up, and their Teacher is out like a light, snoring. Perhaps his mouth is half open and on his chin lay a bead of drool. Dark clouds are gathering on the horizon. Then an argument breaks out over who should wake him up. The skies grow darker, and they are passing the point of no return. 'You wake him up.' 'No, *you* wake him up.' Meanwhile he goes right on snoring. Just then the first bolt of lightning arcs into the water 'on the other side.'"

A woman came up to me after the service and said she would prefer not to be asked to consider whether Jesus ever snored. I get it. So does Mary Oliver. She knows that *when something different crosses the threshold—the uncles mutter together, the women walk away, the younger brother begins to sharpen the knife. Nobody knows what the soul is.*

There is a lesson here. There is hope for the future of the church here. The poets are not trying to help us identify Jesus. They are trying to place those of us who never met him alongside those who did—to see if we too might be amazed and frightened. The Bible is not a dictionary where one looks up answers about God. It is a twice-told tale, and so are our sermons. Instead of training our searchlight down another dark alley in search of his true face, we might want to consider a different kind of search. Instead of preparing for the next round in the never-ending quest for the historical Jesus, why don't we consider a quest for the historical *follower?*

Why were those first Jesus People so strange, so peculiar despite all their differences? Why were they both bewildering and threatening to the status quo? Why haven't we worked just as hard to identify those who were first given the derogatory title of "little Christs"

(Christ-ians) as we have to define the inviolate nature of their Lord? The noble effort to separate the Jesus of history from the Christ of faith has been helpful, but now we need a quest to separate the followers of history from the believers of faith.

What are those uncles of Oliver's poem muttering about, if not this "peculiar" troublemaker? Why do the women walk away, if not to keep the peace, as women so often feel called to do? As for that young brother sharpening his knife, surely he knows that all this talk of love will only last so long. Then real men will have to do what real men do. And while we're at it, what is the soul anyway?

Poets know that most people spend their lives tired, frightened, and clueless. They know that fatigue is the enemy of faith. *It comes and goes like the wind over water—sometimes, for days, you don't think about it.* Think about what? Perhaps that our lives would be radically different if we were fully awake—not just in moments of ecstasy, *after the sermon, after the multitude was fed,* but in between those moments when we feel *the soul slip forth like a tremor of pure sunlight?*

So many Christians today are so intoxicated by the idea of being "right" about Jesus that when it comes to following him, we forget to do something much more important. We forget to *warn* people. We neglect to tell them not to get into the boat to begin with and then expect smooth sailing. We fail to be honest with them about how little difference the creeds and doctrines make compared to setting out on a journey with someone whose claim upon their lives will turn out to be *a thousand times more frightening than the killer sea.*

Crazy Is as Crazy Does

Dear reader, I hope that you do not find the word *crazy* to be offensive when used to describe Jesus of Nazareth. It is not meant to be irreverent or dismissive or even shocking in the service of selling a book. It is meant to be true—as in *real*. The writer of Mark's first portrait of Jesus is believed to have invented the gospel as a literary form. What's more, he probably did so in the aftermath of the destruction of Jerusalem and the Temple in 70 CE. This means that for about four decades, the church had no distinctively Christian reading material.

The authentic letters of Paul had been circulating, of course, if you could get your hands on one or if you could read. The Jesus People had several decades of accumulated oral tradition, as followers remembered and told stories. They may also have had fragments of the earliest collections of "sayings" sources that would become Thomas and Q.[5] But who was going to preserve the *story* of Jesus, shaped as a compelling narrative argument that both the Greek mind could appreciate and skeptical Jews would find persuasive?

The gospels filled that void by fusing logos and pathos, reason and passion. Ethos came from writing under apostolic names and by insisting that Jesus was the one the prophets had predicted. And because all meaning is contextual, it is good to remember that the gospel poets composed their portraits at a time of smoldering apocalyptic passion. The Good News could only be heard and considered "good" if someone, somehow, someday could get Rome off their backs.

Now that the Temple lay in ruins, was this a sign that the one who had attacked it had been vindicated? Did the writer of Mark's gospel think that this traumatic event signaled the end of the age, or just the beginning of a new one? We will never know, but this much is certain. The very first attempt to shape the life of Jesus into a cohesive persuasive narrative includes the "land mine" text of Mark 3:21 about his family going out to "restrain" him because people were saying that he had lost his mind. The Greek word *existemi*, translated *beside himself*, actually means insane and witless.

Scholars rightly surmise that when something is preserved about Jesus in the gospels that is not a compliment (or is counterintuitive), then it is more likely to be authentic. Take the example of the disciples abandoning Jesus to his enemies, fleeing in fear right after sharing with him the cup of fellowship that was supposed to be stronger than death. Or consider the baffling story of the cursing of the barren little fig tree, even though it was not the season for figs. Then of course there is the single most memorable episode of all, the so-called cleansing of the Temple, which was really an *attack* on the Temple. That single act alone would have been sufficient grounds for crucifixion.

These stories survived in part because they are vivid, strange, or violent—they don't fit our preconceived images of Jesus—just like the rumors that he was insane. What's more, this accusation of madness is not just included in the first gospel, but remains present in the last gospel as well. In other words, it has staying power across multiple communities. In John, when Jesus asks a crowd why some sought to kill him, they responded, "You have a demon! Who is trying to kill you?" (7:20). Later, in a heated debate that reveals the seeds of anti-Semitism, the "Jews" add insult to injury by asking, "Are we not right in saying that you are a Samaritan and have a demon?" (8:48).

So what was Jesus doing that caused people to wonder if he had lost his mind or was possessed by a demon? In the late nineteenth and early twentieth centuries, there was a veritable outbreak of research into the mental health of Jesus. Granted, the new discipline of psychiatry was full of itself and its potential. A modernist zeal prevailed that promised explanations for all the mysteries of human behavior. Just study the brain more carefully, we were told. Explore the patient's childhood more fearlessly, and the diagnosis will emerge.

Perhaps the most well known critic of Jesus was David Friedrich Strauss. In his first book on the life of Jesus, published in 1864, he opined that Jesus was simply a religious "fanatic." In his second book, The Life of Jesus Critically Examined, he revised the diagnosis to "close to madness." This was disturbing enough to have been noted by Albert Schweitzer, who sought to blunt such irreverent analysis by reminding readers that much of the New Testament is mythological, especially John, and therefore beyond the reach of definitive conclusions about the mental health of Jesus.[6]

This did not stop a whole gaggle of authors from engaging in such speculation, however. They referred to Jesus as "ecstatic" (euphemism for out of touch with reality), a "degenerate" with a "fixed delusional system," "demented," a "religious paranoid," a "megalomaniac," and, of course, a "paranoid schizophrenic," just to name a few. One Danish author went so far as to conclude that Jesus was an epileptic who had a petit mal in Gethsemane and a grand mal at the cleansing of the Temple.[7]

Did Jesus hear voices because he was schizophrenic? Was this a messiah complex before we had a name for it? Lord knows there is enough arguing in the church already. Rather, such investigations into the mental health of Jesus remind us that although our investigations are often aimed at finding the answers to the identity of Jesus, we can easily forget how strange, how countercultural, even how threatening was the behavior of Jesus.

For twenty centuries we have argued about who can identify the "real" Jesus and who is the keeper of his "real" mission. What if we stopped arguing over whose prognosis is correct long enough to consider something much closer to home and a thousand times more frightening than the killer sea, namely, whether following Jesus today in ways consistent with the practice of his first followers would make us susceptible to exactly the same charge—that we have lost our minds?

It's true, of course, that many of those who questioned the mental health of Jesus did it to render claims about him suspect and thus dismiss the gospel as nonsense. But this may be far from the most frightening conclusion. The evidence offered is exactly what you would expect: he has hallucinations and hears voices; his cleansing of the Temple was the act of an unstable man with anger management issues; his cursing of a poor little fig tree for not bearing fruit out of season is irrational and cruel; his vituperative verbal explosions against Pharisees are really a call for violence; his apparently estranged relationship with his own family is the result of their failure to recognize him as messiah; he displays an exalted messianic self-consciousness that he insists on keeping a secret; and finally (for selective literalists), there is his call for self-mutilation, as in his prescription for castration "for heaven's sake" and his counsel to get rid of certain body parts that offend (Matt. 19:12; 5:29–30).

These are more disturbing, of course, if we forget the power of hyperbole and metaphor. This is exactly what happens when theology gets done without a poet in the room. Whether we call ourselves liberals or conservatives, there remains a fatal flaw in the human species, a sin that clings to us as tribal creatures afflicted with a seemingly incurable disease: *we would rather be right than loving.* We would rather be correct than compassionate. We would rather be saved than seek justice. This is why it is so much easier to reach a verdict than to become a disciple. This is why the church is dying.

If you ask a Christian today about his faith, his response will be to tell you what he *believes.* If you ask a Christian today about her witness, she will describe her efforts to persuade others to believe what she *already* believes—as if the gospel were a numbers game. Giving intellectual assent to theological propositions is easy and intoxicating. But it changes nothing. Becoming a visible disciple, in contrast, can be dangerous. To put this in the language of the academy: defending your thesis can get you tenure, but becoming a disciple can get you dismissed. The former comes with a wink and a nod from your peers, whereas the latter comes with a motion, and a second, that someone call security.

In Defense of Insanity

Thomas Merton, a Trappist monk, writer, and poet who stood in the tradition of radical Roman Catholic clergy, once composed a critique of "sanity" as it applied to nuclear strategic planning by the military-industrial complex. He called it "A Devout Meditation in Memory of Adolf Eichmann." The capture and trial of Eichmann, a Nazi official directly responsible for the Holocaust, is the setting for Merton's opening lines and is relevant to our consideration of the "sanity" of Jesus.

"One of the most disturbing facts that came out in the Eichmann trial was that a psychiatrist examined him and pronounced him perfectly sane. I do not doubt it at all, and that is precisely why I find it disturbing." He continues:

> If all the Nazis had been psychotics, as some of their leaders probably were, their appalling cruelty would have been in some sense easier to understand. It is much worse to consider this calm, "well-balanced," unperturbed official conscientiously going about his desk work, his administrative job which happened to be the supervision of mass murder. He was thoughtful, orderly, unimaginative. He had a profound respect for system, for law and order. He was obedient, loyal, a faithful officer of a great state. He served his government very well.[8]

Merton goes on to note that apparently Eichmann slept well, had a good appetite, and only seemed "disturbed" when he actually visited Auschwitz, where even Himmler had gone "weak at the knees" at viewing the very human results of his work. But apparently not a single Nazi believed that any of his comrades had lost their minds. They were proud of their jobs and deeply patriotic. "We equate sanity with a sense of justice, with humaneness, with prudence, with the capacity to love and understand other people," Merton says and goes on, "We rely on the sane people of the world to preserve it from barbarism, madness, destruction. And now it begins to dawn on us that it is precisely the *sane* ones who are the most dangerous."[9]

The sane ones? That would be you and me and most of the church, defending as it does the morality of Christian men and women who have helped bring the human race to the edge of extinction. We are the world's largest religion, yet we are primarily passive when it comes to the dangers we face. Do we no longer care about the massive inequities between rich and poor? Are we content to "shop until we drop" in a culture of greed and conspicuous consumption? Do we prefer to ignore or merely delude ourselves about the mindless destruction of the only planet we have because we expect the return of Jesus at any moment?

When sinners convert to Christianity, we rejoice because they have "come to their senses" or have "seen the light." We regard "getting religion" as a move away from unconventional or questionable behavior and toward decent living, predictable conformity, and a life that "would make a mother proud." Whether it is "accepting Jesus as your personal lord and savior," as conservatives put it, or becoming enlightened enough to know that Jesus would vote Democratic and prefer Chardonnay with fish, as liberals might assume, no one thinks of going to church as a dangerous bargain that leads to antisocial behavior. To the contrary, we become as predictable (and often as dull), as any group in society. *Avant-garde* is seldom the term used to describe the "church lady."

In literature and film, not to mention in the continuing verdict of the young, Christians are seen as frightened, judgmental, often anti-intellectual conformists. We appear to have traded original thinking for the comfort of belonging to a community of creeds and doctrines meant to protect us from both our true selves and the real world. It's not that the next generation thinks we have lost our minds in order to be crazy like Jesus was crazy. Rather, that the insanity of the church crowd involves delusional thinking—that we believe things that are not really true in order to get rewards that are not really available.

Week after week we sit in the pews and listen to the words of the man of "melancholy madness" joined to a sermon that is often about positive thinking and wealth management. We are often told that we "need Jesus," but never warned to "avoid Jesus." When we sing "What a Friend We Have in Jesus," it never occurs to anyone that with friends like this, who needs enemies!

Whether we allow adoration to compromise critical thinking, or mistake hyperintellectual apologetics for faith, both conservatives and liberals miss the real demands of taking up the cross. Whatever threatens the status quo must be either domesticated or assassinated. What can't be tamed must be eliminated, especially if it threatens wealth and power. If more Christians saw the gospel as more dangerous than comforting, the church could get back to its real business, which is holy foolishness in the service of love.

Instead, we are now seen as the "sane" ones who go out to "restrain" him by marginalizing the very people who are foolish enough to take his teaching seriously. As Merton put it, "We can no longer assume that because a man is 'sane' he is therefore in his 'right mind.' The whole concept of sanity in a society where spiritual values have lost their meaning is itself meaningless."[10]

Apparently it takes a Christian mystic like Merton to recognize that if the world itself has gone insane, then the last thing we need is the kind of Christianity that we equate with sanity! If such sanity means that we have lost our "capacity to love other human beings, to respond to their needs and their suffering, to recognize them also as persons, to apprehend their pain as one's own," then we are the ones who have gone mad.[11] We are the ones who have lost touch with reality by justifying torture, by stockpiling enough nuclear weapons to make the world's rubble bounce ten times. We are the ones who not only fail to recognize our face in the face of the enemy but also pronounce them "evildoers" in the name of Jesus.

Meanwhile, Christians cling to their precious theological formulas, certain that there is a personal payoff regardless of what happens to God's creation. They "coolly estimate," as Merton put it, "how many victims can be considered expendable in a nuclear war." Why then do we consider the doomsday planners to be "normal," while we insist that the pacifists and the "peaceniks" are the ones who have lost touch with reality?

Perhaps we have forgotten the poet's lesson, that everything gains its meaning from context. Take, for example, the list of reasons why Jesus was once considered psychotic. Perhaps we only see it that way because we are the ones who have lost our minds. *He has hallucinations and hears voices.* How else can one describe that "inner life" which we value as a sign of genuine spirituality except to speak of what we "hear" and "see"? When Martin Luther King Jr. said, "I have *seen* the promised land," we did not question either his eyesight or his sanity. We call it wisdom when the writer in Proverbs claims that "without a vision the people perish." But considering that they see what is not obvious to everyone, isn't that, by definition, a hallucination?

His cleansing of the Temple was the act of an unstable man with anger management issues. Or perhaps it was his enraged final act of dissent against the corruption of religion at its epicenter. Perhaps today he would attack the prosperity gospel or the notion that the more you give, the more God loves you (and the more attention you get from the preacher). Perhaps his target today would be the enormous edifices we build to honor a penniless rabbi. Perhaps in a country with the best stadiums and the worst schools in the developed world, he might go ballistic on us—wondering why we know the cost of everything and the value of nothing. Perhaps he would "go off" one Sunday morning in the narthex of one of our churches and start turning over the tables of the trinket sellers, the prayer cloth charlatans, or the hawkers of shallow, narcissistic books. Perhaps a straitjacket would calm him down.

His cursing of a poor little fig tree for not bearing fruit out of season is irrational and cruel. Or perhaps it was the season for figs, and it was the gospel poets who moved the triumphal entry from fall to early spring so that it would coincide with Passover, as some scholars believe. If this is indeed a barren fig tree and the man of "melancholy madness" is on his way to his own execution, then who can blame him for dealing out one more metaphor about the barrenness of religion? If that tree stands in for all that was corrupt in a system that "brokered" access to God according to rank, privilege, and purity, then to curse it is to curse the system. This is a prophet at work, and he is running out of time.

His vituperative verbal explosions against Pharisees are really calls for violence. Or perhaps he had very particular Pharisees in mind, just as today he would have very particular ministers in mind. As for Jesus and violence, the case is closed—he rejects it at every turn. The oft-quoted line about not bringing peace on earth but a sword and division is surely about higher loyalties, about *choosing*, even within your own family, whether you will be a sane foot soldier for the principalities and powers, or a crazy disciple.

His apparently estranged relationship with his own family is the result of their failure to recognize him as messiah. Or perhaps what is true now was true then: that all families are dysfunctional. Besides, what kind of bargain is it for a mother to lose her son instead of collecting grandchildren? What kind of father handles gossip well about a son who seems to have traded honest work for the life of a wandering rabbi, teaching in parables and eating with sinners? "We hear that boy of yours is a Gentile lover."

He displays an exalted messianic self-consciousness that he insists on keeping a secret. Or perhaps the later gospel writers added such messianic self-consciousness to an otherwise humble man who warned his disciples in the earliest layers of the tradition not to seek a sign—to worship the God he revealed, not the revealer. And most of all, he warned them not to argue about who would be the greatest in the

Jesus Administration. As for keeping it a secret, especially in Mark, perhaps this is the writer's effort to explain why so many people who actually met Jesus did not believe he was the messiah. Or perhaps he is simply being cautious (wise as a serpent, harmless as a dove) in a world where he seems to be constantly under surveillance and leaves no forwarding address.

He calls for self-mutilation, and counsels those who sin to get rid of the offending body part. Or perhaps he knows the power of hyperbole. Surely, the same teacher who introduced us to a God he called *Abba* (papa), the unconditional lover of all humanity who has the hairs of our heads numbered and sees a single sparrow fall, does not really want mutilated people walking around with stumps for hands and bloody sockets for eyes. Religion has always been a rather predictable and boring business, and people have always argued over how many angels could dance on the head of a pin. Jesus taught people who thought they had heard it all before. To get their attention must have been like putting a hypodermic needle in a tombstone.

Ask a room full of pastors today if that doesn't describe much of the church. We still argue endlessly over our precious doctrines in a perishing world. We fuss over music and flowers and whether the minister should drive a red car. So here is how we fiddle while Rome burns: Is it justification by works or by faith? Should baptism be by dunking, sprinkling, or dry cleaning? Should we use one communion cup or many? Should we speak in tongues or not speak at all? Should we use real wine for communion or grape juice? Can there be an American flag in a sanctuary that is a house of prayer for all people? Should women wear skirts or slacks, makeup or no makeup?

While we're at it, what about the role of women in church leadership? What about gays and lesbians? What about politics from the pulpit? Not to worry. We know the answer, and if we don't, the church council will meet next Tuesday to discuss all this and take a vote. Meanwhile, in the time it takes to talk another problem to death, a thousand children will actually starve to death.

In the meantime (which the poet W. H. Auden reminded us is the most important time), we are running out of time. The painful but urgent question that must be answered at this Good Friday moment for the church is this: *What kind of community would bring us back from the dead?* What would transform the Chamber of Commerce at Prayer or the Church of What's Happening Now into a beloved community of certifiably insane people? What would make us irresistibly crazy in a world where more and more people find "sanity" itself to be insane?

What would make this American Empire realize that we are not called to be its compliant acolyte? What would make people stop using terms like the "social gospel," as if there were any other kind? What would turn Christians from cartoons of hypocrisy into an irresistible force for justice? What would bring all the warring camps together, from the most devout Baptists to the most erudite Episcopalians, from the most traditional Roman Catholics to the most nontraditional members of the emergent community? What could persuade us, in the twilight of our relevance and power, to stop fighting over abortion and gay marriage long enough to save ourselves through shared mission?

The answer lies in an odd and unexpected place. It will require us to explore some of the most formative myths that we learned about our ancestors in Sunday school. It will require an archeological dig of sorts, but not through earthly sediment. Rather we must unearth our own true identity buried underneath layers of ecclesiastical *sentiment*.

Our journey forward will require a fearless look *backwards* at the original character of the Jesus movement—from its inception as an underground movement born in the winds of Pentecost to its corruption as a belief system at Nicaea. Nothing will give us a clearer picture of the risks and rewards of discipleship than a fearless look at the first disciples. But be warned: they will seem like strangers to us. They will seem more than odd. They may even seem slightly insane. If "melancholy madness" best describes the man from Nazareth, then how would we describe a modern disciple who is as countercultural and anti-imperial as those first followers of The Way? In Oklahoma, we have a word for such people. We call them "peculiar."

This will not be a ride for the faint of heart. Let's take it anyway.

CHAPTER TWO

The Early Church That Never Was

If Christ were here there is one thing he would not be—a Christian.
—MARK TWAIN

Call it "almost Bible." Or in the words of a country sage from Oklahoma, "the things we think we know that just ain't so." Eve ate an apple in the garden; the serpent was Satan; all the animals marched onto the ark two by two; there are ten commandments; the Immaculate Conception refers to Jesus; there were three wise men; a prodigal son is one who leaves and returns; Mary Magdalene was a prostitute; Constantine created the canon of the New Testament; and somewhere in the Bible it says, "God helps those who help themselves."

Whether conservative or liberal, "everyone is entitled to his own opinion, but not to his own facts," as Daniel Patrick Moynihan is famous for saying. Just for the record, Eve ate of the fruit of the "tree of the knowledge of Good and Evil." The serpent is never referred to as Satan. Clean animals (the majority) went onto the ark in groups of seven. The Ten Commandments have been variously grouped into a decalogue by combining fourteen or fifteen statements. The Immaculate Conception refers to Mary. Nowhere does it say that there are three wise men (only three gifts). A prodigal son is one given to "profuse or wasteful expenditure." Nowhere in the Bible is Mary Magdalene referred to as a prostitute (only, like

Jesus, to having been possessed by demons). Constantine called a council of bishops that resulted in the Nicene Creed, and Ben Franklin is credited with having said, "God helps those who help themselves" in *Poor Richard's Almanac*, although he may have gotten it from Algernon Sydney's 1698 article titled "Discourses Concerning Government."

This could all be regarded as nothing more than Bible trivia if the stakes were not so high. The Bible is used constantly in American public discourse by people who have not studied it and are frighteningly misinformed about its content. So many of the things we were taught about the Bible as children, or have just absorbed uncritically from everyday conversation, continue to form the basis of our understanding of Christianity long after we have become adults. Americans profess to be deeply religious people, yet we know little about our own religious heritage or principles.

In a poll conducted recently by the Pew Forum on Religion and Public Life, people were asked thirty-two questions about the Bible, Christianity and other world religions, famous religious figures, and the constitutional principles governing religion in public life. On average, people answered only half the questions correctly, and those who scored the highest were atheists and agnostics! Among the more shocking results of the survey, 53 percent of Protestants could not identify Martin Luther as the man who started the Protestant Reformation. Among Catholics, 45 percent did not know that their church teaches that the consecrated bread and wine in Holy Communion are not merely symbols but actually become the body and blood of Christ. Among Jews, 43 percent did not know that Maimonides, one of the foremost rabbinical authorities and philosophers, was Jewish.[1] To complicate matters, we don't take kindly to being told that many of the things we believe are simply incorrect. It makes us feel "incorrect" and thus a bit foolish. Serious study of the Bible can be more than a little unsettling, especially if one approaches scripture as if the normal tools of literary criticism should not apply. Ask any brave soul who has ever taught a university class under the title "The Bible as Literature." Students feel as if the rug were being pulled out from underneath them. "Why didn't someone tell us this before?" "Isn't that what we are supposed to believe?" "Why is my professor trying to destroy my faith?" There is something very powerful about letting go (or trying not to let go) of the things we grew up believing. It can feel as though a piece of our soul is cracking off and falling away.

Take, for example, our understandable obsession with the "early church." When the monks of the Middle Ages created their lists of "mortal" or "capital" sins, they came up with what we know of today as the seven deadly sins (also not in the Bible). This infamous list, often the subject of cinema and sitcom, names the darkest compulsions of human behavior. They chronicle our most self-destructive vices. But after thirty years in the ministry, I am beginning to think that in their zeal to conform to the holy number seven, those monks omitted a very important and deadly sin in the church: nostalgia.

The past, as someone has said, is not forgotten; it isn't even past. But what we remember is shaped by our very human desire to attach virtue to the "good old days." The vices of the present prove not only that all is now in disarray but that this "awful" age is inherently inferior to some golden age that came before it. Apparently, if my grandparents are to be believed, they never went to school except under blizzard conditions. Marriage vows between one man and one woman were once sacred and inviolate. Women were once blissfully happy staying home to raise children. And, once upon a time, the church of Jesus Christ was pure, orthodox, and joyfully unified. Everyone knew his or her theological place and stayed in it.

Now before we go further, let me pause to reaffirm the importance of studying the past as prologue to the future. We study origins for a very good reason. Past and future are linked, and every renewal of the church has sought to revisit and recapture what the original Jesus Movement was all about before we messed it up. In the church of my boyhood, the Church of Christ, we called it the *restoration* movement and its followers "restorationists." We took Luther's notion of *solo scriptura* ("by scripture alone") literally, vowing to "speak where the Bible speaks and be silent where the Bible is silent." This meant, of course, that when it came to a lot of very important things, we were silent. Likewise when it came to a lot of very trivial things, we held great debates.

What's more, the idea of returning to a simple first-century form of Christianity is easier said than done. The evidence of the softening of the message of Jesus begins early and is mirrored in the pseudo-Pauline epistles. The earliest strands of the Jesus tradition are more radical and anti-imperial than the later ones. Some of the most offensive comments by Paul, especially about women, were probably not written by Paul. So at what moment can we point to "early Christianity" as something other than a moving target?

Conservatives and liberals alike tend to find what they go looking for in scripture. Pentecostals believe they are reviving the ecstatic and miraculous experience of the church as described in Acts. "New age" groups are just as certain that they have uncovered secret or suppressed esoteric lore. Catholics appeal to "apostolic succession," tracing a straight line of authority from Jesus to Peter to the present pope. As Harvey Cox tells us, "Baptists, Congregationalists, and Presbyterians claim their forms of church administration are identical with those of the New Testament. But there is no road back to the primitive church some Protestants long for, or to the splendid medieval synthesis many Catholics dream of, or to the 'old time religion' American revivalists sing about. Much of this attempt to revert to the 'way it was' is based on fanciful reconstructions of some previous period."[2] When it comes to the early church, *the way it was* is the way it wasn't.

Even though we seem to have gotten part of it right, the evidence is mounting that we got most of it wrong. Granted, whenever the church seems to be in trouble, we have always looked back to the first followers to find a corrective for our institutional nostalgia. The argument has always been that what we should be doing today must be shaped by what the first followers did. Why? Because proximity equals authenticity. The closer we get to Jesus, the argument goes, the more uncorrupted and unified the community will be. This will show us where we have gotten off track and provide the corrective we need for faith and practice. Every reform movement in Christianity has essentially accepted this thesis, making all such efforts to renew the church an effort to "restore" the early church in our time.

The problem with this thesis is not its logic but the unstated assumption that the gauzy, sentimental vision of the early church that we carry around in our heads is accurate. As it turns out, generations of ministers have been taught myths about the early church that recent scholarship has increasingly debunked. Our tendency to oversimplify and romanticize the past has made the noble effort of restoration unreliable for a very simple reason: getting back to the way it used to be is helpful only if we have an accurate picture of how it used to be.

The Way It Wasn't

In his wise and helpful book *The Future of Faith*, Cox distills an enormous amount of scholarship on the early church into a handful of readable chapters. I owe much of what follows to his lucid observations, and he owes much of what he has learned about the first three centuries of Christianity to scholars like Krister Stendahl, Elaine Pagels, Karen King, Allen Callahan, and Helmut Koester. Simply put, Cox now realizes that when it comes to Christian origins, most seminary students do not get an accurate picture of the first followers of Jesus. In particular, he explains how our understanding of the early church is defective in three important respects.

First, most ministers have been taught that in the "good old days" Christianity was a single entity, and only later did various "heresies" and schisms attack this unified body from the margins. Second, we assume that "apostolic authority" (the idea that only the original apostles or their direct successors had real authority) took shape right away, as did the creeds and hierarchies that were necessary to preserve "orthodoxy." Third, we have been taught that the Roman Empire was the backdrop for, but not the object of, the ministry of Jesus and his first followers. He was a purely "spiritual" teacher who had no interest in the rough-and-tumble of earthly politics. That familiar canard, "never mix religion and politics," has served generations of ambitious Christians well, partitioning our religious ideas from our political and economic self-interest.

Now, like the walls of Jericho, our myths about the early church are tumbling down. Thanks to a remarkable explosion of interdisciplinary scholarship on the first three centuries of the church, we now know more about this period than anyone has known before. What's more, these new discoveries from what Cox calls "the age of faith" confront both liberals and conservatives with real challenges.

First, there never was a "pure" or "unified" early church. "Among the various congregations scattered throughout the Roman Empire from Antioch to Gaul, there was no standard theology, no single pattern of governance, no uniform liturgy, and no commonly accepted scripture. In faith all focused on Jesus, but there were decisive differences in interpretation."[3] Today we tend to think that a Christian house divided is a more recent phenomenon. We assume that as time passed, false teachers arose, creeds and doctrines became tests of faith that partitioned the body of Christ, and people forgot their original, true, and undefiled identity. In fact, the Jesus

Movement was a divided and quarreling movement from day one, especially when it came to the divinity of Jesus.

Second, the idea of apostolic authority is a convenient fiction created by ambitious men who wished to become leaders in the new church and invented this idea to sanctify their aspirations by reading it back into a gospel record that actually contradicts it. Paul in particular never claims apostolic authority as a lineage, but only as a result of his personal encounter with Christ. He even denies that his authority as an apostle ("messenger") comes from any previous apostles, and taught that the spirit is what distributes the various gifts needed for each congregation, the greatest of which is love.

Third, and most important for the future of the church, the Roman Empire was never merely the "background" for the ministry of Jesus and his followers. The first followers of Jesus formed a fiercely anti-imperial movement. After all, it was Rome that had executed their Lord (not the Jews) and then sent the next generation into the Colosseum to die. It was in fact this very Empire that the Jesus People intended to replace by living in a kind of alternative, parallel social order that might be thought of as anti-Rome. Oddly enough, we see this most clearly in the bizarre, misunderstood, and much abused book of Revelation.

Despite all the end-times prophecies attributed to the last book in the Bible (including the wildly successful but entirely fictitious "Left Behind" series), the ancient and often disturbing symbolism of Revelation refers not to a vision of the end of the world but to a vision of the end of the Roman Empire. The author of Revelation, a political exile living on the craggy island of Patmos, isn't sending a message that God is going to destroy the earth. Rather he is predicting that God will destroy "the great whore of Babylon"—a code word for the city of Rome, whose emperors were decked out in purple and scarlet. We shall return to this image in greater detail in Chapter Eight.

Granted, those first followers expected Rome to collapse soon, which makes anti-imperial behavior easier to justify and even strangely practical. After all, if the great harlot is about to fall and God intends to replace her with the followers of the Lamb, then living as an underground, alternative community holds the implicit promise of eventual justification. We may be suffering now, but we will be vindicated in glory later. Even so, John's ecstatic vision of this coming age in Revelation is so intense and bizarre that many have wondered if this is a true religious dream or a drug-induced nightmare.

To some of the seven churches he says, "Hang on," to others, "Shape up," but most of the symbolism is written in a code to which we have largely lost the key. Whether he speaks of a scroll with seven seals; seven trumpets; a woman "clothed with the sun, with the moon under her feet, and on her head a crown of twelve stars," pregnant and crying out in birth pangs; or a "red dragon, with seven heads and ten horns, and seven diadems on his heads who will eat the child of the woman as soon as it's born," John is trying to do more than provide endless material for apocalyptic hucksters. He is dreaming of the day when the forces of light and love will finally defeat the forces of hatred and violence. He is a poet, after all—albeit it a very strange one.

He tips his hand early, calling himself a brother sharing in the persecution of Jesus. Is he in prison? And yet he counsels "patient endurance" and says the time is near. One can only wonder if, as the decades rolled by and Jesus did not return, his followers began to lose heart. As their patience wore thin and doubts began seeping into the body of Christ like dirty water into a basement, perhaps the only vision that could sustain such a weary lot had to be more convulsive and violent. How else can we understand this nightmare in which those who are not among the elect, the 144,000, will have to hide from the "wrath of the Lamb"? Isn't this Lamb the Prince of Peace?

In one sense, what John hoped for is what we all hope for—an end to the harlotry of injustice. A new reign of God's shalom where everyone has enough, children survive, the oppressed are set free, and the grip of the evil one is finally loosened and then destroyed. Or to put it in John's metaphor, when Satan is thrown into a bottomless pit, bound, and the angel throws away the key! Even those who have been beheaded for their loyalty to Jesus will reappear (presumable with their heads) as time and the world are made right.

Yet who can blame John for doubting that there is any justice in the world until some cataclysmic reversal occurs—what John Dominic Crossan calls "the great divine cleanup of the world"? His dream may be frightening, but his questions are perennial: When will the poor and needy have enough in a rich society? When will the widows and orphans be cared for with dignity and respect in a patriarchal society? When will the resident aliens be welcomed in a tribal society?

Even so, the violent imagery of Revelation has encouraged all sorts of apocalyptic warriors. They are drawn to its decisive and terrifying images of a final battle between good and evil. Yet how odd this is when one considers the "first coming" of Jesus. It is almost comically nonviolent (he rides into Jerusalem on a donkey). But in Revelation, Crossan says, his "Second Coming has Jesus on a war horse leading a violent attack. We Christians still have to choose."[4]

Such a choice cannot be avoided, whether one is liberal or conservative. We all need to call a truce on the Revelation wars long enough to ask larger questions than those posed by apocalyptic gamesmanship. The larger issue is the nature of God and whether we wish to repudiate violence. Is the God we worship the God of the nonviolent first coming, or the terrifying architect of this divine vengeance portrayed by John and others as the Second Coming? How can Jesus insist during his earthly ministry that no one gets "left behind" and then participate in this apocalyptic slaughter when he returns? Did he get it wrong the first time, or have we still not gotten it right?

In fact, all sorts of uncomfortable but necessary choices are now before us—regardless of our religious affiliation, background, or beliefs. None of us can bask in the illusion of a pure and undefiled early church. But neither can we write off the strange behavior of the first Jesus Followers as simple ignorance or superstition. Many were sophisticated, accomplished, and wealthy. Indeed, another lasting myth about the first converts to Christianity is that they were all impoverished. The sociologist Rodney Stark has reexamined the class structure of the early church and discovered that by no means was it made up entirely of the poor and dispossessed. Not only did Christianity grow most quickly in urban areas, but it included wealthy and aristocratic members, especially women of high status.[5]

What led to the remarkable growth of Christianity for three centuries was not the attraction of competing doctrines but a distinctly alternative lifestyle. Practicing communitarian principles, nursing the sick during plagues, outlawing abortion and infanticide (particularly of daughters), and allowing female converts to marry pagan men whom they often converted created a powerful demographic shift that favored the church. They made a deliberate choice and created an alternative world in which to live. They went underground from the Roman Empire and lived as a self-conscious alternative to its death-dealing ways.

Indeed, those peculiar first colonies that constituted The Way shared much in common with the Underground Railroad movement of early nineteenth-century America. Borrowing the language of established railroading, slaves were helped to freedom by using common words like "stations" and "depots" for homes and businesses that allowed fugitives to rest and eat. They were run by "stationmasters," and those who contributed money were called "stockholders." The "conductor" was responsible for moving fugitives from one station to the next.

This vast network chose to violate the laws against helping
runaway slaves in order to follow a higher law—God's law. The early
church was likewise an underground movement, a growing, largely
secretive collection of "stations" where rich and poor alike chose
to practice a radical form of hospitality, a generous but scandalous
communalism, and to commit themselves at personal risk to nonviolent resistance and the protection of the stranger and the alien.
They were not sustained by the assurance of personal salvation in
the form of a ticket to heaven. It was not conformity of belief that
united them, not hierarchy, not creeds. Rather it was a powerful
confidence that in the life, death, and resurrection of Jesus of Nazareth,
God had changed everything. Hence the only way to be a true disciple was to live as a truly changed human being.

The first Jesus Followers were not, as so many churches are
today, communities of conformity. Rather, they were communities
animated by a common spirit—engaged in the mission of following
their sovereign and no other. In an Empire crawling with gods,
Rome allowed all sorts of local religious beliefs and practices to
flourish, *as long as loyal subjects of the realm also worshiped Caesar*. Whether
it was the Mithraism of Persia, with its ritual slaughter of bulls, or
the Egyptian cults of Isis and Osiris, competing religions sur-
rounded the early Christians—just as they do today.

What is vitally important to remember, however, is that when
these first Jesus People encountered such rival faiths, they responded
in a strange and unexpected way. They did not fashion creeds and
demand that they be taken as vows. Rather they simply refused to
worship Caesar, stopped practicing animal sacrifice, threw open the
doors of their underground assemblies to all who would come,
redistributed wealth, and made the dangerous claim that "Jesus
Christ was Lord."

They would pray for the emperor, but not *to* him. As Cox tells
us, "This defiance of the political religion of the Empire, which led
their critics to brand them subversive, landed many of them in

arenas with salivating lions. In our time, when fusing the cross with the flag has become so popular and religiously saturated nationalisms are on the rise around the world, the early Christian refusal to mix the two is a cautionary tale."[6]

That may be an understatement, because if we forget our own story, we are lost. If we have become indistinguishable from our own Empire, then we have lost our souls. Conservatives have often been accused of being nostalgic about an idealized past; liberals have shunned it so completely as "premodern" that they have lost their institutional memory. Yet these two forces, memory and hope, are the two strongest forces in life. They sustain all communities and carry them forward. It is essential that we know where we came from so that we will know who we are. Likewise it is a sacred obligation to imagine and then build the future we desire—even against the odds.

Sadly, many of us continue to think that "modern" humans have cornered the market on enlightened spirituality. Many progressive Christians today call for social justice and spiritual practice as if these were recent inventions. Both have long histories in the Christian tradition, but we have *forgotten*. Without this collective memory, however, our communities invest their hope in the politics of identity and the arrogance of theological purity. We have forgotten what once held us together, so our vision of a world redeemed becomes little more than a world that converts to our way of thinking. In other words, we play our theological fiddles while present-day Rome burns.

Perhaps, to recall the biblical story of the woman caught in adultery, the time has come to drop the stones of hypocrisy and start thumbing through the scrapbook that is the early church as a "people's movement." Instead of seeing it as a history written by the "winners" and the theological elites, perhaps we need to remember the ways in which ordinary people went about fulfilling the commandment to love God and neighbor in this world. Perhaps the droning doctrinal debates that transformed a community rooted in an alternative ethic into an all-male ecclesial imperium need to become as unimportant again in the future church as they once were in the beginning. Perhaps, as Diana Butler Bass put it, we should emulate Howard Zinn and sidestep issues of orthodoxy to "focus on those moments when Christian people really acted like Christians, when they took seriously the call of Jesus to love God and love their neighbors as themselves."[7]

Before we go further, however, you deserve to know what makes this "back to the future" move any different from all the other "restorations." Once, in preparation for a lecture in Colorado Springs, I was being interviewed by a newspaper reporter about my thesis for the Underground Church. He scoffed at the idea that any effort to "recover" the early church would lead to real change. "That has been tried countless times and always failed," he said. "If you think that 'going back' to the practices of the early church is radical, I have news for you. Same song, ten thousandth verse. Nobody cares."

This assumes, of course, that we know what really went on in the early church. If one recovers what isn't real, then of course it means nothing. But what has changed over the last half century has opened a new window on the early church, allowing us all, conservatives and liberals alike, to peer through that ancient portal and into a lost world of peculiar saints. Four developments in particular, claims Cox, have radically altered our understanding of The Way. In each of them are the seeds of the renewal of the church in our time.

You *Can* "Go Home Again"

The first development occurred when a layer of debris obscuring our view of the early church got wiped away by a most unlikely figure. In 1946, Cox tells us, "a young boy looking for some stray sheep chanced upon a whole library of ancient texts stashed in a cave near Nag Hammadi in Egypt. . . . The best known of the documents by far is the Gospel of Thomas, first published in 1959. When a consensus among scholars agreed that it was just as old as any of the gospels in the New Testament, maybe even older, it exploded a bombshell in early Christian studies."[8]

This collection is a "sayings" gospel (a Coptic translation of what was probably first written in Greek) and has no narrative elements at all. Most entries begin, simply, *Jesus said* . . . , and 114 sayings later we have no passion, no crucifixion, no resurrection, and nothing with which to interpret the life of Jesus. Such collections were common in antiquity, produced when students of famous philosophers would collect the wise and witty sayings of their heroes into *gnomologia* or "words of insight," which they would then recite in the marketplaces and streets of the ancient world.[9] Often dismissed by scholars today as belonging to that ill-defined but inferior genre known as "Gnosticism," the Gospel of Thomas raised far more questions than it answered.

What does it mean, for example, that there was once an early community of disciples who were content to live by a "sayings" gospel alone, as if Jesus were primarily a teacher of wisdom? Isn't it obvious that the distinction we make between "orthodox" and "Gnostic" did not exist until much later, when those judged to hold heretical views were forced to hide their work in caves? And how did the early Jesus Movement develop so differently in various geographical areas without corrective creeds and a hierarchy to enforce uniformity of belief?

The answer may be particularly important for our time, as the church today finds itself sharing more in common with the early church than we realize. Christianity is no longer the dominant way of organizing life in an increasingly secular and pluralistic West. As an institution, it is waning here while growing elsewhere, particularly in the developing world. In American society, Christians can no longer take for granted that every house of worship on the corner is a church. It may now be a mosque or a temple. Some conservatives see this as a threat, the waning of a "Christian nation." Some liberals see it as proof that all religions are really "the same" at heart, varying only in the particulars of style, language, and culture. Both views are too easy and wide of the mark.

The recent discoveries of ancient manuscripts that reveal the existence of many other gospels alongside the four that would eventually anchor the New Testament are unnerving to some, exciting to others, and simply perplexing to most. We also continue to use the word "Gnostic" as if everyone agreed on its meaning. Yet it is a term so imprecise and contradictory that it obscures more than it reveals. In many camps, the word has become simply a dismissive label instead of a way to describe a worldview that profoundly influenced early Christians.

The *second* development challenged one of the central doctrines of the church—apostolic authority. This was not the result of a plot by liberal scholars. Rather, it resulted from the collaborative work of a diverse group of researchers working together across old boundaries. In this new age of interdisciplinary scholarship, those who study religious antiquity discovered that they had come to many of the same conclusions—in particular, that the powerful notion of apostolic authority had been superimposed on the church much later, rather than having been recorded in some objective way by early church "historians."

Those who invented apostolic authority were ambitious men who desired to become leaders of the next generation of Christians. Cox puts it well: "Looking for a potent way to establish their own authority, they seized upon a very compelling idea. They claimed to have inherited their right to rule from the first disciples, and that they themselves possessed 'apostolic authority' because they formed a part of what they began to call the 'apostolic succession.' This was a self-justifying fiction."[10]

This fiction, however, was taught to countless seminarians who taught it to countless parishioners. It forms a central tenet of governance in the Roman Catholic Church. Like all cherished myths, it crumbled not because of some enemy from outside the church but because those who study ancient Christianity from within decided to share their work. They studied both canonical and noncanonical texts and integrated the work of archeologists, art historians, anthropologists, and sociologists. Yet long after evidence for the myth faded, the church continues to act as if its latter-day apostles are walking on solid ground, having been handed the keys of the kingdom, directly above the grave of Saint Peter.

Fortunately, a new generation of seminary students is now learning quite different lessons about the history of the early church. They see it as both complex and compelling, not because these early congregations marched to the beat of an orthodoxy drummer, but because a unifying spirit hovered over this ship of holy fools. That spirit, not an ecclesiastical hierarchy, was the source of authority. It was a spirit of generosity, mercy, healing, hope, and radical hospitality.

In these underground churches were gathered people who had never believed in themselves before. They had never even considered the possibility that they were worthy—or as African American Christians are fond of saying, "precious." In a chaotic and violent world, this radical movement transformed their lives. Not because it promised a heavenly reward for earthly suffering, but because it promised a way of life that lifted all followers, regardless of class or ethnicity, into the joy of belonging to a Beloved Community. They were not, after all, called true believers. They were called "the people of The Way."

This new sect infuriated Rome and led to charges that it was immoral and that it undermined traditional Roman values of loyalty and family. The offense was never described in doctrinal terms, but in terms of Christian devotional practices that were subversive and dangerous. Under the influence of a martyred Jewish peasant, the movement was rapidly expanding across Asia Minor, defying the status quo by living out an alternative existence complete with its own laws and its own patterns of behavior.[11] Empires seldom worry about religious beliefs that have no real effect on the loyalty of their subjects. But when that loyalty is subverted or replaced, those beliefs must be investigated and the believers crushed.

As it turns out, the early church can't even be described as liberal or conservative, because such labels simply do not apply. They fail to capture the true unifying force that held otherwise diverse elements together in ways that baffled and then threatened the status quo. Second-century philosopher and apologist Justin Martyr expressed the radical character of the early Christians with unmistakable clarity:

> We who formerly . . . valued above all things the acquisition of wealth and possession, now bring what we have into a common stock, and communicate to everyone in need; we who hated and destroyed one another, and on account of their different manners would not live with men of a different tribe, now, since the coming of Christ, live familiarly with them, and pray for our enemies.[12]

The third development caused yet another layer to dissolve, like scales falling from our eyes. It has to do with our understanding of history and what is "real." We forget, says Cox, to distinguish between history as a record of the elites and history as a record of the people. While most academics concentrate on the theologians who wrote the treatises and on the bishops who argued about questions of authority, the most important constituency of all gets left out: the vast majority of ordinary people whose lives were dramatically changed by the Jesus Movement. This included women, peasants, and slaves.

Because most were illiterate, what they left behind has not been studied until recently. The artifacts of their existence tell a story.

Scholars looked not just at ancient documents but at "games, graffiti, inscriptions on coffins, what we can learn from dishes, house furnishings, and plates, and even the detritus from ancient garbage pits," Cox tells us, "where archaeologists now say some of the juiciest bits of evidence can be exhumed. When combined with what can be learned about the first Christian centuries from studies of tax law, prostitution (Jesus talked about both taxes and prostitution a lot), and the organization of the Roman military, a much fuller sketch appears."[13]

We have always assumed that as the church moved from resisting the Empire to embracing it, the rank and file followed their leaders like docile sheep. Now a more realistic and dissident picture is emerging. While the bishops and the Roman Empire were getting cozy, the people were so busy just trying to survive that revolts were breaking out all over the realm. Rome's military-industrial complex was very expensive and required higher and higher taxes to maintain. People (then as now) found clever ways to avoid paying them, and order was hard to enforce. Barbarians ruled the realm, and emperors were overthrown and replaced.

"The paradox," as Cox puts it, "is that when the ship of state, like Melville's *Pequod*, eventually sank beneath the waves, the church, like Queequeg's coffin, bobbed to the surface. The papacy eventually became, as philosopher Thomas Hobbes once wrote, 'nothing more than the ghost of the deceased Roman Empire, sitting crowded upon the grave thereof.'"[14]

It would be hard to hear a more timely warning for the American church, which may be likewise little more than a ghost sitting atop our own Empire, now in decline. What's more, few ideas have emerged of late with such force, or been voiced so strongly across such a wide spectrum of theology and practice, as the idea that the church must retain its autonomy against the seductions of Empire. Conservatives and liberals alike recognize this danger, although they would surely emphasize different threats.

Conservatives tend to focus more on individual sins brought on by the collapse of social values and morals, whereas liberals focus more on systemic injustice and violence. But by no means are these mutually exclusive. A "personal relationship with the Lord" is central to the thinking of conservatives, but this presumes that one knows what sort of person one is in relationship with. "Got Jesus?" is a familiar question in our time. To which I always want to answer, "Yes, and now I've got trouble."

Liberals commit a different kind of error when they ask us to be in relationship with something so abstract and incomprehensible that no relationship is really possible. Christianity is not a concept; it is grounded in a person. The incarnation is the distinctive, pulsating center of Christianity, not a set of wise sayings suitable for framing. Having a personal relationship with Jesus and taking seriously his call to live out God's shalom is what can bring us together. Like those biblical scholars who now realize how much they have in common, the rest of us might want to at least consider getting in the same room now and talking to one another. Better yet, we could audit one another's classes.

The fourth development relates to the myth that one can be a Christian and avoid politics. Every minister has heard it said ad nauseam, especially after a sermon that moved from polite abstractions about heavenly justice to concrete applications about earthly injustice: don't mix religion and politics. What that usually means, of course is, "Don't mix them in ways I do not approve or that I find personally indicting."

Whether a liberal or a conservative is making this plea (depending almost entirely on what particular party or policy position has been crowned and sanctified by his or her community), the larger, less partisan point is entirely forgotten: there is a politics of the gospel. Jesus was political. He was a dangerous subversive, not because he wanted to help individuals escape a perishing world and make it "up" to heaven, but because he wanted to bring heaven's justice "down" to earth, especially to free those who suffered injustice and oppression.

Countless seminary students were taught for generations that early Christians had no interest whatsoever in "worldly politics" and were simply learning how to pray and behave themselves until the Second Coming. There was a Big Bad Empire out there, of course, but the persecution of Christians had mostly to do with religious rivals, pagan rulers, and the Jewish elite. Jesus was executed, so the theory goes, because he was *misunderstood*, not because he was a genuine threat to those in power.

The truth is, however, that his enemies understood him all too well. Our separation of religion and politics is a "modern conceit," as Cox puts it. When Jesus taught his disciples "to pray for the coming Reign of God, 'on earth as it is in heaven,' it was all too evident to the current rulers that, if this really were to happen, they would be displaced."[15]

Hence, execution by crucifixion was a political solution to a political problem. Except that it did not end the threat. Indeed, after the Roman goons were sent down to close the "Jesus file," the movement refused to die. It became a community movement animated by the spirit of the risen Lord, now free from time and space. It spread rapidly through the known world, creating a self-conscious alternative to the hierarchy and patronage of the Empire.

Christians refused to participate in the emperor cult and thus posed a threat to the whole system by which Rome held its client states together. Thus the first followers of Jesus were *counterimperial*. That made them, in the eyes of Caesar, *anti*-imperial. The distinction that we now make between religion and politics, however, is a product of the Enlightenment and the separation of church from modern nation states. In the ancient Roman Empire, either you pledged your ultimate loyalty and paid your dues to Caesar or you paid the price.

Today we all live under the threat of a difficult kind of illusion, whether we are liberal or conservative—namely, that the American Empire protects our freedom but does not control our behaviors or impose its values and priorities. Because our history is so uniquely about individual freedom and opportunity, it is difficult for all of us to realize how much of our self-understanding is shaped by the dominant culture. We allow those who have commercialized every aspect of life to tell us what is desirable, how to relate to one another, and what creates and sustains human happiness.

Meanwhile we have been so busy fighting partisan wars in the church that we have forgotten what is most peculiar and subversive about the politics of the gospel, rooted not in left or right, but in the "Good News." The first followers of Jesus did not identify themselves with power but with loyalty to a countercultural set of values and principles. They decided to do things differently, especially by advancing the virtue of *mercy* at a time when classical philosophers considered it to be synonymous with pity and thus a pathological emotion or a defect of character. (It involves providing *unearned* help or relief and therefore could not be just.) Yet because the followers of The Way believed that a merciful God required humans to be merciful, they possessed what Pliny the Elder, a Roman author, naturalist, and philosopher, called an "invincible obstinacy."

The Great Reversal

It is hard to imagine a more important message for the future of the church in our time than this: Christianity was born as a movement of the spirit, animated by faith in what *had* happened in Jesus (what scholars call a "realized eschatology"), what *was* happening in the body of Christ (people had become a "new creation"), and what *would* happen in the future (God's reign of shalom would ultimately be victorious and include both Jews and Gentiles). It was an underground, populist movement so distinct from the joyless brutality of the age that it grew from twelve followers to six million in three centuries.

Then something happened that changed Christianity forever. Not all at once, of course, but by increments that spelled disaster over time. Like the frog immersed in water that is gradually heated until it is cooked to death unaware, the church became a victim of incremental oblivion. We never know what is happening to us *while* it is happening to us, until it's too late.

What began as communities of radical inclusiveness, voluntary redistribution of wealth, a rejection of violence as the tool of injustice, and a joyful egalitarianism that welcomed a "nobody" to worship elbow-to-elbow with a "somebody" *devolved* into what Cox calls a "top heavy edifice defined by obligatory beliefs enforced by a hierarchy."[16] We have argued for seventeen centuries now about *why* this happened—Luther blames the papacy, Anabaptists blame Christians for becoming soldiers, Quakers blame written scripture, Greek and Russian Orthodox leaders blame a fatal squabble over the status of the Holy Spirit in the Trinity, and Catholics blame the "heresies" that led to the Reformation. But the evidence that it did happen is both overwhelming and obvious in our own time. Christians are primarily thought to be people who *believe* certain things, not people who *do* certain things.

Ask anyone to define Christianity these days, and the first words out of his or her mouth will likely be the affirmation of a creed or doctrine—intellectual assent to various propositional statements about the metaphysics and the mission of Jesus and the authority of the Bible. That is, the emphasis is on whether you *believe* what the church has asked you to believe about the meaning and purpose of the life of Christ, not on whether the God revealed to you by Jesus compels you to *live* as a disciple of nonviolent distributive justice. The most immediate response to this distinction, of course, is to argue that beliefs and actions cannot be so easily separated.

Conservatives will argue that only a belief in the divinity of Christ as the Son of God can compel the way of life that is recommended and practiced by his disciples. Without that "belief," there is no true authority to inspire imitation. Liberals will argue that wisdom is wisdom and God is God, and that the enemy of true religion is exclusiveness. So although it is fine to say that Jesus may be called the "definitive" revelation of God, there are other revelations that are just as valid for other faith communities. So can't we all just get along?

This chasm in the church, between Jesus as universal teacher and Jesus as exclusive savior, is vast and would seem to be intractable. But this divide has existed in the church from the beginning, and for centuries we have sought to end the debate by writing creeds to settle the matter, which has only partitioned the family further by drawing lines in the sand. The first followers of Jesus did believe certain things about him, or they would not have gathered in his name to begin with or been sustained by his spirit. But the difference between their simple confessions of loyalty, "Jesus Christ is Lord" (not Caesar), and the modern labyrinth of creeds and doctrines that defines a "true believer" today is so profound and so divisive as to be, dare we say it, unchristian.

I have conservative friends who lead lives of sacrifice and service yet believe things about Jesus that I do not believe. But their lives count for more to me than their beliefs. Besides, they may be right and I may be wrong. I can only hope that they feel the same way about me. Otherwise we are all in trouble. Whether in families or in churches, uniformity of belief has never and will never be achieved. Uniformity of spirit, however, is not only a possibility but the hallmark of the most successful and authentic Christian communities in the land. This is the hope of the Underground Church.

If "beliefs" are nonnegotiable while "spirit" is optional, then it follows that churches will be permanently divided by warring factions. But if the gifts of the spirit are nonnegotiable (as when

Paul writes that "without love" all other accomplishments are in fact failures), then differences in beliefs can exist without the collapse of community. Our "eyes will be on the prize" of loving God by loving neighbor. Or to put it in the words of that early Christian instruction manual called the "Didache," "There are two ways, one of life and one of death, but a great difference between the two ways. The way of life, then, is this: First, you shall love God who made you; second, love your neighbor as yourself, and do not do to another what you would not want done to you."[17]

Perhaps the best thing we can do with the creeds is to consider them landmarks along the way, signposts in the evolution of a movement that sought to resolve disputes and keep the body from flying apart. Some argue that the creeds were inevitable because without them there would have been chaos and disorder. Others argue that the best we can do is sing them as poetry rather than recite them as marching orders. What we must not do, however, is forget that our world is vastly different from the world in which those creeds were created. Strangely, we now have more in common with pre-creedal Christianity than we do with the Age of Belief. If we wish to become, in our own time, the "People of The Way," then we can no longer be the "people of the creeds."

For three centuries, the symbols for the Jesus Movement were the fish and the good shepherd. Bloody renderings of the crucifixion do not appear until the tenth century, with their emphasis on Jesus' suffering and death as an atoning sacrifice. This led scholars Rita Brock and Rebecca Parker to begin their book *Saving Paradise* with these astonishing words: "It took Jesus a thousand years to die."[18] The church, they argue, traded love of this world and the dream of paradise for the myth of redemptive violence—crucifixion and Empire.

Surely the art historians were all wrong, they argued. Surely the images that adorned churches for the first millennium were missing something. Jesus is always pictured as a youth, a teacher, a healer, an enthroned god, and a bearded elder. But he is never dead. When he does stand before a tomb or with the cross, he stands in front of it, serene and resurrected. The world around him is a garden, ablaze with beauty. The images are a vision of the world redeemed through love, not saved through torture. So what changed?

Although what I call the Great Reversal has many causes and many faces, one figure deserves special attention before we move on. Next to Jesus and Paul, he may be the most important figure in the history of Christianity, the symbol of its fall from The Way to the Ecclesiastical Imperium. Love him or hate him, you cannot ignore the fateful event that he engineered by compelling all the bishops of the age to come to his lakeside compound at Nicaea to "work out" their theological differences. If we do not understand what happened there in 325 CE, there is little hope for the renewal of the Western church. For it was there that Flavius Valerius Constantine invented heresy.

CHAPTER THREE

Waking Up in Bed with Constantine

When the kindness of Constantine
Gave Holy Church endowments,
in land and leases, lordships and servants,
The Romans heard an angel cry
on high above them,
This day *dos ecclesiae* has drunk venom
And all who have Peter's power
are poisoned forever.
—WILLIAM LANGLAND, *PIERS PLOWMAN*

Whether you love him or hate him, there will never be an end to the arguments over Constantine. Was he, as some of his contemporaries hailed him, "the thirteenth apostle"? Did he not accomplish what Peter and Paul failed to achieve, namely the conversion of Rome itself into the Holy City? Did he not build grand churches, pay clergy handsome salaries out of state funds, and free them from paying taxes? Did he not create Christian academies and universities, make Jerusalem into a pilgrimage destination, and bring the bloody age of martyrdom to an end? As Quaker church historian Roland Bainton put it, "Swords that had been drawn to punish were now raised to honor."[1]

When Constantine the Great sealed the evolution of the church as a spirit-driven, underground, anti-imperial movement and set the stage for Christianity to become the official religion of the Roman Empire, he changed the faith forever. When he ordered his bishops to convene a great council at Nicaea for the purpose of producing Christendom's most important white paper (the short-form loyalty oath we call the Nicene Creed), he changed the definition of what it means to "believe" forever. Christians were no longer "resident aliens" or "settled migrants." Now they were citizens of an earthly kingdom. Their new constitution was a doctrinal formula, not an ethical imperative. Once these spiritually autonomous assemblies had no creeds at all, save their fierce devotion to Jesus as Lord in place of Caesar. Now they were increasingly led by bishops who insisted on theological conformity. Jesus followers increasingly became Christ worshipers, and Christianity was changed forever.

After Constantine essentially legalized Christianity in 313, the money started pouring in. In short, the church, along with its pastors and bishops, became very wealthy. What's more, the state cut off the funding of pagan temples, accelerating their decline. Even so, this new ocean of cash did not come without strings attached. It flowed from the center of political and military power, not from the glad heart of an individual member of the church. Whenever bishops begin lining up to receive favors from politicians, the consequences are predicable. The seduction of the church by the state had begun.

Constantine made the old city of Byzantium into the new capital of Constantinople. "He poured money into the project, building gold-laden churches, a fine university, and new public spaces. He gave away land to middle-class farmers and free bread to the poor; people flocked to his city, quickly making it the wealthiest, most fashionable, and most cosmopolitan place in the Empire."[2] But Verna Dozier, an Episcopalian educator and author, disagreed, saying, "I have always thought exactly the opposite—it was the state that subdued the church."[3]

Money is the great corruptor, and not just of politics. Although that money was often used to help the poor and fund other acts of charity, the period of the crime of simony had arrived—priests and bishops stealing alms and offerings in order to support their own luxurious lifestyles. After refusing to wear the uniform of any army for two centuries, followers of the Prince of Peace were now welcomed into both the government and the army. In fact, Constantine would make being a Christian a *requirement* for military service. Whereas the first followers of Jesus had believed that the kingdom of heaven was both present and yet to come, now Christians could point to the seven hills east of the Tiber and see a Christian emperor and a court of bishops. Was this the heavenly city? Did the kingdom of God now have an earthly residence, a Roman address?

Conservatives and liberals today look at Constantine very differently. Conservatives tend to see the hand of God in the growth and eventual triumph of Christianity. They see it as a sign that the Empire finally bowed down to the church. This growth and eventual coronation of Christianity by the "principalities and powers" had now produced the first Christian emperor. The truth was now institutionalized and very well armed. God's Christian soldiers were indeed marching onward. The church was never meant to remain small and subversive, so the argument goes.

As the movement expanded, it needed greater authority, theological consistency, and the power to protect itself from "all enemies foreign or domestic." The world's best army would now protect God's only Son, even though this was deeply ironic. It was this very army that had put down the Judean rebellion of the first century, and it was a Roman spear that pierced the side of Jesus. Those who had been dispatched to kill a political revolutionary now protected his followers.

Some might argue that in the cosmic battle between good and evil, good had emerged victorious. Those first Jesus People, given to pacifist and egalitarian tendencies, had finally outgrown their misspent youth. At first they were peculiar and disorganized, but by the fourth century, the teenager was becoming an adult. If one sees the hand of God in this move from pre-creedal to post-creedal

Christianity, from the Age of Faith to the Age of Belief, then this was a graduation, not a capitulation.

Liberals as well as some conservatives (and others who might defy any labels, like Stanley Hauerwas) see Constantine's fusing of church and state as perhaps the most fateful event in the entire history of Christianity. As Barbara Tuchman put it in *A Distant Mirror*, "By Constantine's gift, Christianity was both officially established and fatally compromised."[4] Or, to put it in language familiar to every pastor, "That was the terrible moment when 'spiritual' people became 'religious' people, when beautiful, peace-loving, compassionate followers of Jesus were transformed by edict from a circle of enlightened souls into zealous missionaries, baptizing the world at the point of a sword." That was the moment when the drive to "standardize" the Christian product fundamentally transformed The Way into the Belief System—when orthopraxy was replaced by orthodoxy.

In the church, to hear some people tell it, there was B.C. and A.C. (Before Constantine and After Constantine). In the B.C. era, the church was free to practice its radical, unregulated, and "pure" spirituality—flying under the radar of the Empire as sons and daughters of light. Then a politician recognized the benefits of wrapping the flag around the cross. That's when The Way changed from being a thorn in the flesh of the Empire into its compliant acolyte.

Would that anything this complicated could be made this simple! In fact the marriage of Christianity to the Empire was not arranged, any more than all parties on both sides could be described as "just crazy about the idea." But neither was it a pure love affair without deception, manipulation, or the abuse of power. Sociologist and historian Rodney Stark does not see Constantine's Edict of Milan as having caused the triumph of Christianity, but rather as the response of an astute politician to the rapid growth of the church that had already made Christians a major political force. What's more, conservatives are correct to see this as part of the inevitable evolution from house church to cathedral. But they may not see as clearly the inherent danger in what Dozier referred to as "the third fall," which was, as Diana Butler Bass put it, as "detrimental to faith as the original fall and Israel's insistence on a king."[5] Liberals are also correct to see this as a fateful occurrence that changed the church forever, but they may not see as clearly how the church was already moving toward hierarchy and order—long before Constantine threw his party. The bishops had been casting an envious eye on the Empire for decades, and its increasingly all-male clerical cast had begun as early as the early third century to write that there were "heretics" in the house who had "not been present at the beginning." With these words, the early church father Tertullian (c. 160–225) used apostolic authority to argue that those he called "innovators" be condemned based on the idea that what they taught was not "original." As it turns out, what was condemned *had* in fact been there from the beginning. As Cox puts it, "Chronologically the *Gospel of Thomas* is as 'original' as Mark's gospel and may be even more 'original' than the Gospel of John."[6]

As it turns out, serious scholarship on the early church is an equal opportunity offender. The idea that there may have been five original gospels, not four, troubles conservatives, to say the least. But the dismal view of women in the Gospel of Thomas is offensive to liberals, as is the obvious movement of prominent women in the early church from respected leaders to servants on the sideline. So when conservatives hail the gravitas of the early church's fourth-century "conquest" of the imperial city, they betray their own longstanding belief that church and state should not sleep together. But when liberals assume that at Nicaea, a hitherto undefiled movement of spiritual seekers was raped by the sword of patriarchy, they neglect the evidence that in the absence of a Second Coming and with thousands of new converts, the church had for decades been moving, metaphorically speaking, from folding chairs to pews. If

Rome did indeed seduce the church at Nicaea, the bishops went dressed for the occasion.

The Most Dangerous Leg of the Trinity

For us to understand what happened at Nicaea in 325 CE, we cannot avoid the doctrine of the Trinity, and in particular its third "leg," which has been making church fathers nervous from the beginning. The early church needed to answer the charge that affirming both the divinity of Jesus and the Holy Spirit violated the idea of monotheism. So a Triune God was posited that requires a certain suspension of mathematical logic (one is three, and three is one). Like all postbiblical doctrines, it is argued to be essential by some and beside the point by others. My favorite quip about the Trinity came from my preaching professor Fred Craddock. He said once, "I'm not all that interested in the Trinity. I'm more of a Bible person myself."

Yet regardless of your Trinitarian credentials, what matters to the future of the church is that we remember why it has always been a particular headache to the institution. I'm talking about the Holy Spirit, of course, the prodigal child of the Trinity, the one that leaves for no known reason and then shows up without warning. It was the Holy Spirit that birthed the church at Pentecost in a kind of gusty, pyrotechnic, translinguistic miracle. But it was the same Holy Spirit that was immediately attributed as the cause of drunkenness. It is the most mysterious, the most important, and the most disorienting force in the body of Christ.

The real problem is that the Holy Spirit cannot be controlled by the pen of any theologian. Or to use a metaphor, we often assume that we can write about God and Jesus only by using a "justified" left and right margin. But then after we turn out the lights, confident that the shape of our sentences will be preserved overnight, the Holy Spirit will appear to dance outside the block of the text, or to scramble it. It will write itself into the margins as poetry, jumbled and asymmetrical like an E. E. Cummings poem.

The Holy Spirit will appear in the form of a dream or a vision, often to mock the things we think are important. Whether in simple moments of luminescence while one is rocking a sleeping child or in dramatic reversals on the road to Damascus, the Holy Spirit is like an independent contractor. We need it; we fear it. When it "behaves," we claim it. When it is wild, we say we've never met. In truth, the church relates to the spirit in much the same way that men often relate to women, with an anxious befuddlement. Is this one of your "moods," or is this the voice of Sophia? Is this the gift of emotional knowing, or is this the curse of emotionalism?

Here is the problem. If *anyone* can receive the Holy Spirit, then how will we ever know for sure who is the true prophet, the true teacher, the true follower of Christ? How does the church maintain lines of authority when the spirit can erase them at any time? How do we differentiate between the "legitimate" visions of some and the ecstatic experiences of others? Paul claims to have heard a voice speaking directly to him. He was not the first to make such a claim, and he was certainly not the last. Today, we call such people "charismatic" (from the Greek word meaning "gifts of grace"), and there are millions of them in Pentecostal churches all over the world.

It is quite obvious that Paul is preoccupied with this problem, warning against "super apostles" (the TV evangelists of his day), and reminding his critics that he too had seen heavenly visions and could also "speak in tongues." But he did not show them the door. He did not suggest that they all conform to a single standard, with one exception. *All gifts of the spirit and all prophecies must be subsumed under the law of love.*

This may be as important to the future of the church as any single idea: namely, that *uniformity has never and will never be achieved.* The church can survive a diversity of gifts and styles, a diversity of worship and liturgy, even a diversity of ways to express the ultimate mystery that is God—but *only if love rules*. In other words, a church can survive differences of opinion. It cannot, however, survive a deficit of love.

As it turns out, Paul did not solve the problem, nor did generations of church fathers after him. As Harvey Cox put it, "The tensions between ecstasy and order, between spiritual freedom and group cohesion, between mystics and administrators have persisted for the full two thousand years of Christian history. They show no sign of abating."[7]

Indeed, Pentecostals have become the fastest growing part of the body of Christ, and that growth has shifted from Europe and the West to Africa, Asia, and the developing world. Their worship styles still unsettle the more staid denominations, but they often embody a greater concern for the poor, the marginalized, and the downtrodden than do many more progressive mainline congregations. One does not have to make a case for either religious hysteria or hyperintellectual detachment to realize that in the call of faith, we must balance head and heart. Yet often liberals and conservatives have gotten only half of it right.

In a very real sense, church history is subsumed by the tension between mystics and prelates. Despite the fact that the Roman Catholic Church wrote the book on orthodoxy, it has produced some of the most amazing and unsettling mystics of all time—including unorthodox women like Hildegard of Bingen and Julian of Norwich. Today's Catholic Church has spawned numerous charismatic movements that, like the liberation theology of the 1970s and 1980s, make bishops and popes more than a little apprehensive.

It is not always fidelity to creeds or doctrines that causes concern. Rather, it is about the appropriate chain of command. Who is really in charge? The word *hierarchy* means "rule by the holy." This is why the Holy Spirit is the most dangerous leg of the Trinity, and why the defenders of order make rules and write books. It began as early as the second and third centuries with Ignatius and Irenaeus, and propelled a loose network of diverse Jesus fellowships without creed, polity, or standard rituals toward the inevitable imposition of what we might today call "quality control."

As a matter of fact, the concern for what we call "church order" began as early as 96 CE with the First Epistle of Clement. This letter, which never made it into the New Testament, urges the congregation at Corinth, which had been taken over by a kind of youth rebellion, to reinstall the sacked elders. Creeds are not the issue. They do not exist yet, nor is there any mention of heresy, immorality, or false teachings. Instead, it is a formula based on the example of the Roman army, which is held up as a model of efficiency. First Clement argues in favor of using the wisdom of such a military hierarchy to reinstate the elders to their rightful "chain of command" at Corinth. This recommendation comes only seventy years after that same army had dispatched its legions to execute Jesus.

By the third century, a document appears in Syria called the *Didascalia Apostolorum*, allegedly written by the original apostles. It "exalts the bishops to nearly absolute power over the laity and bestows on them something close to semi-divine status. It instructs laity that the bishop is 'your high priest, teacher, mediator and, next to God, your father, prince and governor. He is your mighty king . . . [He] has received from God power over life and death.'"[8] So much for "power to the people"; so much for the "priesthood of all believers"; so much for washing feet and referring to one another as "friends."

It got worse. Origin of Alexandria (185–254) warned people that they were required to obey even unjust bishops. Cyprian (d. 258) took the idea of Christian unity and claimed that it applied only to bishops, and this idea has lasted a very long time. "Not until the Second Vatican Council (1962–65) did the Roman Catholic

Church modify its language to refer to the whole church as the 'People of God.'"[9]

Now the stage was set for the final act of seduction. Christianity was about to become a parody of itself. The word *faith* would undergo a radical transformation that would permanently subvert the teachings of Jesus and the essence of the movement he founded. The command to "Go and *do* likewise" (loving God and neighbor) would be changed to "Go and *believe* as your bishops order you to believe." Trust *in* God would be replaced by assent to propositions *about* God, and the church would suffer the permanent damage.

Jesus Incorporated

Next to a Galilean sage from Nazareth, Flavius Valerius Constantine is arguably the most important man in the history of Christianity. His life story, however, could not be more different from the Nazarene healer and teller of parables. One was born in Macedonia to wealth and privilege and raised in a palace, the other to peasant parents in the shadow of scandal and obscurity. One's father was a Caesar; the other's father remains something of a mystery.

One watched the brutal execution of Christians as a young man; the other would never have heard the word "Christian," but would meet his demise on charges of blasphemy and then forgive his executioners. One was an ambitious young warrior turned military commander; the other taught and practiced nonviolence so completely that some questioned his sanity. One fought a crucial military battle against his rival and claimed years later that his victory was foreshadowed by the appearance of a cross in the sky; the other suffocated on just such a beam.

Constantine may have been the first emperor to fully grasp the political advantages of amalgamating and domesticating a former religious rival. He was shrewd enough to know that Christian charity could provide a needed social safety net in a city like Rome, with its rampant poverty. A lifelong polytheist, he was happy to believe in many gods, but on the battlefield he knew how to bet on the most powerful one—like any good Roman general. His admiration for Christian morality seems not to have affected his own personal moral choices much, considering that he was almost certainly responsible for the murder of both his son and his mother. Yet his "conversion" to Christianity is offered as proof of the saving power of God's love.

Was he a kind of born-again moment for the Empire, one that retooled a pagan realm into a godly kingdom, or the man who drove the final nail into the coffin of Christianity as The Way—a gentle, underground, nonpatriarchal movement that was quietly, mysteriously "corrupting" the Empire like leaven in the imperial loaf?

The truth is surely more complicated, less noble, and more pragmatic on all sides than any partisan talking head, whether on the left or the right, would have us believe. For one thing, the Romans knew that religion could help hold their far-flung Empire together. Christianity was the new kid on the block. It was growing, and Constantine needed something to take the place of older, declining faiths. He knew little about Christianity, and never took the long instruction for becoming a follower (the *catechumenate*) required of others. He also put off baptism until he was dying. But he knew the potential advantages to his administration. So, did he experience a true change of heart (like John Wesley's, was it "strangely warmed"?), or was he just a shrewd politician playing the God card?

We will never know, but we do know that when he chose to fuse the faith with the Empire and the age of persecution ended, a wave of expedient "conversions" swept over the masses. The cross, once an instrument that Rome used to torture Jesus, now decorated the shields of the soldiers who were the descendants of those same executioners. When Constantine's devout mother returned from a trip to the Holy Land bearing what she believed was a piece of the "true cross," this symbol became (and still remains) the central icon of the faith. It also became an item of high fashion among the upper classes.

As for the bishops, they must have been grateful just to have an emperor who wooed them instead of feeding them to the lions. What they did not realize, however, was that Constantine would declare himself to be the ruler of whole church. When he opened the coffers and started the flow of royal cash to support charity, build cathedrals, and support the clergy, the result was predictable. The clergy bellied up to the bar to get their share (or, better yet, a little more than their share), and all the gamesmanship that goes with the appropriation process followed. Every pastor knows this who has watched family members fight over their inheritance before the body of their loved one is even in the ground. Grief is no match for greed.

One thing is certain. Whenever the government begins to fund the church, it's the people who suffer. At precisely the moment in American church history when we *need* for conservatives to be true to their historic aversion to government interference in religion, we have exactly the opposite problem. So-called faith-based initiatives are allowing direct government funding of religious charities, and it is, paradoxically, religious liberals who are fighting back on the grounds of the separation of church and state.

This is one area where we should all come together as students of history. Look at what government funding of the church in Europe has done to Christianity. The state not only subsidizes churches that would otherwise die but also helps make them impotent by virtue of their dependence on public funds. Yet how can they possibly bite the hand that feeds them? Who dares to criticize the man who signs the checks?

In the early Jesus movement, only members contributed to their local congregation, as did some wealthy patrons. Sometimes one congregation would raise funds on behalf of another, as we know from Paul. But once Rome turned on the royal spigot, the bishops turned on one another. What better way to bring home the bacon than to make sure that those who controlled the purse strings had their favorite bishops?

Think of it as ecclesiastical pork. What better way to improve your odds at largess than to spread rumors about a rival bishop's character or the soundness of his views? Things got ugly in a hurry, and the unity that Constantine dreamed of deteriorated. Even the pagan majority got restless and cranky, complaining bitterly about the emperor's favoritism.

What had been minor disputes among the bishops suddenly grew into full-scale wars. Take, for example, the Arian controversy. What exactly were they arguing about? Essentially, the answer to this question: What is the *exact* relationship between Jesus and God? Was he *just* the Son of God, the divine logos, or was he *coeternal* with God? Arius, a brilliant priest from Alexandria, believed the former, claiming that there was a time "when Christ was not." This sounded wise to his friends, but it sounded like a demotion to his ambitious enemies. Because there is no fight like a church fight, all hell broke loose.

Constantine probably did not even understand the theological argument, but it threatened the unity of his Empire. His pleas to turn down the heat and keep what seemed like a "small and very insignificant" matter in perspective failed. He even suggested that perhaps the bishops had too much time on their hands or were acting in ways that were petty and unchristian. Nothing worked.

So Constantine decided to act like any good CEO and get everyone together in the same room until they agreed with him! We call it the Council of Nicaea, and it was the first assembly of all the bishops in the whole world. But this momentous gathering was not called by the clergy. The bishop of Rome did not arrange it. And it did not take place in a church, but rather at Constantine's own five-star lakeside compound at Nicaea. Needless to say, the host held all the cards. After all, who dares to offend one's host at such a lavish party? The church was about to realize exactly what it means to sell your soul to the Empire.

Think about it. Here was a man not baptized into the faith, who had no formal training and little interest in theology, and yet who hovered over the proceedings from start to finish. To read the descriptions of the elaborate processions that Constantine arranged, how the wine flowed and the feast was catered, is to imagine a kind of theological house party where no one leaves until everyone "gets it." To not get it would be almost rude, would it not?

Constantine's own theological adviser suggested that to solve the Arian controversy, the church should use the Greek word *homo-ousios* ("same substance") to describe the relationship of God to Jesus. A few bishops were not impressed, noting that the word does not appear in the Bible. Others just felt uncomfortable trying to wrestle the mystery of the incarnation to the ground, metaphorically speaking, to break its arm. But in the end, the whole scene overwhelmed the dissenters, and Constantine got most of the bishops to go along. Only Arius himself and two other bishops withheld their support. Guess what their reward was for thinking for themselves? Constantine promptly exiled Arius to the remote province of Illyricum, forgetting his own counsel to keep these "small and very insignificant" matters in perspective. The other two bishops were executed.

Then he announced that if any writings by Arius should be discovered, they were to be burned, or the "criminal" who refuses to do so shall be put to death immediately.[10] Having once referred to the Arian controversy as "too sublime and abstruse to be settled with any certainty," Constantine now turned one's position on the matter into a matter of life and death. Christians that once were once killed for refusing to bow down to the emperor could now be killed for refusing to accept his version of what a Christian should believe! It brings to mind the shortest passage of scripture in the Bible: *Jesus wept.*

The days that followed Constantine were dark, bloody, and increasingly corrupt. The bishops continued to argue among themselves, but could now deploy the power of the state against their theological enemies. According to Philip Jenkins, even violent monks attacked those they believed to be heretics. These "Jesus Wars" pitted Christians against other Christians, based on disagreements over the nature of the divinity of Christ. At the second council of Ephesus (491), during a theological debate, "a band of monks and soldiers took control of the meeting hall, forcing bishops to sign a blank paper on which the winning side later filled in its own favored statement. The document targeted the patriarch of Constantinople, Flavian, one of the three or four greatest clerics in the Christian world. Yelling 'Slaughter him!' a mob of monks attacked Flavian, beating him so badly that he died a few days later."[11] The whole bloody mess of a council would later be invalidated, given the name *Latrocinium*, or Gangster Synod.

Next, the Jesus Wars moved beyond the Arian controversy to the nature of Mary's relationship to God and Christ. More creeds, more schisms, more excommunications, more violence followed. Creeds had become the new purity laws of Christendom. Meanwhile, the voice of Jesus faded to black, especially his warnings about legalism and our obsession with being right instead of being loving: *Now you Pharisees clean the outside of the cup and of the dish, but inside you are full of greed and wickedness. . . . For you tithe mint and rue and herbs of all kinds, and neglect justice and the love of God; it is these you ought to have practiced* (Luke 11:39, 42).

The Age of Pretending

If the age that began with Constantine can rightly be called the Age of Belief, then what has happened in the last fifty years that makes some theologians believe we have entered the Age of the Spirit? If faith was so synonymous with correct belief that the words became interchangeable for fifteen hundred years, then what new definitions of faith are now emerging? It is still not uncommon when someone in the church recites with certainty what he or she "believes" (usually in the form of creeds or propositions about the nature and mission of Jesus), to hear that person praised as having "a strong faith."

Yet faith is not propositional. It is existential. Therefore, certainty and faith are not only not the same thing, but the former tends to render the latter unnecessary. Leander Keck said once, "When the possibility of doubt is gone, the possibility of faith is gone." A person who is certain about something is a person who needs no faith whatsoever. Some beliefs, in contrast, are more like opinions. We may not be absolutely certain about them, but we say we "believe" that such-and-such is true. In this case, the "belief" becomes a bridge between uncertainty and certainty. Neither of these approaches to faith has anything to do with faith as described by the earliest followers of Jesus.

Faith is a *verb* in the New Testament (*pistos*). It *acts* in spite of any possible certainty. Faith and love are much more primal than beliefs. In fact, we can "believe" something is true without it making any real difference to us, to our lives, or to our way of being in the world. Our faith, in contrast, is not something we argue about. It is something we make manifest in the way we live. In the Underground Church, one's service to the neighbor as a response to one's love of God will always be held in higher esteem than one's position on theological doctrines.

Or consider how the arguments have gone over the existence of God, with books written on both sides using reason to prove what is beyond the grasp of reason. A new generation of militant atheists has found it both easy and lucrative to knock down the religious straw man of their own creation. Many of us do not believe (and have never believed) in the cartoon God that Richard Dawkins, Christopher Hitchens, and others have created and then destroyed with self-satisfied glee. This is the problem with "beliefs." They are easy and cheap. They tempt us to idolatry. They play to our tribal tendencies. They satisfy the ego without moving the heart. Faith is a form of radical trust. It is an *imitation dei* (imitation of God), not a matter of *intellectus conformetur* (intellectual conformity).

If faith is nothing more than "beliefs," and beliefs are nothing more than giving intellectual assent to theological propositions, then we deserve the attack. As long as people outside the church confuse faith with beliefs, we will continue to be perceived as having nothing to offer intelligent and idealistic people who are looking for an authentic spiritual experience and a community of people who care.

Indeed, *beliefs* are the problem in the church, whether one is conservative or liberal. They are the swords we draw to defend our turf and circle the wagons. The religion of Jesus is not the same as the religious systems that were later created *about* Jesus. Yet most people today believe that "losing the faith" means questioning some of the things they have told they must "believe."

Meanwhile, the essential ingredients for the formation of a Beloved Community—like a sense of awe and wonder, the nurturing of an empathetic imagination, or finding ways to be opened minded, gracious, and generous—are considered secondary to the *identities* we claim that are primarily defined by acceptance or rejection of creeds and doctrines. This is true not just for conservatives, who put great emphasis on the inviolate nature of certain beliefs, but for liberals as well, who are often defined as much by what they do not believe as by what they do.

What matters to those who look to history for important lessons is that something was lost in the fourth century that permanently changed the nature of Christianity. If we do not recover that spirit of loyalty to the ethic of the Sermon on the Mount as opposed to saluting the Nicene Creed, the decline of the church will continue. If we persist in arguing across our theological divides in a perishing world, then the church deserves its fate. If we cannot reverse the move away from praxis and toward doctrine that was sealed by Constantine, the church will become, and deserves to become, the relic of another age.

The enduring lesson for the church is that it must never become entwined in the ways of Empire. It must never accept government funds to do its work. Once you are on the receiving end of a gift, your relationship to the giver changes. Constantine was just one of many who commandeered Christianity for his own personal ambitions, as leaders and politicians have been doing ever since.

The Jesus sect that was born as an alternative community within Judaism was later outlawed and then finally persecuted, was an annoyance that became a problem that became a threat. Then, in a move to unite the realm, it was given a seat at the table of power. The underground movement that was once deeply committed to nonviolence became a sanctifying force for endless war, supplying not only "Christian" soldiers but approval of what became "Christian wars." The "melancholy madness" of Jesus morphed into a muscular new religion of bishops, cathedrals built on the backs of the poor, rigid theological hierarchies, and all the abuse that goes with presuming to hold the keys to the kingdom while operating the only elevator out of hell.

It was post-Constantine theologians who gave us the doctrine of original sin (an inherited disease for which the institution that makes the diagnosis also claims to have the only cure) and the blood atonement, the belief that Jesus came to earth solely for the purpose of dying for our sins, a doctrine not fully developed in the church until the tenth century.

Both these ideas now separate conservatives and liberals in an unceasing stalemate. Are we born "bad" and must be "saved," as conservatives assert, or are we born "good," as liberals maintain, but have forgotten where we came from, where we are going, and to whom we belong? Was the death of Jesus on the cross necessary for the salvation of the world, or is this the ultimate form of Child abuse?

If we could somehow know the "right" answers to these things, would we then become people of faith, or just "true believers"— whether on the left or the right? In the end, what does any of this have to do with the true message of Jesus? Conservatives may be looking to extract from the Bible a formula for salvation while liberals search for eternal wisdom, but are either of those things the "Good News"? The late Peter Gomes, preacher to the Harvard community, may have hit the nail on the head with these words:

> The radical nature of the Jesus story is not in the way of his death—the *via dolorosa*—nor is it even in his glorious resurrection, to which we instinctively respond when strangers fill the churches on Easter. The radical dimension of the Jesus story has to do with the content of his preaching, the nature of the glad tidings that he announced to be at hand. It would take a miracle and a man of Mel Gibson's genius and chutzpah to make a film about what biblical writer Thomas D. Hanks calls the subversive gospel. This is the good news that was bad news to many in Jesus' time, so much so that at the beginning of his preaching they nearly killed him, and at the end of his ministry they succeeded.[12]

Until the *content* of the preaching of Jesus becomes the focus of the ministry of the church again—rather than arguments over the postbiblical formulations about the metaphysics of Christ—the church will go on fiddling while the world burns. The abiding lesson of Constantine is that the church must never be owned by anyone, or anything else. He believed that he could shore up his crumbling dominion by trading in the old gods, who seemed to be abandon-ing the realm, and replacing them with Christianity. The experiment not only failed to save the Empire but degraded Christianity almost beyond repair. Cox tells us, "From an energetic movement of faith it coagulated into a phalanx of required beliefs, thereby laying the foundation for every succeeding Christian fundamentalism for cen-turies to come."[13]

At a deeper level, perhaps the Age of Belief might be better called the Age of Pretending. Constantine did not move toward Christianity for the sake of personal transformation. He wanted the perceived benefits associated with it for his own agenda. Dozier says, "When he built churches and enacted laws favoring Christianity, what he sought was not the good will of Christians, but rather the good will of their God."[14] The result was an institution that became more and more obsessed with its own survival and enrichment. Bishops became part of an increasingly affluent segment of society, and they dressed resplendently. Incense, a sign of respect for the emperor, began to be used in worship. The church mirrored the hierarchical structure of the Empire until it became an Empire of its own.

This would all be little more than a footnote to church history if it were not for the fact that Christians today still live in an Empire. What's more, the Empire lives in us. Our interests may seem well served by such an arrangement, especially with regard to our tax-exempt status, our heroic embrace of warriors, or our blind and convoluted biblical defense of free-market capitalism. But something so vital has been lost as to render us almost indistinguishable from the dominant culture. The first followers of Jesus constituted a counter-cultural, even dangerous alternative to the status quo. Now the church is the primary defender of the status quo.

Stranger still, there is hardly any *offense* left in Christianity—even though it was once called the Great Offense. It is easy to become a member of a church, and easier still to opt out of all controversy by making certain that all teaching and preaching focuses on individual salvation or personal spirituality. In a world of injustice and violence, we insist that our preachers never confront our complicity in such a world. Never urge us to make sacrifices or withdraw our support from the very forces of death that beg the church for a blessing. As Dozier put it, "We live in the kingdom of the world and convince ourselves we are only doing it for the sake of the kingdom of God."[15]

The legacy of Constantine, and the compliant bishops who helped give away the soul of the church, truly constituted the third fall. This may sound like just a clever rhetorical device, but there is more wisdom here than cleverness. The third fall traces the broad outlines of our move from trusting God to playing God, from working to redeem life on this earth to our sole fixation with membership in the House of Heaven; from our joyful, oblivious embrace of equality and compassion to our partisan, self-serving ecclesiastical maneuvers. There really have been three "falls."

> First we human beings succumb to the temptation to be God, to know absolutely what is good and what is evil. [Second] Then we decide that the kingdoms of the world have more to offer than the kingdom of God. [Third] From there it is a short distance to proclaiming the kingdom of this world as the kingdom of God. For Constantine and his successors, the plan of God has been fulfilled. Beyond the present political order, all that Christians are to hope for is their own personal transference to the heavenly kingdom.[16]

Perhaps the greatest loss of all in the Age of Belief is that Christianity lost the voice of the people. They became increasingly passive in both worship and in the *doing* of theology. The architecture of cathedrals separated the prelates from the people, reversing the reunion that occurred symbolically in the death of Jesus when the curtain in the temple was torn in two. Theologians with all the power and the luxury of the pen set down the rules and intimidated those of lesser learning or stature. The idea that power corrupts and absolute power corrupts absolutely infected the body of Christ like a cancer.

When brave protest movements dared to challenge the status quo, as Jesus had done, those nonconformists were persecuted and killed. The Sabellians, Socinians, Ebionates, Erastians, Anabaptists, Antinomians, and countless others sought to follow Jesus, but their theology was deemed heretical and wrong. Their lack of "correctness" made them more dangerous than their loving service made them holy.

Ralph Waldo Emerson once said, "The religions we call false were once true." But the irony of this statement is that it can be reversed and still be true. The religions we call true were once false. In 1431, the church burned Joan of Arc at the stake as a heretic. In the twentieth century, she became a saint. What changed? Time not only heals all wounds but also makes us forget that our obsession with being right over fulfilling our promise to love is still the cardinal sin of Christianity.

Let's be honest. The church is no longer a company of outcasts. It is the epitome of decency and order. Most church people today recoil at the idea that they are in complicity with evil and recoil in the presence of anyone resembling a prophet. Just imagine how most mainstream Christians would react to the hot, blasphemous breath of Jesus—falling on our necks as it once did on the necks of the righteous? What good does it do to be first in line if God starts serving at the back of the line? Has anyone made it clear to Christians that there is something truly disturbing about the idea that the first shall be last and the last shall be first?

If confession is good for the soul, then conservatives and liberals alike should admit that our brokenness is more self-inflicted than fateful. We are tainted by pride more than we are redeemed by grace. We are more intoxicated by tribalism than we are committed to radical hospitality. Now we think nothing of asking what God can do for us, instead of asking what we can do for God.

Whether we are conservatives who confuse faith with certainty, or liberals who believe that knowledge alone is redemptive, the clarion call for our time is buried in a line from "Lift Every Voice and Sing," often called the "Negro National Anthem." James Weldon Johnson put his finger on the sickness of this and every age when he wrote in that stirring final stanza,

Keep us forever in the path we pray.
Lest our feet stray from the places, our God, where we met Thee,
Lest our hearts, drunk with the wine of the world, we forget
    Thee.

So begins our search for the way home. So begins this unblinking look at what made us different and dangerous to begin with. So begins our retreat from the precipice of irrelevancy. So begins the kind of shock therapy that may be required now to clear the mind and find a pulse in the body of Christ. The Old Testament prophets warned us long ago to stop substituting empty ritual for earthly justice if we expect the temple to last. Christians are certainly busy doing *something* on Sunday morning. But for all our eagerness to love God and neighbor, what effect have we really had on poverty, divorce, addiction, estrangement, greed, duplicity, arrogance, abandonment, paranoia, pettiness, cruelty, or the destruction of the environment?

Many are still living the myth of the Roman recipe (peace through strength) and once again trying to "purify" the church by demanding obedience to creeds instead of modeling discipleship.

The result is that we are being rightly abandoned by an entire generation of young people. In a recent survey, more than three-quarters of young churchgoers identified Christianity as judgmental, hypocritical, out of touch, insensitive, boring, and exclusive—the antithesis of love. Only 16 percent of those outside the church believe that Christianity "consistently shows love for other people."[17]

The most common way that this dissatisfaction is expressed is with the familiar lament that we "talk the talk, but do not walk the walk." Many young people whom I have spoken to are offended at the most basic level with the church's embrace of violence in all its forms. The world is soaked in blood, and the sanctuary offers no respite. The media tell us who the enemies are, but the church fails to remind us that we are to pray for them, not kill them.

No recovery of the church can begin without addressing the most obvious, the most hypocritical, and the most counterintuitive behavior of Christians today. We are followers of a God of nonviolent distributive justice, but we are practitioners of a God of violent partisan favoritism. We condemn the violence of others while excusing our acts of violence as "necessary for the greater good." We live and practice the fundamental myth of redemptive violence, but only when such violence is directed at our "enemies."

Perhaps it would help to imagine how we would respond if predator drones were circling above New York City and firing missiles at human targets as they walked through Times Square. Or if foreign contractors were roaming the streets of Detroit killing at will on suspicion of any threat, real or imagined. Or if Iran launched an invasion of the West Coast of the United States in response to the threat posed by Israel's "unofficial" nuclear weapons. What if we all watched it unfold on CNN, with bombs exploding at midnight over the city of San Francisco?

Double standards may be the signature of this and every Empire. But if we support such hypocrisy in the name of the Prince of Peace, then we have blood on our hands. Whether you call yourself a liberal or a conservative (or something in between), the real question has not been addressed. *Are you a Christian?* Is there anything you are willing to die for that is not related to natural resources or the purity of the gene pool?

Let's get real.

CHAPTER FOUR

❦

Onward Christian Soldiers?

Were you looking to be held together by lawyers?
Or by an agreement on paper? Or by arms?
Nay, nor the world, nor any living thing, will so cohere.
Only those who love each other shall become indivisible.
—WALT WHITMAN

During the run-up to the U.S. invasion of Iraq in 2003, the deafening silence from the majority of churches in North America was astonishing. Around the world, the largest antiwar demonstrations in human history had taken place, mostly organized and populated by people who did not consider themselves "religious," including many who did not hesitate to confess that they have given up on "organized religion" altogether. Yet there they were in the streets, by the tens of thousands. Most mainstream Christians, in contrast, were either quietly apprehensive or openly supportive of the war. One well-known televangelist made it clear that no antiwar demonstrators could possibly be Christians, because, as he put it, "God is pro-war."[1] This must come as quite a shock to theologians.

To put it mildly, something has gone terribly wrong. The argument that is made every Sunday in countless pulpits by religious and political conservatives is some variation of this: *Although we are called to be peaceful people, we must sometimes kill to protect innocent people and defend our freedoms through God-ordained wars. The Bible is full of examples where God is said to sanction war and even strengthen warriors. According to Revelation, Jesus will return to earth bearing a "sharp sword" smiting nations and ruling them* with a "rod of iron." Although we are called to love peace and to practice peace, sometimes that means going to war until Christ returns and all wars cease.

According to this logic, if war will not end until the Second Coming of Jesus (which is reputedly going to be a rather violent affair of its own), then what was the purpose of the first coming? If modern-day disciples can justify war as ordained by God, then why were so many of the first disciples pacifists? Did those first followers get it wrong? If not, then how did that first band of anti-imperial renegades who refused to wear the uniform of any army end up producing a religion that would one day be twisted to claim God's blessings on God's chosen wars for God's chosen people? These are perhaps the most difficult, complicated, agonizing questions in the life of faith: Is it possible to be a Christian and a soldier? Can violence ever be used to produce peace? Are there "good" wars, which must be fought? Does nonviolence as a practice actually encourage violence in others?

To make things even more complicated, the attitude in Western culture regarding war as an instrument of foreign policy makes life extremely difficult for those who are referred to pejoratively as "peaceniks." In a culture of Empire such as ours, anyone who argues that only nonviolence can ultimately bring lasting peace is often thought to be naïve, passive, even "effeminate." Indeed, sexual stereotypes and soldiering are deeply intertwined. Our definition of masculinity has become a marketing strategy for the recruitment of those whose job it is to wage war. Real men practice the family values of Empire, go on great crusades to protect threats to the homeland (real or imagined), and attach themselves to guns and gun ownership as a quasi-religious imperative.

Even the term nonviolence itself suffers from negative connotations of passivity. Just imagine that we translated light as "non-darkness" or good as "non-evil." The impression we are left with is that something is missing—such as worldliness, the capacity to be sensible and sane, or a sober recognition that because humans are

inherently violent (or acting under the power of Satan, to use conservative parlance), a "nonviolent" human is some kind of aberration. All of life, we are told in a thousand ways, is just one more
move on a battlefield. To live is to kill or be killed. Every transaction
is part of a zero-sum game in which someone wins and someone
loses and that settles it. Except that "it" is never settled.

All wars are fought to end all wars, but war never ends. The victor knows
his days are numbered, and the defeated (or their ancestors) dream
of revenge. This impulse knows no timeline, as long as the stories
are passed down and the hatred is nourished. Martin Luther King
Jr. had this in mind when he called violence a "downward spiral"
and insisted that nonviolence is neither impractical nor uncon-
cerned with results, only that "returning violence for violence
multiplies violence, adding deeper darkness to a night already
devoid of stars. Hate cannot drive out hate; only love can do that."[2]

Nothing brought this lesson home to Americans like the attacks
on 9/11. The enormous outpouring of sympathy from the world,
combined with the promise of the international community to help
find and prosecute those responsible for the horror of that bright
September morning, was no match for the purple rage of vengeance
that engulfed the nation. With scarcely a whimper from the church,
one war was launched and a second was already being planned.
While the nation was still in a state of shock, broad new powers
were given to the executive branch to put national security ahead
of time-honored civil liberties and the due process of law. Everything
changed, but not in a way that most people could fully appreciate
at the time. As Chalmers Johnson says,

> Americans like to say that the world changed as a result of the
> September 11, 2001, terrorist attacks on the World Trade Center and the
> Pentagon. It would be more accurate to say that the attacks produced a
> dangerous change in the thinking of some of our leaders, who began
> to see our republic as a genuine Empire, a new Rome, the greatest

colossus in history, no longer bound by international law, the concern of allies, or any constraints on its use of military force.[3]

Granted, those who argue that violence can sometimes serve a greater good—to stop a true tyrant or end genocide, for example—do make a compelling case. It's why the Catholic Church struggled to develop Just War theory, or "Christian realism." The operative premise is that war is to be avoided if at all possible, but that sometimes it can prevent greater harm. But the result has also been a slippery slope, where all wars, regardless of true motives or tactics, are said to be just and unavoidable. In the church, this has created a kind of moral schizophrenia.

How does one make room at the table for both the soldier and the conscientious objector? Does the idea of inclusion mean that all ideas and behaviors are given equal value? Is this not exactly the dreaded "moral relativism" that conservatives often complain about? This argument is often made about the issue of homosexuality, claiming that there is only one "Christian verdict" on the matter. But nobody seems to make the claim that there is only one "Christian verdict" on war.

The answer does not lie in churches that insist on checking a person's religious or political ID at the door. Our only hope for the renewal of the church is for the body of Christ to recognize that it *is not the Empire at worship*. It is not the Republican or Democratic Party at worship. It is not a collection of people who all look alike, drive the same kind of vehicle, sport the same bumper stickers, or divide creation into those who graduated from the right schools and those who, as the country western song says, have "friends in low places." When we fuse the church with the Empire, eliminating all distinctions between sacred and secular space, we silence the independent voice of the gospel.

One of the most obvious symbols of church-state collusion is the presence of the American flag prominently displayed in the front of most sanctuaries. Just ask any pastor what happens in most churches when someone (especially the pastor) argues that the symbol of a particular nation state should not be displayed in a house of prayer for all people. American exceptionalism is first and foremost a religious idea. If the flag is moved into another part of the church, such as into the fellowship hall or other meeting space where church governance is practiced, the complaint will be a "lack of patriotism." If it is left in the sanctuary, however, the church demonstrates not just favoritism but a form of civil religion, if not idolatry.

What most people do not realize is that the church has become a stepchild of the Empire. It has lost the independent voice it needs to make moral judgments. When the run-up to the next war occurs (as it certainly will), the voice of the church will once again be as fractured as the voice of the larger society. *We will have nothing distinctively Christian to say.* How does one speak truth to power when one party holds all the cards? How do we practice the radical nonviolence that gave birth to the church in a society that has institutionalized violence and glorified war?

With a few notable exceptions, pastors are afraid to take unpopular stands for fear of losing their jobs. Congregations, meanwhile, often erupt in anger when the word "pacifist" is applied to Jesus. Lately we have come to believe that *all* our military adventures are somehow sanctified because we are a Christian nation served by a man of God—therefore "our" God would never lead us astray. Both conservative and liberals fall victim to the illusion that we can easily tell our friends and enemies apart. But this is hardly the lesson of history.

Those on the left know that the record is uneven. Franklin Delano Roosevelt once ordered the internment of all Japanese Americans on the West Coast. President Clinton, who became an ambassador of goodwill after he left office, once engaged in the pathetic parsing of words to cover shameful sexual misconduct.

Lenin announced that "to achieve our ends, we will unite even with the Devil."

Those on the right have divided up the world into the good guys and the "evildoers," embracing dictators like Anastasio Somoza, Ferdinand Marcos, Augusto Pinochet, Jean-Claude Duvalier, Suharto, Hosni Mubarak, and the like as long as some greater good could be accomplished—like fighting communism, protecting free-market forces, or (most important) keeping the shipping lanes open for the oil tankers. The bitter lesson we *never* seem to learn is that today's friendly dictator is tomorrow's wicked tyrant. Again and again, we have assumed that the "enemy of our enemy is our friend," only to discover that we often can't tell them apart.

The church has lost its voice. It no longer has a clear, strong, self-possessed message shaped by the gospel. How does one criticize the state that grants tax exemption, protects the coveted clergy housing allowance, holds the purse strings for so-called faith-based initiative grants? How do you criticize a government that has the power to revoke your tax-exempt status if it determines that sermons have violated the separation of church and state? This is not just a problem for conservatives since the rise of the Moral Majority and voter guides pointing parishioners toward "God's candidates." Recently the IRS investigated All Saints' Episcopal church of Pasadena, California, because the former rector, Rev. George Regas, gave an antiwar sermon two days before the 2004 election. Even though he did not tell anyone how to vote, he delivered a blistering attack on the policies of the Bush administration, especially the war in Iraq. But isn't such speech protected by the First Amendment? The establishment clause of the constitution does not just protect the Empire from the church. It also protects the church from the Empire, so that we do not become its lapdog.

Former president Ronald Reagan established the prevailing military strategy of our time and called it "Peace Through Strength." But he also dreamed of eliminating all nuclear weapons from the face of the earth. Is that a conservative or liberal idea? The twentieth century was the most violent in human history, but some of its most successful movements were not. Nonviolence won the day in the civil rights movement, exposing the opposition as morally bankrupt. Police riots at the Democratic National Convention in Chicago in 1968, along with the killing of four unarmed students at Kent State, led to political changes and galvanized sentiment against the Vietnam War. Israel's policy of beating Palestinian protestors who sought an end to the occupation of the West Bank solidified the need for a negotiated settlement. In Tiananmen Square, a solitary man stood in front of a tank and came to symbolize the indomitable spirit of resistance to the brutality of a regime that slaughtered its own students.

So-called velvet revolutions have reshaped eastern European nations of the former Soviet Union, and the remarkable uprising of prodemocracy forces in Egypt in 2011 has displaced dictators and sparked a revolution across the Arab world. These movements succeeded because they were nonviolent, which made it more difficult for armies to justify attacking their own people. Indeed, nonviolent "people power" is ascendant throughout the world because human aspirations are everywhere the same. Indeed, if the goal is a genuine peace and a lasting "revolution," then the more violence, the less revolution. Hannah Arendt put it succinctly: "The practice of violence, like all action, changes the world. But the most probable change is to a more violent world."[4]

All this would seem like good news to Christians—those latter-day saints who have always been the bearers of "good news for the poor." "Out of Egypt I have called my son" and "Let my people go" ring in the ear of the faithful. "The arch of the moral universe is long," said Rev. King, "but it bends toward justice."[5] Yet the American church is not the dominant voice that amplifies or even prays for such movements. Nonviolent revolutions around the world are frightening and messy.

They are mixed up with the passions of the young. We fear any change that might threaten our way of life or be secretly engineered or exploited by religious radicals. So preachers by and large do not pledge their support for the insurgencies of the world (especially if they are directed at our forces of occupation). They pray for order and stability. They grieve the loss of American lives, instead of grieving the loss of all life.

They even perpetrate the myth that suicide bombers are individual fanatics dreaming of a heavenly reward, instead of voicing the more uncomfortable truth: *these are the final, desperate acts of hatred directed against military occupation.* They pray for peace, but what this really means is the resumption of the status quo. Peace becomes little more, as the Pentagon once described it, than "a state of permanent pre-hostility." They pray "Thy kingdom come," but what they really mean is "My kingdom stay."

My Kingdom Is Not of This World?

One of the most significant dividing lines between liberals and conservatives involves the tension between trying to repair this world and hoping to *escape* it to the next. Does Jesus matter to us here and now, or only later? Did he walk among us to change this world, or did he come to provide the perfect sacrifice for those who wish to leave it (and the unsaved) behind? Clearly the two cannot be completely separated: there are conservatives who care about social justice, liberals who believe in judgment and the afterlife. But the subject of apocalyptic movements has divided the church in ways that make us more accepting of violence, rather than more determined to join forces to reject it.

What is fascinating about apocalyptic movements, however, is that end-times fever rises or falls based on the present quality of life. The more desperate and hopeless people feel, the more appealing it is for them to "depart" this world. The better off we are, the more affluent, the more hopeful, the more stable, the less we long for a heavenly rescue. In other words, those in agony will take the first available train leaving the station, while the prosperous and the contented apply for tenure.

What matters to the future of the church is not for us to take bets on when or how the world will end. Rather, it is to become a force for the salvation of the only world we have. Instead of arguing about the end of history, why don't we study our own history more carefully and recover our own nonviolent roots? If we are going to have a "personal" relationship with Jesus, then we ought to know what might actually happen to us as a result of the company we keep.

The foremost historical Jesus scholar alive today, John Dominic Crossan, gives a single, powerful example of the nonviolence of Jesus. In what he calls a "magnificently parabolic scene" in John's gospel, Pilate confronts Jesus about the kingdom of God. "My kingdom" (replies Jesus in the King James Version), "is not of this world: if my kingdom were of this world, then would my servants fight, that I should not be delivered to the Jews: but now is my kingdom not from hence" (18:36 KJV).

Crossan draws five foundational insights from this single event. First, that Jesus does indeed make a distinction between the kingdom of God and the kingdoms of "this world." This difference is still painfully obvious to anyone who is paying attention. Second, Jesus is "condemned to death by Pilate, who is Roman, in Roman Judea, in the eastern reaches of the Roman Empire. But he never mentions Rome as such, and he never addresses Pilate by name. Third, had Jesus stopped after saying that 'my kingdom is not of this world,' as we so often do in quoting him, that 'of' would be utterly ambiguous." Crossan goes on:

> "Not of this world" could mean: never on earth, but always in heaven; or not now in present time, but off in the imminent or distant future;

or not a matter of the exterior world, but of the interior life alone. Jesus spoils all of these possible misinterpretations by continuing with this: "if my kingdom were of this world, then would my servants fight, that I should not be delivered" up to execution. Your soldiers hold me, Pilate, but my companions will not attack you even to save me from death. Your Roman Empire, Pilate, is based on the injustice of violence, but my divine kingdom is based on the justice of nonviolence.[6]

Fourth, Crossan argues that the crucial difference between the kingdom of God and the kingdom of Rome is that one is nonviolent and the other is not. "This world" refers to the violent normalcy of civilization itself under Roman rule in the first century—to the way things got done and life is ordered. Fifth, Crossan argues that Pilate is the most important interpreter of Jesus in the entire New Testament. He knows the difference between Barabbas and Jesus. As Crossan points out, "Barabbas is a violent revolutionary who 'was in prison with the rebels who had committed murder during the insurrection' (Mark 15:7). Pilate arrested Barabbas along with those of his followers he could capture. But Jesus is a non-violent revolutionary, so Pilate has made no attempt to round up his companions. Both Barabbas and Jesus oppose Roman injustice in the Jewish homeland, but Pilate knows exactly and correctly how to calibrate their divergent oppositions."[7]

Again this might seem like just one more theological argument in the ongoing culture wars. But for all Christians now living in the American Empire (the *Pax Americana*), these questions do not go away regardless of whether you belong to a conservative church, a liberal church, or no faith community at all. The Roman Empire crucified our Lord. How then are we to be faithful followers when we have gotten so cozy with, and in some cases appear to be indistinguishable from, what we could call the "New Roman Empire"? Is the Bible we champion a violent document or a nonviolent one? And perhaps most important of all: *Does the dominant theology of the church, so* focused on the blood atonement, actually encourage and sanctify imperial violence in a "Christian" nation?

It is not just liberals who have cast off old ways of thinking about these things. Some evangelicals and practitioners of the so-called emergent tradition seem open to the possibility that the blood atonement is not a doctrine that must be embraced by all Christians. Is it the biblical plan of salvation, or is it the inevitable result of the marriage of the church to an Empire that worshiped the redemptive power of violence? No one doubts that in the time of Jesus, the Jewish sacrifice syndrome depended on the belief that the shedding of innocent blood could "atone" for sins and reset (wash clean) one's relationship to God. Likewise, for generations the faithful had practiced the ritual of collective atonement in which the sins of a whole community were symbolically heaped on a scapegoat and then driven out of town. But the first followers of Jesus stopped practicing animal sacrifice altogether, in part because they believed that no further "sacrifices" were necessary.

Countless modern Christians have just assumed that the first followers saw the death of the "Lamb of God" as required by God, making his death the predetermined purpose of his life. But those who first experienced the risen Jesus and called him the Christ responded by doing something both countercultural and danger-ous. Rome encouraged the practice of local religious rituals as long as it did not threaten law and order. The sacrificial practices of a client state under occupation were seen as a kind of safety value, shifting attention away from the brutality of the realm and giving comfort to the masses.

So when those first Jesus People stopped practicing animal sacrifice, they put themselves and their movement at risk. Their Lord had gone nonviolently to his own death. His disciples believed that God had raised him from the dead. The "risen" message he brought was "peace." Therefore, the nature and will of the God that is both revealed and vindicated by the resurrection is one of nonviolent distributive justice. Easter is not a transaction for sin but a revelation about God. This God does not *want* sacrifice or empty ritual. This God is the unconditional lover of all creation.

It is no coincidence that it took as long for the idea of the blood atonement to be fully formed as it took for Christian artists to begin to show us an image of the corpse of Jesus hanging on a cross. This icon of suffering and death, so central to Western Christianity, is absent from the art of the church for a thousand years. Why? Because the church considered itself to be *paradise restored* (and restoring) on earth. The only images to be found in the catacombs or in ancient churches were scenes from the Bible, Jesus as a young shepherd boy, or the four life-giving streams of water (Pishon, Gihon, Tigris, and Euphrates) flowing from the throne of God into an earthly garden whose glorious fertility depicts what was lost in the Fall. These images depict life, abundance, peace, and heaven coming down to earth—but no crucifixes. *No dead Jesus for a thousand years.* This is not to say that the suffering of Jesus is unimportant; indeed it bears witness to the depth of his capacity to love. But the church celebrated the living Christ, which brings to mind the words of Luke: "Why do you look for the living among the dead?"

If we are going to look to the past to learn lessons about how to renew the church in the future, then this discovery should be as startling as it is hopeful. Early Christians did not think of heaven or paradise just as something beyond this life. It was, first and foremost, in this world. It is made possible by the spirit of God that permeates those at worship, who glimpse paradise around the communion table. In the Beloved Community, they practiced hospitality and generosity on behalf of the well-being of all the "saints." Early Christian art makes this fantastically clear. The earliest images are of paradise restored and Jesus as the new ruler in place of Caesar. In glorious scenes of lush abundance, humanity is liberated from oppression beneath a dome of stars in the midnight sky. The images of the departed saints are everywhere, in purple robes of nobility or white robes of baptism. They wear wreaths of victory on their heads while bars of streaming golden sunlight fall from heaven on verdant meadows. Paradise was the dominant image of the early church.

Again, we are concerned with more than just art history here. If the early followers of Jesus considered themselves to be resident aliens who gathered to worship in places where they could glimpse paradise restored, then what does this mean for the church of the future? If nonviolent distributive justice was the response of the first Jesus People, then where are the resident aliens in our time? Why did we change both our theological priorities and our earthly practices?

Most of us have been taught to understand Christianity as right belief (orthodoxy), and the history of the church as the unfolding story of the search for and defense of that "truth." Hence the ecclesiastical debates, the holy wars, the endless fracturing of the body of Christ into a million pieces—it has mostly been the result of our disagreements. In short, we have been more concerned with being right than with being loving.

But what if the essence of the Underground Church is to proclaim that Christianity is primarily about the creation, expression, and practice of redemptive communities that see the life, death, and resurrection of Jesus of Nazareth as the anti-imperial restoration of paradise? What would we be left to argue about that could possibly be more important than the love and compassion we are called to embody? What disagreements between liberals and conservatives could possibly keep us from working together to heal a broken world?

These are the questions that will dominate the rest of this book. But first we must begin with confession. We are a violent, violent people. What's worse, when we look at the church, we often don't see anything but the violent status quo in search of divine sanction. When a born-again president refers to an invasion as a "crusade";

when Christians describe the hanging of Saddam Hussein as "awesome" and as a "mighty victory for God"; when millions flock to see a movie like Mel Gibson's *The Passion of Christ*, taking children as young as twelve to see a film rated R for violence, we have made a statement to the world about what we think the gospel is all about.

The singular and extensive focus in that film is the graphic violence of the crucifixion. Like the pornographic addiction to violence in our culture at large, it not only distorts the mission and message of Jesus but also further erodes the church's credibility. Most dangerous of all, however, is the divine sanction that the film gives to violence itself as a means to an end. The message is that God engineers some violence in order to accomplish what only pain can gain us. In other words, *violence is redemptive*. Violence *saves*.

Students of history know all too well how this idea has added to the bloody tides of history. The heresy killings, required to restore "honor" to the institution; multiple crusades and inquisitions; the slaughter of countless pagans, including children, witches, native people, political enemies—it all adds up to this irrefutable fact: *Christians have killed more people for religious reasons* (or for cultural ones masquerading as religion) *than anyone else*. It does not matter if you are a liberal or a conservative, a true believer or an infidel—this historical reality belongs to all of us. As we conduct the "global war on terror," we must all remember how much terror has been rained down by those who conquered and murdered in the name of the Prince of Peace. Paschal was right when he said that "men never do evil so completely and cheerfully as when they do it from religious conviction."

What's more, no other single fact has led so many to turn against organized religion. Watching the left and the right parse the meaning of the commandment "Thou shalt not kill," for example, to mean "murder" or "only in self-defense" or "to defeat the enemy" or "to end the suffering of an animal (or even a human) that is terminally ill and in great pain," often does more harm to the integrity of faith than simply admitting: we are lost. We fall so far short of what Gandhi called *ahimsa*, what early Christians called *agape*, what Albert Schweitzer called *reverence for life*, that to find our way back we must begin with confession and end with a clarion call to *be dependably different* in the world. In short, the church should be, first and foremost, *a nonviolent community standing against the unchallenged and acceptable violence of the Empire.*

Immediately, of course, we face a serious objection. We must begin by admitting that the Bible itself is often violent and that the God of the Bible is often the one who either commands violence or endorses it. This is part of the story, but it is not the whole story. Besides, in the end it is not the Bible that we worship. As Brian McLaren reminds us, the Bible is a library, not a constitution. The mystery to which this epic and uneven narrative points us is the object of our worship, if indeed "object" is the right word. All worship should begin in wonder and end in humility. But too often it begins with idolatry and ends in violence.

The Evolution of God

Richard Dawkins, a militant atheist from Oxford, has made quite a name (and a lot of money) for himself with his contention that religion is the most dangerous force on the planet. What's more, he wants everyone to know that all religious practitioners are the most ignorant, pathetic members of the human family. He once sent out this very clever message to his Christian "friends" in America to promote a magazine called *Free Inquiry.* A portion is included here, complete with British spelling.

> Dear Friend,
> If you live in America, the chances are good that your next door
> neighbours believe the following: the Inventor of the laws of physics
> and Programmer of the DNA code decided to enter the uterus of a

Jewish virgin, got himself born, then deliberately had himself
tortured and executed because he couldn't think of a better way to
forgive the theft of an apple, committed at the instigation of a talking
snake. As Creator of the majestically expanding universe, he not
only understands relativistic gravity and quantum mechanics but
actually *designed* them. Yet what he really cares about is "sin," abortion,
how often you go to church, and whether gay people should marry.
Statistically, the chances are that your neighbours believe all that—and
they can vote.

In other parts of the world, there is a good chance that your
neighbours believe you should be beheaded if you draw a cartoon of a
desert warlord who copulated with a child and flew into the sky on a
winged horse. In other places, there's a good chance that your
neighbors think their wishes will be granted if they pray to a human
figure with an elephant's trunk.

Even if your neighbours don't hold any of those mutually
contradictory beliefs, they probably take it for granted that we should
unquestioningly respect those who do. And the huge majority of
American and British newspapers and periodicals go along with this
abject kow-towing to what their educated editorial staff must know, in
their heart of hearts, is nonsense.[8]

Where to begin? First, by extending to Dawkins the "unques-
tioning respect" that he would deny to all the idiots he sees around
him. Second, by reminding him that it wasn't an apple and it wasn't
stolen. Third, to ask if they still teach metaphor at Oxford. How
about symbolism? Or better yet, the meaning of myth?

There are, of course, all kinds of people who have given religion a bad name, more by what they *do* than by what they believe.
The easiest way to dismiss anyone in the world is to argue that what
he or she believes is nonsense. And because all kinds of people
believe all kinds of nonsense (Dawkins has surely heard that some
people think the monarchy is nonsense), it is cheap, easy, and lucrative sport to make a kind of cosmic seating chart based on intellectual prowess. Blessed are the very smart people, for they shall

inherit the earth. In a way strangely identical to those he fears, Dawkins divides the world into the good guys (hyperintellectual snobs) and the "evildoers" (superstitious religious fanatics).

It might come as a surprise to Dawkins to learn that there are people who have given their life to the idea of faith and to the importance of faith communities who are not fanatics. Yet neither do we find it either adequate or realistic to believe only in that which can be weighed, measured, and observed. We do not find the infinite and mysterious nature of the universe to be dignified only by grand abstractions, but also by the most mundane and concrete discussions about how humans should actually behave, make choices, and live in relationship to one another.

It is also strange, and more than a little disconcerting, to hear someone foster more fear and loathing for the neighbor. Instead of encouraging us to love the neighbor despite our differences (not to mention praying for the enemy next door), Dawkins urges us to pity the idiot living next door. Worse still, we are reminded that this mistake of creation can vote. What's more, we should assume that the most violent and fanatical elements of Islam represent all of Islam. Look with disgust, Dawkins urges, upon those faith traditions you know nothing about, and judge their adherents as both fanatic and simpleminded. And by all means, Dawkins urges us, do not participate in the media's conspiracy of legitimacy, as open hostility and insults will surely bring us closer together. Indeed, he seems to be saying that we should go deeper into the chasm that separates the human family by first making a cartoon out of the "other" and then concluding that the "other" is indeed a caricature.

It is not news that the Bible is both the most powerful and the most misunderstood collection of writings in the world. Or that it is the most purchased and revered but least read or seriously studied book in the world. Yet without knowledge of the Bible, one cannot be considered literate. Young people watch classic movies and fail to realize that even the titles are direct quotations from scripture: *Lilies of the Field* (Matt. 6:28), *Inherit the Wind* (Prov. 11:29), and *Through a Glass Darkly* (1 Cor. 13:12). Most people have heard of the Ten Commandments, where the connection is obvious, but miss the biblical basis for films like Steinbeck's *East of Eden* or Connelly's *Four Horsemen of the Apocalypse*. Many contemporary films are likewise built on biblical themes, although in ways that may be less obvious without basic biblical literacy: *The Truman Show, The Green Mile, Pulp Fiction, The Apostle, The Shawshank Redemption,* and *The Silence of the Lambs* and its sequel *Hannibal,* just to mention a few.

When we say "for crying out loud," we refer to Jesus on the cross. When we offer an "olive branch" for peace, we are remembering the story of Noah.[9] But there is another, more serious problem with biblical illiteracy. The Bible can be selectively used to justify violence and oppression against the very human beings that the biblical prophets, including Jesus, wished to free. From start to finish, there is both a *micro* and a *macro* message in scripture. Individual passages cannot be said to speak for the whole arc of the Bible, which evolves toward justice and mercy. We should judge the scriptures by Jesus, not Jesus by the scriptures.

It begins in Genesis with both accounts of creation, and moves immediately to paradise spoiled by the sin and the first murder. The epic stories of the patriarchs gave us the Torah, the defining law of Moses that interprets all things Jewish. There are "former prophets" who stretch the story between the death of Moses and the Exile, and then "latter prophets" and finally "writing prophets," who redefined Judaism by speaking unpleasant truth to the power. They were the *conscience* of Israel, and they dispel the myth that Judaism is all about legalism and ritual purity. Isaiah, Jeremiah, Amos, and Micah all composed stunningly beautiful visions of the covenant restored and the coming reign of justice.

Those Jewish prophets redefined the meaning of religion, excoriated those who went through the ritual motions of faith but lacked simple compassion. They pushed the children of Israel to escape tribal limitations in thought and action, and brought down barriers between Jews as the chosen people and everyone else. But to say that the Bible is a mixed blessing is an understatement. Its pages are littered with a partisan God who does special favors for his favorite children by splitting the Red Sea (imagine how the mother of an Egyptian soldier would hear that story, for example) and dropping bread from heaven to feed the chosen while the enemies of God are the victims of horrific plagues.

It has all the marks of a history written by the winners, including the myth that the Promised Land was not already inhabited or that God had "deeded" portions of it in the divine will, by having already allowed their ancestors to live on it hundreds of years earlier. God is apparently in the land grant business, and moonlights as an assassin. How strange that in the poetry of Genesis, God creates the world and calls it all "good," but then gets petitioned constantly to bless the slaughter of one part of that creation in order to assist with the ambitions of another!

Did God change? Or did our understanding of God *evolve* over the centuries? One thing is certain: *all the good stuff did not begin with Jesus.* The Jew from Nazareth stands in a long line of remarkable Jewish prophets who saw, as John Shelby Spong tells us, "love as the primary nature of God, saw social justice as the goal of God and saw the necessity of having the covenant marked not with power images exclusively but with their responsibility to do justice, to love mercy and to walk humbly with their God."[10]

Minority voices were already questioning conventional religious wisdom, asking, Why do the righteous suffer? Why is the world not fair? The "comforters" of Job assumed that all his calamities were the result of secret sins for which God was punishing him. They urged him to confess and call God off. But he refused, and his voice brought us a new understanding of God—beyond Lawgiver and Judge and toward a mystery that deserves radical trust.

The larger point is that we are the ones who are evolving. A local storm god at Sinai is not the deity that can bring humanity together. Whenever God is thought to be a *partisan*, a deity working on behalf of a particular people or party, religion turns dark quickly. The innocents must die because God wills it as a means to an end. Women can take a backseat to men because we continue to fear and mistrust them. Jonah must not preach to the Arabs of Nineveh, or they will repent and receive God's mercy also. A Moabite woman named Ruth cannot marry Boaz and give birth to the father of King David because this pollutes the gene pool.

Fortunately, none of this is God's last word, because, as we like to say in the United Church of Christ, "God is still speaking." Over time, voices of inclusion were heard alongside voices of tribalism. In the wonderful tradition of *Midrash*, God continues to speak in new ways that evolve along with human understanding. Fred Craddock, renowned professor of homiletics, used to teach his students this rabbinical saying: "An hour of study in the sight of the Holy One (blessed be He) is as an hour of prayer." In both the head and the heart, a new vision of God was evolving—one who loves all humanity and welcomes all people.

When Jesus came along, gathered disciples, announced the reign of God, healed the sick, and taught in parables, the evolution of our understanding of God continued. Because he wrote nothing down, all we know about him comes from the writing of Paul, his imitators, and other epistle writers, followed by the gospels and the acts of the apostles—written decades after his death, and not by eyewitnesses. This is disturbing to many conservatives who would rather think of the New Testament as a largely historical account. To many liberals, such writings become pure fiction. Neither position captures the essential message of the gospels as portraits created by and lived out in community.

One of the most important ways for the church of the future to talk across its vast theological and political differences is to shift the focus away from our usual debates over how historically accurate are the recorded sayings of Jesus (and therefore what they really mean with regard to his divinity). We should focus instead on what it means that particular communities with particular problems were determined to preserve both the memory and the message of Jesus in order to inspire and influence the way his followers should actually behave. Their unity came not from a list of identical beliefs but from a united, anti-imperial, underground set of behaviors that set them apart from "this world." At the top of the list: they would do no harm where harm could be avoided.

Blessed Are the Peacemakers

That's the motto my grandmother had stitched and framed and hanging on her wall—one of those noble devotional sentiments known as the Beatitudes. But she and I never discussed how one actually goes about becoming a peacemaker, or whether there is anything dangerous about it. We liked the idea, and we left it at that. Meanwhile, the world went right on turning as it always has. The strong robbed the weak and called it business. The weak feared the strong and called it life.

When the twentieth century dawned, there was great hope among some that humankind was in the process of evolving beyond war. Some even called it "the Christian Century," and that became the hopeful name of a progressive magazine. Not only did war not cease, but the technology of killing advanced to the point where all life can now be destroyed in a nuclear holocaust. Our existential reality is beyond denial. We live in a world in which we can destroy what we did not create and snuff out the future that we have borrowed from our children. Hence, the practice of nonviolence is no longer just the optional pastime of religious eccentrics. It is our only hope.

As a young man, Leo Tolstoy served in the Russian army during the Crimean War. But in his later life, he decided to take the commandment "Thou shalt not kill" seriously and reject so-called Christian realism. Just War theory was a slippery slope, he believed, so he became a kind of principled anarchist, opposing not only all participation in war but also the workings of government, which serve to institutionalize violence and glorify it. He too, like Constantine, was hailed as the "thirteenth apostle," but for exactly the opposite reason. He saw the marriage of church and state as having produced the bastard child of endless war. A Christian cannot kill, period.

To say the least, Western Christianity honors Constantine, not Tolstoy. The media industry devoted to glorifying war and hallowing soldiers is omnipresent—especially now that we have an all-volunteer army, and war is outsourced like everything else. Unlike the first followers of Jesus, those who oppose war today are immediately accused of not supporting our "brave men and women in uniform." They are seen not as true conscientious objectors but as ungrateful and unpatriotic. We live by the convenient false dichotomy (testified to by countless bumper stickers) that support for soldiers is inseparable from support for the war they are fighting. Indeed, even in the church, we seem unable to explain why opposition to war is the best way to support soldiers.

Perhaps even more insidious is the manner in which we now kill. A man can leave his wife and children in the suburbs, drive to an undisclosed location, and enter codes into a computer that will unleash laser-guided bombs from unmanned predator drones. They will strike "targets" that he will never see, pulverize houses that are invisible and in which he has never been served tea, and scatter the torn flesh of children over a field he has never walked on.

After this mission is completed, he will join his friends for lunch or perhaps play a round of golf in the afternoon. Then he will head home, where there may be a Bible prominently displayed on the coffee table. He will delight in seeing his own children home from school, and knows no higher obligation than protecting them and providing for them. On Sunday he will drop them off at church, concerned for their moral development. If he decides to stay for the service, he may hear a message from the Sermon on the Mount— something about praying for our enemies and those who persecute us. So many of us attend church to look respectable that we fail to anticipate anything resembling disorientation. To quote Albert Camus, "We gain in cleanliness, but lose in understanding."

Here then is the Grand Canyon, so to speak, that separates liberals and conservatives. To a conservative, the antiwar activist is hopelessly naïve. The world is a dangerous place and sometimes requires violence or the threat of violence to keep the peace. Liberals, in contrast, insist that the empathic imagination requires that we become the person we are killing and break the endless cycle and futility of war by taking risks for peace. Conservatives quote Chamberlain as a warning against appeasement. Liberals quote Gandhi: "An eye for an eye makes the whole world blind." Even at the church coffee hour, the house is divided.

What remains unresolved in this standoff is not whether there is a valid argument on both sides but whether or not there is a Christian response to violence that transcends individual opinion. If not, then we have agreed to make the message of Jesus infinitely malleable. Each camp hunkers down in mutual suspicion and misunderstanding, and by default the church allows the partisan politics of war and peace to supplant the politics of the gospel. We know that it is polite to allow everyone to have an opinion, and to respect it. But being a person of grace and tolerance is not the same thing as believing that all ideas are created equal. One can make a convincing argument using the scriptures we have that Jesus of Nazareth was a pacifist. To argue the opposite, that he understood violence as sometimes redemptive and war as sometimes unavoidable, requires an argument that directly *contradicts* the words attributed to him in the Bible.

In a world saturated with violence, there is a choice we all must make, conservative and liberals alike. Do we add divine sanction to violence, or do we respond consistently as faith communities to mitigate the ways of death everywhere in the world? Can we, despite our differences on specific issues, live a more consistently nonviolent vision? If we take seriously the words from Deuteronomy, "Choose life so that you and your descendants may live," does this apply only to the issue of abortion? Or also to wars of choice, to violent video games, to the violence that is perpetrated against women and children in a patriarchal society? Does it apply to all forms of violence that can result from situations in which some have power and others do not? Does it apply to our treatment of gays, of immigrants, of our Muslim sisters and brothers in a time of fear? Does it apply to violence against the earth?

Can these forms of violence, most often critiqued by progressive Christians, coexist with more traditional conservative views on abortion and illegal immigration? Perhaps the ultimate pacifism is to do no harm where harm can be avoided, regardless of what one's particular position on these issues may be. Can we give each other enough space and respect in the body of Christ to work together to reduce the scourge of violence in our society? The violence that conservatives wish to illuminate in abortion cannot then be ignored or sanitized on the battlefield. Our "culture of death" is pervasive and is not just limited to certain hot-button issues.

The Underground Church of the future must be unmistakably committed to nonviolence even if there are internal arguments about how this commitment is to be lived out. At the very least, we must move beyond the notion that pacifism is a form of weakness whereas militant realism is a sign of strength. Gandhi's commitment to *ahimsa* did not mean meek submission to the will of the evildoer, but just the opposite. One was to pit one's whole soul against the will of the tyrant, and that means that even a single individual can defy the Empire. Far from weakness or cowardliness, the practice of what Gandhi called *tapasya*, which is a willingness to suffer oneself and not to shift that suffering to another, including the opponent, takes great strength.

Diana Butler Bass recalls her visit once to St. Martin-in-the-Fields Episcopal Church in Philadelphia, where she gazed upon an extraordinary stained-glass window containing a long-forgotten message. It depicts a man sheltering someone in his cloak. It illustrates the beautiful, radically Christian practice of hospitality, but the message goes deeper. The figure in the window is St. Martin, who converted to Christ while a soldier. One day, while he was guarding the city of Amiens, he met a naked beggar on the road. Although he was not yet a baptized Christian, he took off his cloak, tore it in half, and covered the beggar—a practice commanded in the Sermon on the Mount.

The next night, Jesus appeared to Martin in a dream, thanking him for this simple act, which was spiritually equivalent to covering Jesus himself with the garment. As often happens, the garment itself became the stuff of legend and was rumored to have miraculous power. But the most miraculous point of all was missed. When Martin was eventually baptized, he asked to be released from the army. "I am Christ's soldier," he maintained; "I am not allowed to fight."[11]

Today we might think of him as a conscientious objector. But he was simply following early Christian practice. Before the fourth century and the rise of so-called Just War theory, Christians were not allowed to be soldiers in anyone's army. As Butler Bass puts it, "The strong consensus of the early church teachers was that war meant killing, killing was murder, and murder was wrong."[12]

A long list of church fathers, including Justin Martyr, Irenaeus, Hippolytus, Tertullian, and Origen, all specifically condemned participation in war. So-called peace churches—such as the Church of the Brethren; Mennonites, including the Amish; and the Religious

Society of Friends, or Quakers—have been committed to nonviolence ever since and continue to this day. Often they are considered
to be out of touch with mainstream Christianity. But they do not
see it that way. Indeed, it would seem unfaithful to these communities to do anything unnecessarily violent in the name of the Lord.

Christians distinguished themselves from the rest of the Empire
by their self-sacrificing commitment to nonviolence. Today the situation is completely reversed. In mainstream Christianity, being a
conscientious objector is considered optional and is often viewed
with suspicion, if not contempt. Exactly the opposite response
comes from clergy and laity alike when a member of the congregation is a Christian soldier "marching as to war." He or she is not
only considered worthy of immediate and unqualified praise but is
sent forth with prayers and petitions for special protection.

The first followers of Jesus could not be soldiers for a second
reason, as Butler Bass points out. They believed that the gospel
forbade them from performing acts of worship to the state, the
gods, and the emperor. They saw being a soldier as requiring actions
that constituted idolatry. After all, the Empire was murdering
Christians (among others), and Tertullian pointed out that their
tokens of victory, especially the crown of laurel leaves, symbolized
death, and the spoils made possible at the expense of other human
beings. "Is the laurel of the triumph made of leaves, or of corpses?
Is it adorned with ribbons, or with tombs? Is it bedewed with oint-
ments, or with the tears of wives and mothers?"[13]

Scholars are now united in this important finding: for at least
two centuries, once a Christian was baptized, he could no longer
consider military service. Just imagine a baptismal ceremony today
that included language prohibiting the initiate from ever enlisting
in the armed forces. Imagine being immersed, lifted out of the
water, and pronounced a pacifist for life. Imagine that this was not
just a sacrament for the "remission of sins" but for the "renouncing
of violence." Imagine being warned against baptism as an irreversible step that would make it impossible for you to ever be one of

"the few, the proud, the Marines." That would be the unmistakable mark of the Underground Church.

In the landscape of Christianity today, we regard the Quakers and Mennonites as quaint appendages to the body of Christ. But in this respect, at least, they are the ones who have it exactly right. Nonviolence is not optional for Christians. It is essential. There will be no recovery of Christianity as a vital and transformative force in the West without a return to our pacifist roots. *This is the first and most important characteristic of the Underground Church.* It is a principle of origin, a founding characteristic, and the essential recovery of a sacred tradition—as unmistakable and nonnegotiable as it is profoundly subversive.

We insult the gospel and a cloud of witnesses when we act as if violence can be a negotiable article of faith. When violence of any kind is anything other than a last resort (and even then with the certain knowledge that the gospel has been compromised), we give aid and comfort to the death-dealing ways of the Empire. When modern Christians are among the most vocal of warmongers, and God is called on to sanctify our wars, the critics of the church are handed their best argument.

A second argument against the church, nearly as strong, requires that we reexamine the meaning of one of the most important words in our religious vocabulary. When we say the word "faith," most people hear the word "beliefs." Then it is open season on whether those "beliefs" are true or false or even plausible. In the Underground Church, however, we will seek to recover faith as a verb and reject it as a noun. A person of strong faith will not be confused with a person who is absolutely certain about the answer to all religious questions. On the contrary, she will be the manifestation of something much more mysterious and compelling: radically embodied trust.

To this new definition of faith, which is really the recovery of something very old, we now turn.

CHAPTER FIVE

Faith as Radically Embodied Trust

Faith is a terribly caustic substance, a burning acid. It puts to test every element of my life and society; it spares nothing. It leads me ineluctably to question my certitudes, all my moralities, beliefs and policies. It forbids me to attach ultimate significance to any expression of human activity. It detaches and delivers me from money and the family, from my job and my knowledge. It's the surest road to realizing that "the only thing I know is that I don't know anything."

—JACQUES ELLUL

Faith may be the most misunderstood word in our religious vocabulary. Without careful consideration of its use in the New Testament as a form of trustworthy action (*pistos*), we will continue to interpret "faith" to mean the strength and certainty of one's "beliefs." In everyday speech we refer to "getting faith," "keeping faith," and "losing faith" as if faith were a measurable quantity, poured in or leaking out. More is always better than less. After all, to shame someone who is deficient "in the faith," don't we say, "Oh ye of little faith"?

In the church we often hear some variation of the following conversation:

"Do you know Joe?"

"Yes, he teaches Sunday school, and he is a deacon. He is a man of very strong faith."

"What do you mean by strong faith?"

"Well, Joe has no doubts whatsoever when it comes to the fundamentals. The virgin birth, the miracles, the blood atonement, the bodily resurrection, the Second Coming, the infallibility of scripture—you name it, he is absolutely certain about all of it. I am sometimes a bit of a Doubting Thomas myself, but not Joe. Joe is a man of very strong faith."

How odd that the word *faith* and the word *certainty* should be so joined when absolute certainty eliminates the need for faith. Absolute certainty, by definition, is orphaned from grace. It needs nothing beyond itself. It is entirely self-possessed. Certainty turns truth into dogma and goes through life in search of question marks that can be turned into periods—or better yet, exclamation points. When a person knows something "without doubt or reservation" as the lawyers like to say, then that person needs no faith whatsoever.

It is this confusion of faith with certainty that has turned countless seekers into religious cynics. Writing for the *Guardian* newspaper on the morning of September 12, 2001, Richard Dawkins made it clear that he believes we should stop regarding faith as "harmless nonsense." If people need a "crutch for consolation, where's the harm?" But now, with smoke still rising from that mass grave at Ground Zero, he continued:

> Revealed faith is not harmless nonsense, it can be lethally dangerous nonsense. Dangerous because it gives people unshakable confidence in their own righteousness. Dangerous because it gives them false courage to kill themselves, which automatically removes normal barriers to killing others. Dangerous because it teaches enmity to others [who are] labeled only by a difference of inherited tradition. And dangerous because we have all bought into a weird respect, which uniquely protects religion from normal criticism. Let's now stop being so damned respectful.[1]

What is revealing about this comment is the use of the term "revealed faith." The writer can assume that when most people hear the word "faith," they think of something that is objective and propositional. They do not understand faith as a way of being in the world that invests in the idea of redemption, but rather as a set of divine instructions that calcifies into blind obedience. Instead of a "leap of faith" that equips us to love beyond reason, this "revealed faith" is a heavenly suitcase full of laws and self-righteous rage. It motivates "true believers" (in this instance) to commit mass murder in exchange for a heavenly reward.

No doubt such fanaticism exists in every religious tradition in the world, including Christianity. I live in Oklahoma City, and was calling roll in a public speaking class at the university less than a mile from the Alfred P. Murrah Federal Building on April 19, 1995. Without a cloud in the sky, we heard what sounded like thunder, followed by a strange roaring. The Bible-toting superpatriot Timothy McVeigh, hoping to start the second American revolution, had just set off a bomb that killed 169 people, including 19 children. Two of my parishioners were at work in the building but survived. On the Sunday following, they were both sitting in their favorite pews, seeking the strength of community and the resilience of faith.

If you were to ask either one of them what faith had to do with what McVeigh did, they would say nothing at all. Fear and hatred, yes. A clash of cultural values, yes. The desire to find and destroy an enemy who is thought to be responsible for all that is wrong with the world, yes. But faith? Can something be called faith which is born of hatred and justifies the murder of innocent life in the name of God? Are these so-called beliefs merely human projections, as Ludwig Feuerbach would say, where "God is man writ large"? His definition of faith reveals the church's dilemma: "Faith is essentially intolerant . . . because with faith is always associated the illusion that its cause is the cause of God, its honour, his honour."[2]

It is clear that Feuerbach conflates beliefs with faith—but so do millions of Christians. If the two are indeed synonymous, then faith can be, and often is, intolerant. If religious beliefs are propositional certainties given divine sanction (and God cannot be wrong), then how can we even have a civil conversation about faith? But believing and having faith are not the same thing. Beliefs are claims made that something is or is not the case. In religion these claims are made about God and then elevated to the level of dogma (that which a particular religious tradition considers essential to believe in order to be considered one of the "faithful"). To this day in England, for example, a Christian is known as a "believer."

Faith, in contrast, is an *orientation* toward the mystery of God, best understood by many as unconditional love, not a list of claims that one can know with certainty what that mystery is or wants, or even whether it exists! Faith, oddly enough, requires faith. It is a form of *trust*, the ultimate form of trust in fact. Because we trust in spite of what we cannot know, faith shares more in common with trusting than it does with believing.

When the great Danish philosopher Søren Kierkegaard sought to define faith, he described it as a "leap." What we leap across is the chasm that separates faith from the possibility of certainty. Another metaphor Kierkegaard uses is that of a person trying not to drown in the middle of the ocean. Our desire to "know" things about God with certainty is represented by our frantic attempt to tread water, which is ultimately futile. It is only when one lets go, surrenders, and floats on top of the water that it is possible not to sink.

German philosopher Friedrich Schleiermacher revolutionized Christian theology as Immanuel Kant had revolutionized philosophy by pointing out the impossibility of knowing "things in themselves." In a time very much like the present, when the intelligentsia urges that we give up on religion altogether, Schleiermacher recast religious "feeling" (das Gefuhl) as integral to humanity. This *feeling* was not beliefs, per se, or just a fleeting emotion, but rather our deepest direct experience of the world, of the infinite, or, in religious terms, of God. Thus he gave us one of the most enduring of all definitions of faith as differentiated from beliefs. Faith, said Schleiermacher, *is the feeling of absolute dependence.*

Doctrines and dogmas, Schleiermacher believed, were simply the community's articulation of this fundamental experience. "Believing" in them as an intellectual activity does not make one truly religious. Not surprisingly, the criticism he encountered is the very same objection that remains to this day, namely that such "feelings" are ultimately subjective. Who is to say, therefore, that *your* feeling that God has ordered you to commit mass murder is not equal in validity to *my* feeling that Francis of Assisi deserves to be called a saint? If all human ideas can be equally attributed to God, then we have no grounds on which to condemn anything done in the name of God—that is, unless there is some *revealed* truth, something objective, something preserved by the community that is the church (or temple or mosque), which stands apart from strictly human constructions.

Here is a point of convergence for liberals and conservatives around what seems like an impossible divide. Whereas conservatives have often claimed inerrant scripture or infallible tradition as authoritative, liberals have often retreated into a kind of postmodern ethical relativism that forbids them to judge any idea as better or worse than another idea—just different. So let's be clear about something. In the Underground Church, we do not expect complete doctrinal agreement, but neither do we believe in a world of equally valid ideas or behaviors. Peace is better than war because life is better than death. Children need protection. Either all of us matter or none of us do. Idolatry is the mother and father of all sin. Loving the neighbor, not one's opinion of the neighbor, is closer to the heart of God. Welcoming the stranger is not optional. But how dare we *make* these claims? And how are they different from "beliefs"?

Oddly enough, it is the Bible itself (often the object of idolatry) that condemns the notion that ritual dogmatism and cultic pomposity have anything to do with faith. In both the older and newer testaments, faith *attacks* the idea of "religion" (as in the organizations and rituals associated with the practice of faith) as a travesty and a perversion. How odd that Dawkins has something in common with the prophet Amos, who denounces cultic pomposity (5:21). Likewise in those scathing letters to the churches of Asia Minor in the book of Revelation, the theme of *observance does not equal obedience* reflects the teachings of Jesus in the Sermon on the Mount about outward displays of piety not matched by simple compassion.

Some of the greatest Protestant theologians of the twentieth century—Karl Barth, Paul Tillich, and Dietrich Bonheoffer—joined in this relentless critique of "faith as religion" by making it clear that faith is *against* religion. "The message of the Bible," wrote Barth, "is that God hates religion." What "we must say [of religion] is that it is the one great concern of *godless* men."[3]

Again we are instructed by Kierkegaard, who spent the whole of his eccentric life trying to explain in his writing the difference between *concept* and *capacity*. In his essay "Attack upon Christendom," he relentlessly exposed the truth about the longest journey a human can ever taken—from the head (concept) to the heart (capacity). Instead of thinking of faith as a *confirming* force, Kierkegaard speaks of it as disorienting. It *undoes* us, by sweeping away all other attachments except God. When faith becomes a form of neutral energy, like some sort of additive that we pour into the human tank so that we will get wherever it is we are going faster and with fewer knocks, it can be truly dangerous. Religion, writes Barth, is "unbelief, and is not acquitted by any inward worthiness." Religion, Barth declares,

> is a *grasping*. . . . Man tries to grasp at truth [by] himself. . . . But in that case he does not do what he has to do when truth comes to him. He does not *believe*. If he did, he would listen; but in religion he talks. If he did, he would accept a gift; but in religion he takes something for himself. If he did, he would let God Himself intercede for God; but in religion he ventures to grasp at God.[4]

Grasping at God. What a marvelous way to distinguish between religion as something we seize for our own purposes, and the gift of faith, which is a transcendent reality that defies definition. Religion can actually harden the heart by "insisting on its own way," to quote Paul, whereas faith is an *orientation* toward the mystery of love. Religion is like the myth of the tower of Babel (where we try to take heaven by storm and fail); faith is like the mystery of Pentecost (where the spirit descends and transforms from within). It was Augustine who wrote, *Si comprehendis, non est Deus* (If you think you understand, it's not God you're talking about). As Fred Craddock put it in one of his lectures, "We are all walking around a mountain too high to climb." Faith, according to the writer of the letter to the Hebrews, "is the assurance of things hoped for, the conviction of things not seen" (11:1).

On a personal note, I wrote this book in what I thought might be my father's final days of life. He had had a series of heart attacks, and it appeared that death, with its yellow face, was sitting outside his door. What I experienced at the hospital was that even between two preachers, nothing dries up faster than *words.* Here was a distinguished professor of English literature, a Shakespeare man, entangled in the tubing and machinery that keeps us alive. Here was his son the rhetorician and author. But what descended between us was silence. If this were the last conversation, what should I say? Just that I love him? Or that I lifted a few dollars off his dresser as a kid and need to confess it? When we stare into the abyss, the idea of faith as an intellectual construct doesn't just evaporate. It mocks us. It reminds me of people who stand at the edge of the Grand Canyon and talk about the weather or lower back pain.

So I just told him that I loved him, more than he would ever know. And we wept. And in the sound of that weeping was the music of the spheres. As ministers we had consoled others at such moments, many times. We always went dressed for the occasion and bearing a pocket full of words. But at a time like this, the words we might have offered to a stranger weren't there when we reached for them. Instead there was a hole in the pocket where the words used to be. The name of that hole is faith.

Far from the idea of certainty based on the evidence, faith seeks to change the evidence by its relentless posture of leaning toward God, as if you will fall into God's arms one way or another. Indeed, on the one hand, whenever "faith" insists on using a closed belief system to define the "other" as deficient based on doctrinal differences, it has betrayed its own nature. On the other hand, whenever it becomes just another word for the idolatry of reason, we fall short of what makes faith a gift. In the Underground Church, faith will be a form of radically embodied trust, and that will confuse everybody. Labels like liberal and conservative fall away in the presence of someone who embodies trust instead of trying to win arguments. Trust, together with forgiveness, is the way human beings act like God. It is a derivative of grace.

It bears repeating that Christianity was not born a religion. It was born a collection of hearts on fire. These Jesus People were not debaters. They were not fighters. They were not just another society of the elect. They were people who believed in the radical notion of universal access to God—not just access but also limitless love, as witnessed by the incarnation. So they worshiped on their tiptoes. They leaned "up." Their faith was a love song with two refrains: (1) love God and neighbor, and (2) do not do to another that which you would not want done to you.

Through a Glass Darkly

A person whose faith is based on trust rather than certainty is easy to spot in this world of self-important nonsense. First, she is humble. She is slow to judge. She gives the benefit of the doubt. She sees through the bravado of others, around the corners of the ego and into the heart of their brokenness—just as she understands her own brokenness. A person of deep and authentic faith will stand out in the Western world like a woman wearing the hajab to a meeting of the Humanist Society. She will unsettle those for whom religion is more important than faith, just as did the woman who anointed the feet of Jesus with her tears and wiped them with her hair. She will be intrinsically modest, but not to achieve accolades for her modesty. Rather she will come as a person who *listens*, who knows that she does not know, and who trusts in the power of trust itself. "Authentic faith can never rest content with itself; it can never extinguish its own existential antithesis, doubt; and it can never assume that it has arrived at its destination—that now it 'sees' face to face and not as through a glass darkly (1 Cor. 13:12)"[5]

At the university, I teach a class titled "The Ethics of Communication." When students ask me what the class is about (so they can decide whether or not to take it, because they have a grade in mind that they "must make"), I tell them the truth: *it's a course about lying.* Never mind the more academic-sounding course description: "We will study the ethical implications of the way human beings use symbols to send messages, with an emphasis on deceit." The truth is that it's really a course about lying—why we do it, what the moral philosophers have had to say about it (surprisingly little), and what the consequences are to everything we value in the world, including ourselves. Students can't help but be curious. It's a chance to take a course on a subject about which they are (or so they think) already experts!

The course uses narrative as a vessel for moral lessons about lying. We study the myths, legends, parables, and fairy tales across cultures that seek to explain the power that lying has to undo the world and everything in it. Students are surprised to learn that the most common fairy tale in the world is some version of the most famous of Aesop's fables, "The Boy Who Cried Wolf." The Greek storytellers were obsessed with the idea of reputation and credibility (what we today often call "character"). What happens to a person who has squandered his own believability? When trust is gone, they pondered, has the person actually ceased to exist?

The most intense moment in my class always occurs when we discuss, not the vast variety of deceptions or their rationales, but their *consequences*—especially to human relationships. I ask the students to think about a moment in their lives when someone they loved lied to them. Reading their faces (some of which are like an open book) tells me that it is an extremely painful but universal human experience. The room fills with an urgent silence. The eyes go down, and for what seems like an eternity, no one says anything.

"Tell me what happened after the lie?" I continue. Silence.

"What was lost?"

More silence. Then, almost in unison the answer ripples across the room: "Trust."

That's what they *all* say, as if they had been coached. But they haven't.

"The trust is gone."

"And how do you get it back?" I ask. More silence, even more awkward than before.

"What if it's true," I continue, "that nobody knows *how* to get it back? That there is no formula available from any source—not from a clergyman, not from a psychologist, not from a philosopher, a sage, or a shaman of any kind—that can restore trust in a relationship after it has been lost. If you think the formula for Coca-Cola is a well-kept secret, then consider this. Nobody has any idea how to put trust back into a relationship where it has been lost through lying. And this might not be so important, except for one little thing." The word "little" is left hanging.

"What is the most important ingredient in all human relationships?"

Now the students have moved beyond all reticence. With one voice they say it: "Trust."

In the Underground Church, the word "trust" should largely replace the word "faith" in both worship and practice. In one simple rhetorical act, we will neutralize centuries of ingrained connotation that conflates faith and belief. Trust will be the defining characteristic of the Underground Church, not institutional doctrine. The idea of certainty will be replaced by the idea that we are most fully alive when we give one another the benefit of the doubt.

In our liturgies of worship, song, and prayer, we will speak not of our faith in God but of trusting God. Not of our faith in Jesus but of our trust in The Way of Jesus. We will not recite creeds or participate in the rhetoric of triumphalism. Rather, we will create communities in which the primary relationship (divine trust) will be mysteriously demonstrated by the ways in which we trust one another. If the final act of grace is to make a person gracious, then the final act of trust is to make others trustworthy.

Consider that laboratory of human behavior known as the church meeting. Think how often you have prepared for such meetings by making assumptions about the "agenda" of those who are present. You try to guess "what so-and-so is up to" and then you arm yourself against it. Unless of course you agree with it, in which case you make plans to join the battle against all who might oppose it. But like almost everything else in this culture, the model is competition and conflict. Often the first question that someone will ask after a contentious church meeting is, "Who won?"

Strangely, it seems commonplace in the church to start a meeting, not with prayer, but with opening statements, as if we were in court. Or we forget to pray before meetings because we have devalued the power of prayer outside of worship. Or if we do pray, it is little more than our way of winking at God, to enlist divine favor on behalf of a predetermined outcome. What is conspicuously absent, however, is what is most desperately needed:

trust. Trust is a visible manifestation of grace, yet churches are often full of people who do not trust one another.

Time and time again in my own church, I have seen both the cancer of mistrust and the miraculous power of giving the benefit of the doubt (or BOD for short). After preaching a sermon about how often in my own life I have been wrong when I made assumptions about someone else's behavior (usually because I was reacting defensively or failed to understand what was really going on in that person's life), I revealed the code that my wife and I have adopted for taking each other down a notch when we start assuming the worst. If I begin to describe some imagined conspiracy or some nefarious uprising in the congregation, or relate the story of a comment made after church that may have been a dagger that went in and out of the robe without notice until I got home, Shawn will say, "BOD, Robin."

When someone at church begins to run someone else down or to imagine some dark scenario to explain that person's behavior, we have all been advised to adopt BOD as the default setting for relationships in the Beloved Community. We say it in meetings now, and in social gatherings. When special meetings are called to discuss controversial programs or decisions, we ask for everyone to give everyone else the benefit of the doubt. To begin such meetings, we pray, and then we address the controversy head-on, instead of talking around it. Then we try to do something counterintuitive— and as befits the Underground Church, subversive.

We begin by complimenting what some might call the troublemakers. We thank them for caring enough about the church, and what's best for the church, to be present and to express their opinions. It is quite remarkable what happens when people are not boxed in, and the object of meeting is not to "win" but rather to find our way forward in love. Even when we completely disagree with someone or with a certain position, we remind each other that every person present must care deeply for the church and for its future. Because strangely enough, even if he doesn't, he begins to—because we *assume* he does. This is precisely why trust is not only a derivative of grace. It acts like leaven in the loaf.

One of our highest and most sacred obligations in the Underground Church is to look for the good that's not there yet, until we see it. We are not just a gathering of like-minded folk who share a similar theological or political orientation. We are not a social club, a lonely hearts club, or a place to assuage guilt or drop off problem children to be turned into good little Christians. The church is a place where we make one another into what we expect from one another. When radically embodied trust replaces intellectual assent to theological propositions, we slowly but surely create people who possess and practice radical trust. Contrary to our culture of hyperindividualism (where every man or woman rises or falls in isolation), this is as countercultural as it gets: to prove that the Pygmalion effect does not sleep in on Sunday mornings. Joy is not just contagious. It is reproductive.

The Fertility of Trust

In the late 1960s, a controversial educational study took place called the Oak School experiment. It figured prominently in an equally controversial book, *Pygmalion in the Classroom: Teacher Expectation and Pupils' Intellectual Development*. I read that book in college as part of my preparation to become a high school English teacher, before taking a different path. At the time I remember thinking that the Pygmalion phenomenon, as it is called, was no big deal, just another social scientific proof for what common sense can deliver. Looking back, I realize that those findings were as remarkable as they were unsettling for one simple reason: truth doesn't just enlighten us; it *obligates* us.

In this famous experiment, teachers were led to believe that certain students (who in fact were selected at random) were exceptional. They were likely to show signs of a spurt in intellectual growth and development. They were "tagged," if you will, so that when the teacher looked at those students, she saw "great potential." At the end of the year, the students so identified showed significantly greater gains in intellectual development than did those in the "control group" (those who had not been identified as exceptional). In some cases, the gain in IQ was twice as high as among those not identified as gifted.[6] In short, the teacher's belief in the exceptional capacity of some students became a self-fulfilling prophecy. It became a form of radically embodied trust.

One can only imagine what happened throughout the year. The exceptional students must have been called on more often and given more challenging tasks to do; in classroom exercises and discussions, they felt those various forms of validation that a teacher telegraphs to a "favorite student." This is how it works. When the hard questions are asked and no answer is forthcoming, teachers have a fallback plan—a default setting that involves a handful of the best students. Those students can be trusted to "get it," and over time they begin to thrive on that expectation. Meanwhile, the other students "get it" (that they don't get it) too. We quickly learn that we are all located somewhere in the great hierarchy, ranked in so many ways by the messages we receive from a world of authority figures.

The most interesting response to this experiment, however, was the *resistance* to it by some in the educational establishment. Perhaps there was (and is) something truly frightening about realizing that we are all constantly *creating one another*. By the choice of a single word, by a glance, by finding one lost face in the crowd and recognizing it, by saying something that is *encouraging*, we project our evaluations of the worthiness (or lack thereof) on every human being we come into contact with. Those projections have real results, from crippling to empowering. As it turns out, this was not just another educational experiment with results to be read at a conference and discussed in break-out groups. Instead what was discovered constituted an uncomfortable but profound moral imperative.

Teachers have good reason, after all, to believe that they treat all their students exactly the same. Don't we all live by this myth? Parents can be even more vociferous in their insistence that they treat all their children exactly the same. Pastors give theological lip service to the idea, burdened by the impossible demands of the gospel, while finding ways to avoid even running into certain people on Sunday morning. I know. I've done it myself.

In educational circles, if one expects little from one's students, it affects both what is taught and how it is taught. The expectation that students can't handle much, or are not too bright, leads to the kind of teaching that brings exactly that result. Again, this is essentially a matter of trust, as it presumes that the students either can or cannot be trusted to do more. When they are, and the bar is set higher, they frequently achieve what is expected of them. Sometimes, in fact, when they are asked to do impossible things, they do them, not understanding that they are impossible.

In the end, anyone in a position of authority (such as a pastor) who is responsible for the growth and learning of other people has to be very careful about thinking that he or she can determine what is possible or what individuals can "handle." We constantly send messages about what we think is possible, no matter how often we say that "with God all things are possible." What's worse, we can trap people at a certain level of spiritual development by our perception that they are not destined to do, think, or say new things.

In the Oak School experiment, a lesser-known but equally important finding involved the so-called lower-track students (those in the control group who were not expected to shine). When some of them began to show marked improvement, the teacher

evaluations actually declined. In other words, the teacher refused to
see their progress because they were not supposed to *make* progress.
As one of the authors of the study put it, "If the world thinks little
of you, it's going to punish you if you begin to succeed."

The Pygmalion effect does not just suggest that teachers work
on their teaching style, aiming to mitigate the latent clues they send
that some students can't be taught or are bound to fail. It brings us
all to admit that the way we relate to one another is not incidental
but *constitutional*. It means that superb teachers can teach the "unteach-
able" (and they prove it all the time). But it also means that any
teacher who is certain about who can learn and who can't, who
knows who will succeed and who will fail, should get out of the
classroom. As for the church, what then are we to make of pastors
who do not trust their own congregations? What does it mean that
so many clergy go off to seminary to learn things that they later
refuse to share from their pulpits?

I once heard a story from a New Testament scholar about how
mistrust in a congregation can cause the bough to break. He had
been invited by a Sunday school class to lecture in a very conservative church in Arkansas. Some church members complained that
the scholar was too liberal and that, as a member of the controversial Jesus Seminar, he could not be trusted. Others wondered why
he would even want to speak in such a conservative church, where
the audience might be very hostile. But the people in the Sunday
school class wanted to *learn*, and among the members of that class
was the matriarch of the church. Every church has one.

His lecture was about recent discoveries in New Testament
scholarship, about the so-called Q gospel, whose existence is pre-
sumed but not verified, as a source for material found in both
Matthew and Luke but not in Mark. He discussed evidence in the
New Testament that Jesus became more supernatural over time, and
the impact of the discovery of the so-called Gnostic gospels at Nag
Hammadi, which included the Gospel of Thomas. Many scholars

believe it is as old as any of the four gospels we have, and have even started calling it the fifth gospel. But it is very strange indeed, and gives us a very different picture of the mission of Jesus. The Sunday school class was betting that many people in the church had never heard of the Gospel of Thomas (or of any of the other gospels that didn't make it into the Bible). They trusted that people could make up their own minds.

At the end of the lecture, during the Q&A, the matriarch of the church rose to address, not the scholar, but the pastor.

"Did you know about the Q gospel?" she asked him.

"Yes," he replied.

"Where did you learn about it?"

"In seminary," he responded.

"So why didn't you teach us about Q?" she continued. He gave no answer, so she pressed him further.

"What about the Gospel of Thomas? Have you heard of it before?"

"Yes ma'am, I have."

"And where did you learn about Thomas?

"In seminary."

"So why didn't you share that information with us?" The room had grown quiet and more than a little bit tense. "I don't think our guest scholar made this stuff up. We studied the Gospel of Thomas in our Sunday school class—all 114 'sayings' of Jesus. We were shocked to discover that it's called a gospel but doesn't have a passion narrative, a crucifixion, or a resurrection. What's more, in the Infancy Gospel of Thomas, Jesus was quite the little magical hellion. He kills one of his playmates for taunting him. Did you know that?"

"Yes, ma'am, I've studied that so-called gospel."

"In seminary, I suppose," she continued.

"Yes, ma'am."

"Why didn't you tell us about it?"

Frustrated and uneasy, he looked away, out the window, and said, "I didn't think you needed to know."

Not long after, a meeting was held in the church to discuss, among other things, why the congregation sent ministers to seminary in the first place. As for the current minister, he was fired. The charge? It was as simple as it was fatal. Lack of trust.

Mortal Mistrust

If trust holds human relationships together, and lack of trust destroys them, then what forms of mistrust are destroying the church in our time? One is the so-called battle for the Bible, in which conservatives and liberals square off to defend either a literal or a metaphorical reading of scripture. The second is a kind of theological mistrust that describes God as loving, accepting, and forgiving and then acts as if God's judgment and wrath were to be feared. Both are examples of mistrust. Some might even say that given what they have done to damage the church, they are forms of "mortal" mistrust. In other words, they have killed the spirit of love and compassion in our churches.

First, we mistrust the story that we have inherited, by manipulating it instead of listening to it. Conservatives insist that if scripture is not essentially historical, containing an accurate account of what "really happened," then it has no authority. The scriptures must be understood as infallible or "inerrant," as they convey the word of God. Liberals counter that reading the Bible literally is the greatest impediment to finding its essential message. The word myth continues to confound us all. Some still hear the word and think it means untrue, fanciful—a fairy tale. Others hold the view of Joseph Campbell, that a myth is a story whose truth is too large to be contained by mere facts.

Second, we mistrust God by assuming that God can be understood in the language of human experience, using the symbols of power that make sense to us. It is the primary complaint of today's crusading atheists, who refer to it as the "God delusion." We continue to use language about God that makes the idea of the ineffable seem as commonplace as a stoplight or a can of tuna. In the time of Jesus, the rabbis would not even dare to say the name of God out loud, lest it sound too familiar. Or they stripped out the vowels of the names of God in a kind of linguistic blush. The Almighty is beyond time and space, beyond comprehension, what William James referred to as a "More," beyond knowing or naming. The God of human reckoning, however, is too often like what the poet William Blake called "Nobodaddy"—an angry, jealous, capricious deity in the sky.

The library of books that constitute Holy Scripture, written over nearly two thousand years, translated multiple times, and covered with human fingerprints, is not the object of our worship. When we read or listen to the Bible, we are all listening to ancient conversations not intended for us. We are, as Fred Craddock put it, in the posture of "overhearing" voices not addressed to us—as if on our knees listening through a keyhole between two worlds. Across that threshold is a chasm of time and space, culture, worldview, and language. The obstacles to serious Bible study are so formidable that either everyone should go to seminary before attempting it, or every minister who does go should make a solemn promise to go on studying for a lifetime—and then not to leave the congregation sitting out in the hall. The language of the Bible is at the center of American life, and is often a tool of American politics, but almost nobody has any idea how we got it, what's really in it, or why a little bit of biblical knowledge is more dangerous than none at all.

Whenever we engage in the use of the Bible to acquire power over others or to engineer exclusive communities that claim "true and absolute knowledge" of the meaning of each and every word of scripture, we fail to trust in the work of the spirit that moved those who left us a record of that remarkable conversation. And we fail to trust in the process of interpretation, because deep down we mistrust the ambiguity of dialogue itself, preferring something more authoritative, like edicts or rules.

In the Underground Church, the Bible will be at the center of the life of the Beloved Community because it tells the story that formed us, reforms us, and continues to astonish us. But we will not make an idol of the scriptures, any more than we should make an idol out of anything. Our trust shall be reserved for what is beyond human contrivance, beyond sectarian agendas, beyond the grasping at God that represents the worst of religion.

Growing up the son of a preacher, I heard stories about the well-intended but, in the end, deeply mistrustful antics of American fundamentalists. We were Protestants, not Catholics, so it was important for us not to do what the Romans had done—that is, make a god out of tradition. So we decided to make a god out of the Bible! Authority, as they say, must be lodged somewhere. But as so often happens, we can fall victim to the idolatry of our ideas by placing our trust in something other than God. That's what I mean by "mortal mistrust." To illustrate this, I offer two stories, both true, each examples of mortal mistrust. One is strange but sad; the other is tragic.

The first is a story of how we mistrust scripture, by asking something of it that it was never intended to deliver. It's a story told to me by my father, who grew up in the noninstrumental Church of Christ (so called because no instruments are allowed in worship because none are mentioned as part of worship in the New Testament). Dad was "delivered" to the task of preaching as a teenager when the elders laid hands on him. His gifts were already apparent, and in that tradition, going to seminary was not a requirement. In fact, it was widely viewed to be a liability. "Cemeteries" is what some of the bull elders called them, as that is where one goes to "bury one's faith."

While teaching at Harding College, my father also preached in the small town of Beebe, Arkansas, a town that few readers will recognize, but some of whom many remember as the place where thousands of blackbirds once fell mysteriously from the sky on New Year's Eve and littered the ground. The residents of Beebe would have preferred some other form of notoriety, and some even speculated that the mass bird kill was a sign of the coming apocalypse. As it turns out, it may have had something to do with fireworks, but more sinister explanations were hard to resist.[7]

It was my father's first Sunday to preach at Beebe, and after taking his seat while communion was served (ministers in that tradition do not do the serving as would a priest), he heard a distinct popping sound as the bread carriers worked their way from the back of the room. When the tray reached him, he understood the reason for the popping sounds. The bread was so hard that when a piece was broken off, it popped, sometimes sending fragments skittering across the floor like tiddly-winks. Oh well, he thought, sometimes you leave the oven on too long and burn the bread, right?

He said nothing that first Sunday, only to return to more popping bread the next Sunday, and then again on the following Sunday. He decided to ask for what is called a "men's business meeting" (no women allowed, of course). They gathered at the front, after the service; when asked about the popping bread, they stared at their boots and seemed slightly embarrassed. Finally, one of the elders said that he could explain it.

"We had a preacher here once who told us that the Bible didn't say that Jesus 'bent' the bread, but that he 'broke' it. He warned us that to be absolutely faithful to scripture, we should be able to hear it 'pop,' and that would prove that we were following the example of Jesus at the Last Supper."

Years later, my father referred to the dear people at Beebe as constituting the "cult of the audible bread breakers." Not to pass judgment on them, for they were only doing what the preacher had told them to do, but as a reminder that we can approach the scripture out of fear, rather than trust. What would happen to them, after all, if they ignored this mandate from a preacher of the gospel? If he was so certain, then why not follow this strict mandate, just to be safe? They were not preachers, after all, but simple men who feared not getting it right.

It was the preacher who should have trusted the story, instead of searching the text for new legalisms. It was the preacher who should have known that everywhere you look in the gospels, it is Jesus who shows no patience for such legalism—especially if there was a thirsty child nearby. It was the preacher who should have brought them a larger vision, instead of making them think that God is the True Legalist. Or if not the preacher, then perhaps a brave member of the congregation could dare to make a bold comparison. What if burned communion bread shares something in common with burnt offerings? What if both would bring the ire of the prophet Amos, who would "take no delight" in them or in our solemn assemblies? Surely what the world needs is not the right sound when breaking bread but a church that lets "justice roll down like waters, and righteousness like an ever-flowing stream" (Amos 5:24).

The second story is much more painful. It is a story of how we mistrust the love of God and make it, instead, as narrow and impoverished as our own.

A pastor whom I know received the dreadful news that a young man in his congregation, Rick, had been diagnosed with terminal cancer. Rick was in college and not particularly religious, but he remembered the strict teaching of his boyhood church. He had not been baptized and was terrified that this meant he was not "saved" and would go to hell. The pastor looked at his wasted limbs, his eyes bright with cold fear, and thought of the nature of the God he preached, a God of grace and mercy.

Although words at such a moment are excruciatingly difficult, the pastor talked about his deep trust in the love and mercy of God, and told the young man that the arms of God were around him day and night. Do not be afraid, he told him. You are caught up in his love.

"Thanks" the young man replied. "I'm all right."

Later the same day, my friend learned the reason for Rick's sudden terror. A much-publicized evangelist had come into town for a gospel meeting, heard of Rick's plight, and decided to pay him a visit. The family had not asked for the visit, but their decency made them vulnerable, so when he knocked on the door, they opened it. When he asked to be left alone in the room with Rick, they granted the request. The evangelist asked Rick if he had been baptized, making it clear that all the law and the prophets hung upon the answer.

Rick whispered in pain, "No sir."

The evangelist told him in a somber tone, both deeply felt and utterly devoid of feeling, that if Rick died unbaptized, he would go to hell. If he were to be baptized, he would not have to be afraid of meeting God when he died. He prayed for Rick to make the right decision, and then left.

So which counsel was correct? The reassurance of his pastor or the frightening prospects described by the evangelist? Rick spent his days not only in pain but also deeply conflicted. One morning, after a fit of coughing and with death's yellow face staring at him through the window, he asked his mother to call the pastor. She requested that he come to the hospital and baptize Rick by immersion (the only acceptable form of baptism in his tradition). The pastor agreed, now also deeply conflicted.

Rick had no idea what the ritual of baptism meant, but he feared the consequences of not going through with it. By this time, the logistics of a baptism by full immersion were complicated, to say the least. The hospital staff would need to secure a large tank, loaned from the physical therapy department. Lowering Rick into the tank would be painful, as would be the trip from his room to the basement where the tank was located and filled (mercifully) with warm water. Lifting him off the bed caused Rick excruciating pain, and he cried out so loudly that those assisting him lost both will and strength—starting and stopping several times, wishing they could abandon the task altogether.

The ride on the elevator was painful, as was the task of getting Rick into a sling that would swivel out over the tank and lower him into the water. Even some of the experienced therapists winced at his screaming and stood back to watch in silent fascination while he appropriated the grace of God.

Once on the sling, Rick was all alone. The pastor knew that he was supposed to "say something" (this is both the blessing and the curse of the profession), so he did. But what a strange scene it was, speaking the words of baptism, of rebirth, into the ear of a dying man whose pain was serenaded by the clicking and grinding of machinery.

When he was lowered into the water, he was too weak to keep it out of his mouth, so he came up strangled and close to drowning. Some of the technicians left the room. The pastor helped dry him off, and then the tortured trip back to his room began. Rick died three days later.

This is mortal mistrust. This is anti-grace. This is the anti-gospel. This is the final insult to the idea of a God of unconditional love, forgiveness, and grace. If any decent person would know better than to put someone through this, then how can we possibly assume that this is the will of God? Perhaps no single aspect of religion has so alienated so many people as the idea that we are asked to worship a God whose love, not to mention common sense, seems more limited than our own. Never mind the loving father who runs to meet the prodigal son and welcomes him home without so much as a stern lecture or the stony silence he deserves. Perhaps the sad truth is that we have a loving father gospel in an elder brother church.

In the Underground Church, we will not circle the wagons to keep out those with whom we disagree, as if faith and prayer can ever be used as weapons. We are called instead to embody radical trust, giving everyone the benefit of the doubt, including the enemy, the stranger, even the peculiar and subversive words we call scripture. But most of all, we need to trust the unfathomable mystery that is God.

In an age of public ridicule, glorified gossip, humiliation as entertainment, and the bullying epidemic, the peculiar saints of the Underground Church will commit themselves to *encouragement*. Paul's warm and affectionate words to the church at Thessalonica should be heeded by all: "Therefore encourage one another and build up each other, as indeed you are doing . . . encourage the fainthearted, help the weak, be patient with all of them. See that none of you repays evil for evil, but always seek to do good to one another and to all" (1 Thess. 5:11–15).

Faith as radical trust is marked by an unearthly patience and by a deep and abiding belief that what we sow in love shall be harvested long after we are gone. Arguments over "beliefs" pale next to the practice of planting trees under whose shady branches we will never sit. One can only imagine what might happen if despite our theological differences, we felt compelled to work together rather than to persuade others that we are right and they are wrong. Indeed, the angels might begin to sing, and the kingdom might come on earth as it is in heaven.

What have we got to lose? Certainly not our faith.

CHAPTER SIX

Renewing the Church Through Shared Mission

The biggest change on the religious front is that young evangelicals are leaving their roots. Can we put aside our elitism? Can we reach out to them? If we can, this could be a time of tremendous growth and renewal for our congregations.
—CAROL HOWARD MERRITT

The religious tradition of my grandparents was very conservative, but none of the Meyers kids were raised to be fundamentalists. To the contrary, we were raised in the liberal Protestant tradition of Harry Emerson Fosdick. I grew up believing that the Riverside Church in New York City, on the upper west side of Manhattan, was the closest thing to a Mecca of progressive Christianity that this preacher's kid from Kansas would ever see. And to be honest, I was drawn to this remarkable church on numerous occasions while in graduate school and throughout my ministry. I reveled in Riverside's focus on the social gospel and was moved by the amazing preachers who spoke truth to power from its splendid, storied pulpit. I dreamed of being a Riverside preacher myself one day.

That's why it came as such a shock to discover that what we idolize is so often an illusion. As a recent candidate for the pulpit at Riverside, I discovered that the rumors I had heard were true—that for years the church has been torn by internal dissent, profoundly crippled by both racial and theological divisions. In recent years it seems to have the dubious distinction of having set the standard by which contentious and petty church meetings could be judged.

Church members have fought over how money should be spent, whether funds have been misappropriated, and what theological traditions and worship styles should prevail. Granted, all churches argue over these things, but at Riverside, with its powerful people and personalities, the infamous "church fight" took on a whole new meaning. You know that things are bad when only lawyers from each side of a dispute are talking to each other.

Fosdick, the church's founding minister, had a nervous breakdown while tending the flock at Riverside. Ernest Campbell resigned after a fairly brief tenure, unable to tolerate the power struggles that afflicted his tenure. Once, in the middle of one of Campbell's sermons, the Black Panthers commandeered the worship service, took control of the chancel, and demanded to be heard on issues of race, poverty, and reparations. Jim Forbes, the church's first African American minister, spent years dealing with bitter quarrels among those who felt the heart and soul of Riverside had been lost, its great liberal witness and theological distinctiveness compromised by a more evangelical approach.

William Sloane Coffin Jr., perhaps the most memorable prophetic voice at Riverside, spoke often about his unceasing battles with a men's Bible study group. He described the chasm that separated that landmark gothic tower atop the highest spot in the city of New York from a dark, dysfunctional side that operated in what he called "the bowels of that place."

The point here is not to embarrass Riverside, although I can imagine that members or friends with whom I am now acquainted might see it that way. My point is not to hang out their dirty laundry, given that all of this is public knowledge, but to remind the reader that we are all the victims of our particular idealized stereotypes. Human nature is such that when we deeply admire someone, or something, we fill in all the blanks with positive attributes. When we are true believers, there is often a naïve capacity to imagine that things are as good on the inside as they appear on the outside. Life is one long series of honeymoon periods that must give way to a more complicated and compromised reality called marriage.

This was painful to me not because Riverside doesn't matter but because it does. It is so important to so many people that we would prefer the illusion that the whole church is as bold and gracious as its pulpit. Riverside, after all, paved the way for the sanctuary movement in America. It has been in the vanguard of the civil rights, women's rights, and gay rights movements. Loving the tradition and history of this church and having been so profoundly influenced by its message made it particularly difficult for me to realize that, to adapt the words of a country western song, liberals get the blues too.

In the middle of my interview with the search committee, sensing the pain of those who were struggling valiantly to save the church from itself, I wondered aloud if perhaps Riverside might be "a victim of its own grandeur." There followed a moment of awkward silence. This is exactly what I now wonder about the liberal Protestant tradition itself, or what is more widely called progressive Christianity. Is it a victim of its own grandeur? Are we simply hoping to bring back the "good old days" when Fosdick preached that seminal sermon, "Shall the Fundamentalists Win?" and later when two million people listened to him on the radio? Or are we frozen in the heady days of the 1960s when Dr. Martin Luther King Jr. mesmerized the nation with his call for racial and economic justice?

Time not only heals all wounds but also makes us forget how things really were. Fosdick was the object of vicious attacks by fellow clergy, and King preached a sermon at Riverside one year before he was assassinated that condemned the hypocrisies of the Vietnam War and the morality of systemic economic inequality. It brought condemnation from, of all places, the *New York Times*. In an editorial the next day, the *Times* called it "Dr. King's Mistake." He should not leave his true calling, this "liberal" paper argued, which is integration, to meddle in foreign affairs or economic issues. Once again we are reminded that the words of a prophet can be an equal opportunity offender. Conservatives and liberals alike have oversimplified both the questions and the answers.

Do we see the speck in our neighbor's eye but not the log in our own? We now live in a postmodern, post-Christian, post–Religious Right context in North America. Mainline and progressive churches are still not entirely sure what to make of the so-called emergent movement, except to lament that it seems to be where their young people have gone. While we argue over music styles, dress codes, and whether God approves of any musical instrument in the sanctuary that must be plugged in, we may have missed the point. We try to laugh it off, making jokes about how power corrupts and PowerPoint corrupts absolutely—but in the end, we may be the ones who are missing the point.

Many of those who make up the emergent community are former evangelicals and fundamentalists. They have a deep appetite for relevance and for social justice. They are searching for meaningful interpersonal relationships in the age of social media and speed dating. They value open and inclusive approaches to Christianity and "are less interested in having all the answers than in living the questions. Emergents wish to participate in communities of faith that take the Bible seriously, but not always literally. Emergents believe that following Jesus isn't just about getting to heaven when they die, but is about partnering with God to bring heaven to earth in the here and now."[1]

If that sounds surprisingly like the credo of many so-called liberal or progressive congregations, then welcome to what's happening. The gospel isn't being reinvented. It is being rediscovered, and that always means new forms of worship. Unfortunately, we have let differences in form blind us to otherwise remarkable similarities in content. This doesn't mean that all mainline congregations need to incorporate a band into their worship service or to replace the cross with a giant screen. It means that the children of baby boomers who still desire a community of faith value *authenticity* over *orthodoxy*. What is often ignored about emerging forms of worship is that in addition to being more participatory and multisensory, they often include a renewed interest in ancient Christian practices and symbols. Not only have they not thrown the baby out with the bathwater, but some are actually reintroducing us to the baby!

Let us confess that we are creatures of habit who resist change, and perhaps nowhere more so than in church. It is amusing to think how well adapted we are to technological change, joking about every gadget becoming obsolete the moment we purchase it, but in our spiritual lives we expect nothing to change. Some still regard pipe organs as the only instrument that can stir the soul. Others are suspicious that any emotional involvement in worship is a slippery slope toward "emotionalism." Perhaps the sad state of the mainline church in our time is a testimony to a kind of arrested spiritual development. Perhaps the knocking sound we hear at the door comes from the next generation, trying to rouse us from our slumber.

Part of the problem is that we live such isolated lives. We have managed to wall ourselves off from our neighbors and are encouraged, especially by the media, to live in suspicion and fear. We have formed communities of political, theological, economic, and racial purity—until we have all become cartoons in one another's minds. We have our enemies list, the "other," but the truth is, we don't really know one another.

One of my next-door neighbors asked my wife once if it was true what she had heard "about your husband—that he is a liberal." In Oklahoma, the L-word is often used as an epithet.

"Yes," Shawn responded, "he is a liberal."

This elderly and respectable woman, who has been our neighbor for twenty-five years, paused and said earnestly, "But he seems like such a nice man."

So it goes. But in all honesty, it goes the other way too. Not long ago I was invited to have a conversation about my book *Saving Jesus from the Church* with members of the Fifth Street Missionary Baptist Church in Oklahoma City. It was the first such invitation I had ever received to speak in a black church in my hometown, and I must admit to wondering if someone had made a mistake. Did they get their books mixed up? There is a Joyce Meyer, a TV evangelist—perhaps they think we are related? Or maybe (this was a dark thought of which I am not proud) it is a setup, a kind of theological ambush. Maybe they intend to let this white liberal have it for publishing a book with a cover that shows Jesus with duct tape over his mouth. And then for good measure say, "Reverend, God made Adam and Eve, not Adam and Steve."

I crossed Lincoln Boulevard that Saturday morning knowing that, racially speaking, I was going to the "other side"—a term Jesus used in the gospels to describe a journey into Gentile territory. Once inside the church, I was told, "Pastor Coleman is waiting for you," and was led to his modest office. He was a large, jovial man, without an Oklahoma accent. He was transplanted from Chicago, a graduate of one of the most progressive seminaries in the country and a great admirer of Harry Emerson Fosdick. He had spent thirteen years struggling to adapt to the ultraconservatism of Oklahoma, and was introducing his congregation to authors whom he believed were doing important work in biblical scholarship and prophetic ministry. He named Marcus Borg, John Dominic Crossan, John Shelby Spong, and Philip Gulley—whose book *If the Church Were Christian* the congregation had just finished studying. In the words of Rev. Coleman, "My people ate it up. We love Philip Gulley."

I suddenly felt discombobulated, which in some circumstances may be a sign of the presence of the spirit. Then the associate pastor and the president of the congregation walked in and said that it was time for prayer. We joined hands, and they prayed for me to find the right words to say. They asked the Lord to "help me tell the truth." They prayed for me and "for my voice" to be strong and clear and courageous. I felt like a boxer about to go into the ring, lifted by melodious petitions from these spirit-filled trainers. Hadn't we just met? To be honest, I was feeling, at that moment—well, very white.

You haven't been prayed for until you have been prayed for in the black church. I felt light, as if I had actually lost several pounds during the prayer, and then tiptoed into the hall where a crowd waited that was as engaged, as curious, as thoughtful, and as gracious as any I have ever spoken to. They wanted to learn, but they were not angry. So many of the white, hyperintellectual crowds I speak to these days are just angry, certain that the world is ending and hopeful that before it does, they can at least pass a resolution that predicts it.

The result of that experience is that Mayflower and Fifth Street Missionary Baptist Church are now planning joint activities, and Rev. Coleman has joined the board of the Oklahoma Institute for Biblical Literacy, headquartered at Mayflower, whose purpose is to bring important biblical scholars into the church to teach the people in the pews, so that pastors and laypersons alike can continue to learn. It is, after all, for the health and vitality of the local church that the seminary exists, is it not? Scholars do their work not just for other scholars, but so that nonscholars can also learn, correct?

But the most important lesson for me was to be reminded again how often we are victimized by our assumptions. If the command is to love God and neighbor, it helps to know the neighbor. Better yet, it helps to do something with the neighbor that transcends doctrine and tradition—and even (heaven forbid) styles of worship. I heard a woman in my congregation say once that she would never go to a church "where people raise their hands during worship."

I remember thinking that perhaps others were at that moment swearing never to go to a church where everyone sits on them.

That's when the parable of the Pharisee and the tax collector came to mind. I have prayed the stock prayer of the Pharisee many times without realizing it, thanking God that I am "not like other people: thieves, rogues, adulterers, or even like this tax collector [which in my case might be a fundamentalist]. I fast [from dogmatic certainty] twice a week. I give a tenth of my income [or better yet, half my superior intellect]." Why then does the tax collector, a professional sinner with no advanced degrees, go home "justified," rather than the Pharisee? I don't like this parable. Not one bit. It reminds me that spiritual pride cuts both ways, and in the end I am still confronted by the "other." It all comes down to the other.

I've heard some very nasty things said about liberals (after all, I live in Oklahoma). But I've also heard some very nasty things said about conservatives (after all, I live in Oklahoma). What I don't hear, and too seldom see, is the power of love to get the Pharisee and the publican together in the same serving line at the homeless shelter. The real question for our time is this: Why would we rather be right than loving? If the Sermon on the Mount represents the Great Reversal, and Paul's most dangerous words in the Bible are *Do not be conformed to this world, but be transformed by the renewing of your minds, so that you may discern what is the will of God—what is good and acceptable and perfect* (Rom. 12:2), then why do I enjoy conformity so much when it suits me? Why do I find it so pleasant, so self-affirming, and so lucrative?

In the Underground Church, the defining characteristic of a follower of Jesus will be nonconformity to what the Bible calls the "principalities and powers." But not just for the sake of nonconformity, lest we all become conforming nonconformists. The idea here is not just to "stick it to the man," as my friends used to say in college, but to embody a way of being in the world that disassembles even our defining assumptions and prejudices. We are not called to be "mad prophets decrying the hypocrisies of our time," as Coffin used to say, but mad prophets decrying even our own hypocrisy! Better yet, mad prophets living out a vision that is as self-indicting as it is "other" oriented. Put more simply, to save the church, liberals and conservatives (and everyone in between) need to find concrete ways to work together across our theological and liturgical divides— lest they define us, instead of love. I have grown more than a little weary of arguing about doctrinal differences while people starve to death.

If the Church Were Christian

I left the Fifth Street Missionary Baptist church with Rev. Coleman's words still ringing in my ears: "We love Philip Gulley." Good Lord, I thought to myself, Philip Gulley is a Quaker, and we all know how strange they are. No ministers, a lot of sitting in silence, and a stubborn (some might even say naïve) commitment to nonviolence. But if they are so strange, then why do I seem to be drawn to Quakers, and never fail to mention my admiration for them in every book I write? Was I a Quaker in a former life, or is it something much simpler, namely *simplicity* itself, that is so appealing?

Perhaps what stands out is the way in which they are counter-cultural without being obnoxious. It would be hard to imagine a more important question for the Underground Church than this: What if the church *were* Christian? Not Roman Catholic, Baptist, Presbyterian, Methodist, Congregational, Pentecostal, or any other proud variety of nondenominational or "Other"—but just *Christian*. What if the political orientation was neither left nor right, but something much more radical—namely, the subversive politics of the gospel?

If the church of the future can be renewed by its capacity to share mission work across theological, liturgical, and cultural

differences, then our Christian identity will have to matter more
than our denominational loyalties. If, for example, one just takes
Gulley's chapter titles and rolls them all together into one para-
graph, they describe perfectly what will go on in the Underground
Church. Listen:

> If the Church were Christian, Jesus would be a model for living, rather
> than an object of worship. Affirming our potential would be more
> important than condemning our brokenness. Reconciliation would be
> valued over judgment. Gracious behavior would be more important
> than right belief. Inviting questions would be valued more than
> supplying answers. Encouraging personal exploration would be
> more important than communal uniformity. Meeting needs would
> be more important than maintaining institutions. Peace would be
> more important than power. We would care more about love and less
> about sex. This life would be more important than the afterlife.[2]

Very well. But the question, as always, is how. Not what is
Christian, but how is one Christian, in this time and in this place?
Fred Craddock argues that in the entire enterprise that is Christianity,
"Every 'what' deserves consideration only as it serves the overarch-
ing question of how to be Christian."[3] So what would it look like
for people to act this way? What would be the consequences? Are
we supposed to give up our identities completely, or simply not
allow them to hold us apart from one another? What about those
areas in which compromise is not possible? Do we have to pretend
to believe things we do not believe?

To begin with, if Jesus is our model for living rather than an object
of worship, then most of things we fight about in the church disappear. Most of our quarrels are theological, not ethical. There have
been and will always be arguments over the divinity of Jesus (as
there were from the beginning), but not so much about the virtues
to which he calls us. If Jesus is a means to an end and not an end
unto himself, then the proper object of our worship is God. It was

Hans Küng who said that it is in "service to [humankind] that service to God is proved." In the Underground Church, we will worship God by following Jesus, and we will follow Jesus by loving the neighbor—period.

If a conservative church opens a shelter for battered women and invites others to join them in volunteering, cleaning, providing financial support and child care, then what is to stop a liberal church from becoming a partner? One objection might be the differences between the way conservatives and liberals might understand the root causes of the abuse or about the necessity of conversion to Christianity as a solution. Let it be. One can and should refrain from any activity that is a violation of one's beliefs, but nothing stops us from performing acts of simple human compassion. When we model the way of Jesus, we do not need to argue with others over formulas for salvation. Given the desperate needs around us every day, why can't we "do justice, love kindness, and walk humbly" with both those who worship Jesus as God and those who don't?

During the second century, there was a great epidemic in the Mediterranean world, known as the Plague of Galen (165–180), in which hundreds of thousands of people perished, filling the streets with corpses. Christians tended to the sick at great personal risk, and the challenge of doing so set them apart from others. Because they did not fear death, they remained in cities that others had fled in fear. What's more, they tended to everyone who was sick, regardless of class, tribe, or religion—unlike the Roman pagans. The early Christian preacher Chrysostom put it simply: "This is the rule of most perfect Christianity, its most exact definition, its highest point, namely, the seeking of the common good . . . for nothing can so make a person an imitator of Christ as caring for his neighbors."[4]

If affirming our potential is more important than condemning our brokenness, then in the Underground Church we will emphasize "original blessing" over original sin. We will not save souls so much as we will trust in the power of love to restore them. If reconciliation is to be valued over judgment, then any mission project that affirms human dignity rather than condemning human depravity should provide us all with an opportunity for ministry. If fear is the weapon, we should walk away. But if love is freely offered without strings attached, we should gladly join in the project.

If *gracious behavior* is more important than *right belief*, then the mark of the Underground Church will be unmistakable. This will be, metaphorically speaking, the tattoo that adorns the body of the Beloved Community: we are saved by grace, not by particular doctrines of grace. If we are followers, if we are imitators of Christ, then feeding the hungry, clothing the naked, tending the sick, counseling the troubled, visiting the prisoner, making a world fit for children—none of it should be offered as part of a theological quid pro quo. To do so reduces faith to a transaction and a misuse of power. Trust in the redemptive power of the *loving action itself* powers the Underground Church.

In the small mountain town of Jinotega, Nicaragua, Mayflower maintains a year-round medical mission to deaf children. This is the second-poorest country in the Western hemisphere. In addition to bringing doctors and nurses from all over the country to perform surgeries to restore or improve the hearing of these children, Mayflower has purchased and restored a large home in the center of town that serves as a shelter and boarding school for twenty-one deaf children. We staff the boarding school with teachers of sign language who teach these children, some of whom were simply abandoned in the market by their parents as an impossible liability and then scooped up off the street by a good Samaritan.

They come to us without the most basic capacities for self-care, social interaction, or self-esteem. They come to live at what is now known throughout Jinotega as the *Albergue Mayflower* (the Inn of Mayflower). As I write, my wife is there over spring break, working with other artists to paint colorful murals on the walls that surround the compound. Others are doing electrical work, painting bedrooms, and building a computer lab. Work trips occur three to four times a year, and all expenses are paid out of pocket by those who volunteer. The latest project was to open a bakery, to be run by a local entrepreneur, whose rent will support the work of the school. The bread that is baked and sold there, we believe, is the Eucharist itself.

This project, which had its roots in a sermon about the disciples being told by Jesus to "push out into deep water and let down their nets" is now a $100,000-a-year operation, with a full-time on-site manager and a staff of local workers paid by Mayflower. At no time do we attempt to convert any child (most of whom are Catholic) to our brand of Christianity. We are there to make Christianity itself visible. We want to be part of the Underground Church movement, and as such, we leave all denominational and doctrinal require-ments or strategies for evangelism behind. Our presence and our witness is our evangelism.

If inviting questions is to be more valued than supplying answers, then we have invited more than our share of questions in Nicaragua. Why do you do this? What difference does it make? What claim do these children have on your life? In all honesty, we are lousy at answering these questions—perhaps because deep down we are too busy asking ourselves the same questions. It all comes back to trust. Some things are compelling even without an adequate explanation, like love itself.

If encouraging personal exploration is more important than communal uniformity, then why not agree to a Bible study that is outside your tradition, or even your comfort zone? Why not discuss with other churches what it means that Christians know so little about Islam? Is there a mosque in your area that you could attend? Would you, if the situation required it, hide an innocent Muslim family in your church after a terrorist attack? The last half of the twentieth century was shaped by the enduring guilt of the Holocaust. What plans have we made to stop the next one?

If meeting needs is really more important than maintaining institutions, then why are so many local congregations unable to look around themselves to find partners in ministry? It is often astonishing to discover that churches on the same block have no idea what mission work the other is doing. What if they are doing something that works? What if they are doing something we could do also as partners? In some urban areas, gang members outnumber church members, but efforts to get them inside to meet the enemy and perhaps put down their weapons have been stalled by a long-standing rule that forbids pizza to be consumed in the parlor. What about illegal immigrants as the "strangers among us"? Isn't it true that many people want them to cut their grass and then go away? They have names. They have children. They have hopes and dreams of their own. Will the church have a response when the persecutions and deportations begin?

Often the members of a small and struggling church will respond to this challenge by saying that they don't have the money or the bodies to do anything more than they are already doing. The real question may be about what they are doing now, and whether it is focused inwardly to keep the doors open, or outwardly to engage the community as a force for healing and hope. Indeed, the "we are too small" argument is exactly why shared mission and cooperation with other communities are so important. Not only can we do more together, but we will learn from one another, be inspired by one another, even come to realize how many of our dreams are shared together: a world fit for children, the best possible schools, safe neighborhoods, neighbors who care for one another, and resources for those among us who fall sick or into despair. Whether as an individual or a beloved community, everything changes when you cross the room to talk to the stranger.

If peace is more important than power, then how will the Underground Church embody this defining characteristic of The Way? Could we agree across our traditions that violent video games have no place in our churches (or in our homes either)? Would we be able to embrace and defend a conscientious objector in our congregation with as much enthusiasm as we praise our soldiers? What about our national obsession with sporting events that celebrate gratuitous violence? Is this what happens when followers of the Prince of Peace partition their faith completely from the games of the dominant culture?

If one of the distinctive characteristics of a Christian is to be nonviolent, to have reverence for life, for healing, and for wholeness, then why are we all just as "fanatic" about brutal contact sports as the most pagan fan among us? The evidence is mounting that head injuries will disable countless young men and women with concussion-related afflictions in the future, yet we purchase and watch video compilations of the most "memorable hits" on the field and cheer them in super slow motion. The rise of blood sports like extreme or cage fighting is a disturbing regression to public spectacles of pain and even death. We spend hours in the church discussing theological ideas and distinctions, but in prime time our voice is conspicuously absent. In our increasingly Roman culture, the church looks and sounds like one more compliant customer. Can we even have this discussion, or do our sporting events and our athletes constitute our real religion?

If we really cared more about love and less about sex, then would Christians of all persuasions boycott pornography, or just keep it in the closet? The overt sexualizing of young women in talent contests and beauty pageants and by the fashion industry remains fundamentally incompatible with our professed belief that beauty is the effortless manifestation of inner peace. This is not a conservative or liberal issue. This is the marketing of human flesh to a willing American Empire that deludes itself about being "Christian"— when in fact it is profoundly Roman. Who better to resist the objectification of women through noncooperation than the members of the Underground Church?

Finally, if this life is really more important than the afterlife, then why is the church still obsessed with the afterlife? Why do we continue to manipulate the ultimate fear, the fear of death, and use it to gain power over other people? We should trust that there is a reason for our lives without claiming to know what we do not know—what happens to us after we die. Life after death can no more be proved than disproved. "For nothing worth proving can be proven, nor yet disproven," as Tennyson said.

Perhaps in all our fear of death we fail to consider something worse—that we would live forever. As Coffin put it, "Life without death would be interminable—literally, figuratively. We'd take days just to get out of bed, weeks to decide, 'what's next?' Students would never graduate, faculty meetings and all kinds of other gatherings would go on for months. Chances are, we'd be as bored as the ancient Greek gods and up to their same mischievous tricks."[5]

Besides, death is the great equalizer, mocking our pretentions about race, class, nationality, sexual orientation, and religious identity. Death gets us out of the way so that God can have another go at it with fresh recruits. Otherwise the world would have quickly become overpopulated by immortals. Besides, our gospel teaches us not to fear death, which has lost its "sting" as Paul put it, but we do. Yet without death, we would never live, and the only way to have a good death is to lead a good life. Then we do not have to rage against the dying of the light.

If the sacredness of our lives does not depend on certain knowledge of an afterlife, then why don't we work together to defend and celebrate that sacredness without requiring such knowledge? Trust, not certainty, is what defines our "faith." Trust is most needed if we are to view death as a friend, not an enemy. In this death-denying culture, few things could unite us more across various religious traditions than to come to terms with death as entirely natural. As Paul put it, "No one lives unto himself alone, and no one dies unto himself alone. If we live, we live unto the Lord; and if we die, we die unto the Lord. So whether we live or whether we die, we are the Lord's" (Rom. 14:8).

We may not know what is beyond the grave, but we know who is beyond it. "And Christ resurrected links the two worlds, telling us that we really live only in one. . . . The abyss of God's love is deeper than the abyss of death."[6] As for growing old gracefully, which we have a very hard time doing, let us remember the words of Albert Camus: "To grow old is to pass from passion to compassion." Eternity is not a gift that is conferred at death, but a present endowment. As the great rabbi Abraham Heschel put it, with God, "time is eternity in disguise."

Building Bridges

As Diana Butler Bass has noted, it is unfortunate that the word *hospitality* has been taken over by the hotel industry. It was once the dominant and distinctive marker of the first Christians, who welcomed those whom Jesus called "the least of these" into the heart of the beloved community. Far from a commercial transaction, or even a move designed as part of a reciprocal relationship, hospitality involves inviting, not friends or family members or rich neighbors, but "the poor, the crippled, the lame, the blind, and you will be blessed because they cannot repay you" (Luke 14:12–13).

Although these days when we speak of hospitality we think more easily of Martha Stewart than of Jesus, this much is certain. "While contemporary Christians tend to equate morality with sexual ethics, our ancestors defined morality as welcoming the stranger. Unlike almost every other contested idea in early Christianity, including the nature of Christ and the doctrine of the Trinity, the unanimous witness of the ancient fathers and mothers was that hospitality was the primary Christian virtue . . . hospitality equaled Christian morality."[7]

Wendell Berry warns us that one of the first responsibilities of living the life of the spirit is what he calls "the joy of sales resistance." "We live in a time when technologies and ideas (often the same thing) are adopted in response not to need but to advertising, salesmanship, and fashion. Salesmen and saleswomen now hover about us as persistently as angels, intent on 'doing us good' according to instructions set forth by persons educated at great public expense in the arts of greed and prevarication."[8]

Advertisers are what S. I. Hayakawa called the "sponsored poets" of our society. They are among the most creative people in our culture, and they think nothing of stealing our best words. Hospitality is now something sold as a luxury at great price. It is not a gift but a transaction. Once the radical practice of welcoming the stranger into the heart of a community that both protected them and affirmed their intrinsic value, hospitality is now just another rung on the great economic ladder of life. The more money you have, the more hospitality you can purchase. Those people who scurry around after your tip are trained to make you feel most welcome.

How then did it happen that churches have become among the most inhospitable places in our communities? The convenience store is open 24/7, but most churches are locked down in the middle of the day. The message is that we don't wish to be bothered by intruders—and that we fear them. Come back on Sunday morning, and then only if properly dressed and somehow able to distinguish between the visitor's gallery and a pew owned by a pillar of the congregation. Sit there by mistake and you will know the meaning of the word *inhospitable*.

One of the most obvious divides in the church today between liberals and conservatives can be seen in our definition of morality. Evangelicals place the emphasis on individual sin (primarily sexual), whereas progressives focus more on institutional sin (primarily economic). The former is thought to be synonymous with "morality"; the latter is thought to be a largely secular, political matter. Such a distinction would not have been made in the early church. The first followers of Jesus defined morality as *welcoming the stranger*. As for economic injustice, the first followers of Jesus had a way of dealing with poverty that has long been forgotten—a subject to which we shall return. It bears repeating, however, that the unity was not theological. It was *ethical*. As we know, they argued about all sorts of things (the nature of Christ, the Trinity, circumcision, and so on), but there seems to have been no argument whatsoever about this: *hospitality was the primary Christian virtue.*

After all, the church began in people's homes, and included offering shelter to widows, orphans, and traveling missionaries and preachers. At the center of the life of the early church, however, was the fundamental human sacrament: food, shared in community. It was offered to the poor, so that they could live. It was offered in funeral banquets, so that people did not have to suffer alone. Together with the making of clothing for those in needs, the church offered the world the basics of life. Women were primarily responsible for these simple acts of hospitality, as they continue to be in churches today. How ironic then, that according to our story, women were last at the cross and first at the tomb—yet in some churches they are still not allowed to preach or hold positions of authority. Without women there would be no church. This is not a liberal or conservative position, but rather an historical reality.

After Christianity became the religion of the Empire, and many protested by establishing monastic communities in the desert, hospitality remained the cardinal virtue. The idea was not just to be nice; rather it was to view the welcoming of every stranger as the welcoming of Christ himself. Many historians believe that hospitality accounted for more conversions than did martyrdom. "'Only look,' they said, 'look how they love one another.'"[9]

Only look? Fair enough. Let us look at the treatment of the stranger in our time. Our greatest fears today involve two groups of "strangers"—Muslims and undocumented immigrants. A controversy erupted over plans to build a mosque near Ground Zero. A pastor in Florida got fifteen minutes of twisted fame by planning to burn a copy of the Koran. In Oklahoma, with its surprisingly populist roots, serenaded by Woody Guthrie, we have evolved into the reddest of the red states. Once the end of the line for the Trail of Tears, we are now attempting to pass the meanest anti-immigrant laws in the nation. One would make it a crime to feed or provide transportation to an illegal immigrant or his family. Another would deny public education and all public services to the children of undocumented workers. Still another would have children carry a special ID card that would brand them as the children of such workers. Why not just sew a Mexican flag on their shirts?

Then there is the sheer hypocrisy of it all. After a recent epic hailstorm in Oklahoma City, thousands of damaged roofs were repaired, and all the crews were Hispanic. Among them were certainly undocumented workers who streamed north to find work, yet they were hired. The economy cannot function without them. Their work ethic is the strongest that I have ever seen, and we use them to do the hardest manual labor. Then we are so afraid of them that we ask them to disappear when the sun goes down.

At a recent gathering of churches concerned with the treatment of illegal immigrants in Oklahoma City, reporters were present from across the country. (They know what is about to happen in Oklahoma.) My associate Chris Moore and I were the only white, mainline clergy in attendance. In fact, other than a woman from our congregation, we were the only white people there. In a strange and sad conversation, members of that Catholic parish on the south side of Oklahoma City came up, one after another, and asked us to explain why we were there. "We've never seen white people at these meetings before. We wondered if you were INS agents posing as pastors."

At a mosque only blocks from Mayflower, tires were slashed in the parking lot, and more than once someone has attempted to set the building on fire. So much for welcoming (or even tolerating) the stranger in our midst. So much for hospitality. And there is no need to state the obvious—most of this hatred comes from professing Christians. They apparently believe all the right things, but see absolutely no connection between what they profess and the most basic forms of human dignity.

The days ahead in America will be trying, especially because economic hard times amplify the darkest of human fears and accelerate the turning of the stranger into the scapegoat. In the Underground Church, no matter what name is on the outside of the building, no matter what its theological tradition or worship style, we will stand with the stranger. Otherwise we should abandon the name Christian.

Our coalitions should be built around the collective practice of the original and subversive Christian virtues. Churches should build bridges and work together on issues of peace and nonviolence, radical hospitality, and economic justice. When wars are brewing, Christians ought to be the most resistant constituency in the land. At the very least, we should insist on compliance with Just War theory, even though many will argue (and at the deepest level, they are right) that all war is fundamentally incompatible with Christianity. Why? Because war is sin.

But we will need to do more than just march or give speeches. The Underground Church lives up to its name by being conscientiously noncompliant. We will do more than protest. We will organize support systems for those who wish to leave military service as conscientious objectors. We will work with the traditional pacifist communities (Quakers, Mennonites, and so on) to recover pacifism as a core Christian value, not the quaint aberration of "fringe elements." We will be at least as concerned about violence in movies as we are about sex in movies.

When it comes to hospitality, we are going to have to do more than just put a generic ALL ARE WELCOME message on the wayside pulpit in front of the church. Besides, who can blame people, especially our gay sisters and brothers, for simply not believing it? Hospitality is more than just a goal; it is an attitude that is embodied in the way people are greeted, whether they are accommodated (especially if they are disabled), and whether they are offered help in navigating an unfamiliar space. If there are special customs or songs (benediction responses or other "in-house" rituals) that will be confusing or unfamiliar, a deacon or other church member should offer to explain the "mysteries of the place." Everything that is familiar to regular worshipers is unfamiliar to visitors. Simple graciousness is required, and that means paying attention to visitors and using one's empathetic imagination. Regular attendees should ask themselves a simple question: What if I were that person, in this strange place, for the first time?

When it comes to economic justice, the Underground Church should begin by partnering with other congregations to pay a living wage to all its employees. With shrinking congregations and limited budgets, this can be very difficult for some churches to manage, but it should be our goal. A church budget is a theological statement, and we pay for what we value. Church employees must be paid, of course, but if this consumes most of the budget, then something is wrong. What we often forget is that we can practice hospitality with our money. We can use it to lift others up and to heal. Remember, the Latin root for *hospitality* is the same as for *hospital* and *hospice*.

The vast majority of traditional parish churches are a long, long way from the goal of spending as much on mission as they do on "keeping house." But we could all agree to move in that direction. If every church in this country spent as much on others as it spends on itself, the amount of money that would go for programs that help people would be staggering. At a time when government services are being cut, the church has a moral obligation to help fill that void. Granted, some of the consequences of following Jesus are riskier than others. Some communities will not be ready for some of the ideas that follow. But we call it the Underground Church for a reason.

Let's Get Real

In the days ahead, decisions will have to be made about when it is moral for members of the Underground Church to break the law in order to follow a higher law. There is a long, rich tradition of Christian disobedience, and as a result of such holy dissent, we have often made the world a better place for those without a voice, without power, without hope. All of us are citizens who are subject to the law, of course. But some of us have also sworn allegiance to a higher law that is often at odds with the Empire. If this were not the case, Christians would not have been persecuted and killed, nor would Jesus have been executed as a political revolutionary.

One of the insidious results of having sold our souls to the Empire, both the Roman one and now the American one, is that we are beholden to it for protection; we are also on the receiving end of its wealth. The church can no more criticize its own benefactor than an employee can criticize her boss—even if she thinks that the boss is doing something terribly wrong. Add to this "captivity" the dominant theme that this is a "Christian nation," with all the trappings of civil religion, and the church's capacity for civil disobedience is virtually eliminated.

In particular, the granting of tax exemption for churches and the use of government funds for so-called faith-based initiatives put the once anti-imperial church in the back pocket of the Empire. Among the most radical of ideas being floated these days is that we should not be tax exempt and should never accept government funds for any church project or mission—no matter how worthy. To do so compromises our ability to resist the Empire when such resistance is called for. Tax exemption is a form of government subsidy. Faith-based initiative grants are a direct investment of public funds for religious purposes. Conservatives and liberals might have very different reasons for resisting this entanglement, but both can resist it by not taking the money!

Here is an example of being subversive in a way that transcends the labels of left and right. The danger, of course, is that we will debate these matters past the point of no return. Human beings have a habit of knowing that things are wrong, but doing nothing to stop them until it is too late.

When one of the foremost advocates for religiously based pacifism in the United States, A. J. Muste, wrote his classic essay, "Holy Disobedience," he included this chilling reminder of what happens when we wait too long:

> In the introductory chapter to Kay Boyle's volume of short stories about occupied Germany, The Smoking Mountains, there is an episode which seems to me to emphasize the need of Resistance and of not waiting until it is indeed too late. She tells about a women, professor of philology in a Hessian university, who said of the German experience with Nazism, "It was a gradual process." When the first Jews Not Wanted signs went up, "there was never any protest made about them, and, after a few months, not only we, but even the Jews who lived in that town, walked past without noticing any more that they were there. Does it seem impossible to you that this should have happened to civilized people anywhere?"
>
> The philology professor went on to say that after a while she put up a picture of Hitler in her classroom. After twice refusing to take the oath of allegiance to Hitler, she was persuaded by her students to take it. "They argued that in taking this oath, which so many anti-Nazis had taken before me, I was committing myself to nothing, and that I could exert more influence as a professor than as an outcast in the town.

She concluded by saying that she now had a picture of a Jew, Spinoza, where Hitler's picture used to hang, and added, "Perhaps you will think that I did this ten years too late, and perhaps you are right in thinking this. *Perhaps there was something else we could all of us have done, but we never seemed to find a way to do it, either as individuals or as a group, we never seemed to find a way.*[10]

So goes the argument that I have often heard in church. I can do much more as a minister if I always work within the system, if I "go along to get along." But the day is coming (and coming soon) when people will have to decide whether to shelter an undocumented worker in order to keep him from being deported and his family broken up. When such a "stranger" stops by the church to ask for food and a ride, do we follow the law that forbids us to help, or follow the higher law of Christian hospitality?

Do we continue to pay taxes to a system that is perpetually at war and that has adopted the right to wage preemptive war based on the perception of an imminent threat from nonexistent weapons of mass destruction? What about states that execute inmates using tax dollars? Is this not just as offensive to some as public funds used for abortions are to others?

It has been half a century since the church was a truly irresistible force for social change and justice in this country. Not since Martin Luther King Jr. have we heard the call to resist unjust laws, and answered that call in language as unapologetic and biblical as that of King's "Letter from a Birmingham Jail." Written on the margins of a newspaper in which a number of Georgia ministers had denounced the civil rights campaign he was leading, Dr. King responded to charges that he was an extremist by reminding us all that Jesus was an "extremist for love," that Amos was an "extremist for justice," that Paul was an "extremist for the gospel." The question is not whether we will be extremists, wrote King, "but what kind of extremists will we be. Will we be extremists for hate or for love?"[11]

Where are the extremists for love in the church today? Here and there we have seen outbreaks of moral indignation, mostly by special interests calling rallies to press grievances or to plead for a cause. But the infinite power of corporations and the media to marginalize such movements and distract us with lies and fear mongering always prevails. Now that corporations have the constitutional rights that people have to free speech, and even more rights than people have to make unlimited secret campaign contributions (thanks to a disastrous Supreme Court Ruling in *Citizens United v. Federal Election Commission*), the imbalance of power has only widened. We love to recoil at the word "fascist," thinking that it can only apply to jackbooted thugs. But the classic definition of fascism is "control of government by special interests, with the blessing of the church."

What if the church no longer gave its blessing?

CHAPTER SEVEN

Leavening the Imperial Loaf

Heaven's Imperial rule is like leaven that a woman took and concealed
in three measures of flour until it was all leavened.
—MATTHEW 13:33 (KJV)

This verse from Matthew may be the most subversive parable in
the New Testament, although it sounds harmless. It may also be
as authentic as any utterance by the historical Jesus in the gospels.
Scholars have good reason to believe that this "one-liner," or simili-
tude, comparing the "kingdom of God" with a woman making
bread, is Jesus of Nazareth at his most provocative. Surely they must
be kidding?

Isn't the parable of the good Samaritan or the prodigal son what
comes to mind when we think of Jesus the Teacher at his best? Why
would this brief and thoroughly domesticated little ditty be considered so radical? We learned it in Sunday school as part of a pair
of teachings that included the story of the mustard seed. The lesson
seemed obvious enough for the average third grader: *out of humble,
even hidden origins can grow great and powerful things*—which we all knew
was just a metaphor for the church. We started small but then grew
into something great, just like the mustard seed grows into a great
shrub (and then miraculously, in Matthew, into a tree). Likewise a
pinch of yeast causes a larger amount of bread to rise. What a perfect
little devotional parable for a meeting of the Ladies Guild.

Like so much of the gospels, the true meaning of the words of
Jesus have been lost across a chasm of time, language, culture, and

the well-intentioned editing of nameless scribes. When it comes to what has been "lost in translation," this parable is exhibit A. It occurs in both the Gospel of Thomas and in what scholars call the Q gospel. Considering that no gospel named Q exists in the Bible (and no manuscript has ever been found), the reader has the right to ask what this means. Historical Jesus scholars have known for two hundred years that there are passages in Matthew and Luke that are almost identical but don't come from the earliest gospel, Mark. This has led most scholars to conclude that both gospel writers borrowed material from an additional "sayings" source beyond the oral tradition, and they named it Q (from the German word *quelle*, or "source"). Because the Gospel of Thomas is also an ancient collection of the sayings of Jesus, this parable is independently attested in two very early Christian documents. It has been of more interest to biblical scholars than to most preachers. It should be of great interest, however, to the Underground Church.

Because the parable's language is so heavily influenced by the King James Version, words like "leaven" and "three measures" remain difficult for most moderns to understand. Most translators do not know what to do with the idea that the woman "hid" the leaven in the dough, because the Greek is hard to decipher. So they have the woman either "mixing" or "kneading" the dough, which makes more sense to us. As for "three measures," a modern listener misses the significance here, even though it is a very large amount of flour—about fifty pounds.

To the ancient listener, however, the connotation would have been obvious and unmistakable. A first-century Jew would hear an echo of the words of Genesis 18:1–8, when Abraham's three "visitors" are provided hospitality, and he went to the tent and said to Sarah, "Make ready quickly *three measures* of choice flour, knead it, and make cakes."[1] These three angels, one of whom is Yahweh, come as part of the prophecy of the birth of Isaac, an idea so fantastic that it made Sarah laugh. No wonder that when the impossible child was born they named him Laughter, which in Hebrew is pronounced Isaac.

So more than just a large amount of flour is at work in this verse from Matthew. The whole thing is improbable if not impossible—not to mention the fact that the main actor is a woman. Add to this the action of hiding the leaven, often translated "yeast," and the parable moves even further underground. Remember, the plight of most women in the Roman Empire was unfavorable, to say the least.

In a male-dominated patriarchal society, women were subject to their husbands or fathers. They were at a distinct disadvantage when it came to the purity codes and were often looked on with superstition and fear. There is nothing unusual about a woman baking bread, but as the symbol of the sacred activity of God, it is highly problematic. Indeed it would have been a scandal.

What's more, the Greek words used for "hiding," or "concealed," is krypto (Luke) or enkrypto (Matthew), which both have negative connotations. These are the root words from which we get our English word encrypt, known to all computer users as the verb form of our word encryption, or to keep secret by means of a code. It is how we send information that we wish to protect. The more important the information, the more important it becomes to protect or secure it—in short, to hide it. The words of Jesus from Mark come to mind: "To you has been given the secret of the kingdom of God, but for those outside, everything comes in parables" (4:11).

The phrase "until it was all leavened" speaks of the process by which leaven works on dough until everything is "corrupted." Once set in motion, the outcome is both inevitable and irresistible. But why would scholars refer to this process as "corruption"? How can a huge quantity of bread quietly rising to feed a hungry world possibly be a bad thing? To our ears it is not. But if we were first-century Jews, the answer would be so obvious that no one would even think to ask the question. In the ancient world, the process of leavening frequently stood as a *metaphor for moral corruption*. The Jews, after all, did not celebrate the feast of the leavened bread, but of the *unleavened* bread.

In their defining event, the children of Israel escaped Egypt by taking their dough before it was leavened, "with their kneading bowls wrapped up in their cloaks on their shoulders" (Exod. 12:34b). To celebrate Passover, Moses gives very specific instructions about who can partake of the feast of unleavened bread, and forbids the eating of leavened bread. For seven days no leavened bread should be eaten or "seen in your possession, and no leaven shall be seen among you in all your territory" (13:7). In short, all leavened bread had to be cleaned out of the house.

Leaven makes bread rise, but it also makes it rot. It makes it swell, just as a dead body swells (or road-kill, to bring this closer to home) due to fermentation. Corpses were a powerful symbol of impurity, hence the power of Jesus calling some Pharisees "unmarked graves that people walk over without realizing it."

There are several examples in the New Testament that prove this common understanding. Jesus warns the disciples concerning the leaven of the Pharisees and the leaven of Herod (Mark 8:15). They had just asked Jesus for a sign (a miracle, which he refuses to perform), and such a request corrupts the whole enterprise. Matthew refers to their teaching as the "leaven of the Pharisees" (16:12); for Luke, it is their hypocrisy (12:1). Paul twice quotes the proverb, "A little leaven leavens the whole lump"—once in Galatians to warn against a person who is demanding that they be circumcised (5:9) and again in his first letter to the Corinthians when he refers to the "leaven of malice and evil" and contrasts it to the "unleavened bread of sincerity and truth" (5:8).

Preachers know that certain words can be depended on to produce certain effects in the listener. We call them "trigger words." Today, among a liberal crowd, we might say something about the "military-industrial complex" or "corporate lobbyists" and assume one reaction; trigger words for the conservative ear might be "big government" or "socialism." Most of us have heard this familiar American proverb, "one rotten apple spoils the whole barrel." This may come closest to explaining how a first-century Jewish audience would have heard the word "leaven."

Leaven was a trigger word in the time of Jesus, and everyone would have "gotten" that it signified "rotten." Today we might speak of a virus, either of the body or on one's computer. But the effect is *negative*, out of all proportion to size, and once it begins, it cannot be stopped. Like the mustard seed, something tiny and hidden can infect your whole garden. The effect is inevitable and unstoppable— it will be taken over by what is actually a noxious weed. Once established and set in motion, it is almost impossible to "weed out."

So what appeared at first to be a harmless little parable is in fact a dangerous one. This parable, understood in its original context, captures the essence of the Underground Church. As followers in this subversive movement, we are neither dissuaded by the odds nor naïve about how long it takes before the "corruption" is complete. What is strange and radical about understanding the church as a form of moral corruption should be obvious. We have so long associated purity with religion and held that "cleanliness is next to godliness" that the idea of being leaven (and thus corruption) in the loaf of the Empire is the furthest thing from our minds.

Perhaps the time has come in the church to turn away from the idea that we can just "think positive thoughts" or sing one more verse of "Amazing Grace" while carrying water for the emperor. If we are salt and light, then what does it mean that we have lost our "saltiness" or failed to chase any of the darkness from the room? It means that most people in church see themselves as salve, not leaven—as sugar, not salt. We want to fix what is broken or heal whatever festers. We want to overcome corruption by being incorruptible, not by corrupting it!

We grasp only half of that ancient saying by Jesus correctly, choosing only to be as "harmless as doves" but not as "wise as serpents." We want to talk about the ways in which the world is infected with sin, with dis-ease, but when was the last time that a preacher urged us to infect the infection? In fact, the whole idea of fermentation is a little creepy. Isn't that how people make beer? Well yes, but not all forms of rot are rotten. Moldy bread, after all, gave us penicillin.

You see, the truth is that the church has a reputation problem. No one considers the church in our time to be a threat to the Empire. The last time we systematically challenged the status quo was during the civil rights movement. We pass resolutions now and organize marches, but the Empire knows that in the end this is a good bargain. It knows we need to "blow off steam." This proves that we live in a free country and that "democracy works." Then we can return to business as usual, and for the Empire, business as usual is the good news.

In the Underground Church, however, we have good news that comes in the form of bad news. It is good news to all those who have been left out, and bad news to all those who have designed the world around a closed table. For starters, we will need to do more than just talk about a "paradigm shift." We need to be one—small, hidden, irrepressible, and confident that we can corrupt at least three measures of the imperial loaf.

Sharing the Good Bad News

Let's first admit that we are so accustomed to speaking of the gospel as "Good News" that it is nearly impossible to imagine that it was not (and still should not be) good news to everyone. So much of the church is now so infected with the power of positive thinking that when we hear the announcement of the arrival of the kingdom of God, we assume that it should be accompanied by an Aaron Copeland fanfare. Isn't this the Glory Train pulling into the station? Hasn't evil now been put on notice? Didn't the angels just receive a promotion? Won't the lame now begin to walk? Won't the blind now receive their sight? Won't the prisoners be set free—or does this only happen in real life when the prisons are overcrowded?

Our problem is that we have adapted the announcement of the coming of the kingdom to our present understanding, instead of considering it a challenge to everything we think we know and believe. Granted, this is not a new problem. Every generation has failed to hear what is truly radical about the gospel, preferring to domesticate it according to "accepted community standards." If someone were to offer a devotional from Luke 4 at a meeting of the local chamber of commerce, for example, wouldn't everyone just assume that when Isaiah speaks of proclaiming "the year of the Lord's favor," it means that the Lord favors free enterprise? Or that when he says he "has not come to bring peace but a sword," what he is really talking about is "the few, the proud, the Marines"? Or that when he speaks clearly against divorce, what he is really talking about is gay marriage? Or that when he commands us to love our enemies and pray for them, he is really just talking about good sportsmanship toward members of the opposing foot-ball team?

In the church, we are drowning in a sea of shallow sentimentality. The gospel is presented without teeth, and by definition, the toothless cannot chew on anything of substance. Worship feels like one continuous appetizer without a main course. Sometimes the most memorable moments in church occur when the real world intrudes, either by design or by accident. I have always had a fantasy about rearranging a line or two in the annual Christmas pageant. A new script would be provided to the shepherds (played by unruly boys) and the angels (played by girls whose mothers insisted on it). Instead of a safe little spectacle performed mostly for parents, one of the shepherds breaks from the script and brings a new message:

> Be afraid, be very afraid—for behold I bring most of you bad news of a deep sadness for all the important and powerful people. For to you this day is born a subversive savior, who will be leaven in the loaf of the Empire. A teenage mother has hidden this leaven in the midst of scandal and obscurity. This will be a sign for you: you will find a child wrapped in bands of cloth and fermenting in a manger. By the time you understand what it all means, three measures of the existing order will already be corrupted. A multitude of the heavenly host will praise God, saying, "Glory to an unclean God in the lowest heaven, and on earth peace among those whom he has leavened!"

Imagine the response from the audience. People might put down their cell phones and camcorders long enough to say, "What version is that?" Or consider what might happen in an Easter sermon if the preacher were to announce, not Good News, but Very Frightening News. Instead of "He is risen!" what if he said, "Oh no, he's back!" What if instead of angels singing we heard multinational corporations groaning, slumlords fuming, payday loan crooks reeling—in short, all the Herods of the world muttering about how crucifixion isn't what it used to be? Think of it in Empire-speak: "We ask for a simple favor—go down there and close the damn Jesus file! And this is what we get? We give our men the best equipment and training, and we get some sort of counterinsurgency? What do 'you people' want?"

To get a glimpse of how countercultural the parable of the leaven is, consider the Greek word that we translate as "kingdom of God." It is *basileia*, from which we get the English word *basilica*, which was the Roman word for a very large public building. In the ancient world it had to do with royal administration, so the *basileia* is essentially the Roman Empire itself. To say the least, such rule was not benevolent. The great gift of Augustus to his people was the *Pax*

Romana, the peace of Rome. "But it was pax only if you were Romana; otherwise it was oppressio, oppression."[2] The audience listening to this parable would inevitably hear basileia as "empire," so what we translate as "kingdom of God" would have been heard and understood as the "empire of God." It had a negative connotation, but that's where the parable gets its leverage. The empire of Caesar is being replaced by the empire of God. Jesus employs the term empire as an activity, not as a noun for the ruler, emperor, or king. Such references to God as king or emperor were common in the Hebrew Bible, but the idea of the empire (as a process or activity) of God was not.

When we hear the word "kingdom" today, we usually think of Walt Disney and the Magic Kingdom. It is a fanciful, otherworldly place, but it is certainly not negative. No one thinks of corruption when he or she hears the term "kingdom of God." But to the first listeners, this parable basically says that the empire of God is like moral corruption that a woman took and concealed (she acts subversively) in three measures of flour (an amount so large as to signify an event as significant as the birth of Isaac) until it was all leavened (until in the "great divine cleanup of the world"[3] there is enough for everyone). She begins the process by which distributive justice will one day be realized and the messianic banquet will be served.

For this reason, the movement, which must now begin in all our churches, the movement of the spirit that we are calling the Underground Church, must take this ancient and misunderstood parable as its signature text. Not just because of its ancient and authentic credentials, but because it captures the essence of the first Jesus People. They were subversive and profoundly anti-imperial. If members of the Underground Church thought of themselves as leaven in the loaf of the Empire, then this is bad news to all who are invested in the unleavened status quo. It means that instead of appearing to the outside world as a harmless cartoon, like the Church Lady from Saturday Night Live, Jesus People need to be considered a real threat again, like a virus that can't be quarantined. Instead of being described in conventional terms like "salt of the earth" (which today has come to mean the humble, patient, and nonconfrontational), followers of The Way are redefined in the Underground Church as a kind of self-germinating, Empire-corrupting collection of holy fools.

Members of the Underground Church will not blend into the dominant culture, but will do subversive things for the right reasons. We will hide ourselves in three measures of the world's weary madness and set in motion our peculiar form of fermentation. Our power will come not from denominational identity or theological purity but from one simple, nonnegotiable, radical idea: *the power of love is ultimately greater than the love of power.*

In this deceivingly simple parable from Matthew, the Underground Church possesses both a model and a method. A woman takes subtle, hidden action, and against the odds something improbably wonderful happens. Consider for a moment how counterintuitive this is. Many churches these days are so deeply into survival mode that their members wish to control the outcome *before* they take action. They prefer the probable to the improbable, and opt for certain outcomes over fermentation—not to mention the fact that many of them still won't let a women do the leavening!

Conventional wisdom says that we can't afford to spend too much time and money on mission if we are going to survive [argues the dying church]. But this begs the questions: If we are not doing mission, then for what purpose are we "saving" ourselves? Wouldn't it be better to die pushing out than to die circling the wagons? Wouldn't you rather be digging in your garden when the world ends than cowering in a fallout shelter?

Not all churches are going to make it, of course. But far more would not only survive but prosper if they would just consider practicing the gospel's own radical equation: *we gain our lives by losing them.* We plant seeds and then we trust the process of germination over which we have no control. As Fred Craddock reminded us, nobody stands over a seed and shouts, "Come on now, grow!" We invest a little of our infectious love in the community, and it germinates. People begin to come to us, but not to be inoculated. Strangely, they wish to catch this virus, to be exposed to this highly contagious notion that either all of us matter or none of us do.

It is remarkable that in the church, of all institutions, there is so much resistance to change. Every pastor knows the Seven Last Words of the Church: "We've never done it that way before." Yet the beloved community of the Jesus Followers was born doing things that had never been done before, and, as Diana Butler Bass says, with the exception of children, "Jesus insists that every person he meets *do* something and *change*. The whole message of the Christian scripture is based in the idea of *metanoia*, the change of heart that happens when we meet God face-to-face."[4]

After thirty years in the ministry, I can say with real conviction that almost every good thing that happens in a church happens when people move toward God without knowing how anything is going to turn out. And almost everything bad happens when people move away from God because they are afraid. We want peace, of course, but we think that peace means tranquility. We want security, but we think this means that there is some amount of money that represents economic tenure. We want to be "saved," but continue to understand this as a personal, individual transaction. So it is that we find ourselves lost at home, seeking after something whose essential character we have completely forgotten—namely what a Christian *does*, not what a Christian believes. We have embraced orthodoxy and forgotten orthopraxy. Our collective sickness is not unlike a form of ecclesiastical Alzheimer's.

When someone says the word "justice," today we think of a criminal proceeding followed by appropriate punishment. (Will justice be done?) But if the call of Jesus is to worship a God of distributive justice, then there is no getting around the fact that this means that everyone in the world must have enough. Calling this "socialism" is a scare tactic because it harks back to totalitarian movements of the twentieth century. Making sure that everyone in the world has enough should be called "church."

Justice means that everyone is welcome at the table, which means that a closed communion table is the anti-gospel. Taking the gospel seriously means that praying for the enemy, if practiced, would be the most countercultural activity on earth. Turning the other cheek is an idea that we have lampooned, but it breaks the downward spiral of violence into which the world is now imploding. Just remember, for example, what happened in Hollywood right after the horror of 9/11. Filmmakers agreed to stop making movies about things blowing up and people dying in mindless spectacles of violence. Now we are back to normal, which means we are sick again.

A woman in my church who was studying the parables of Jesus in a Sunday school class recently challenged me to use a parable as a text for my Easter sermon. She knew that I would find this hard to resist and said, simply, "Robin, try preaching a *parabolic* Easter sermon." So I took the dare and preached on the resurrection using the parable of the leaven. I wondered if anyone had ever done this before, but the more I thought about it the more I liked the idea: Easter as a form of moral corruption. I wondered if it would be my farewell sermon.

Rome knew that if you had a problem with some*body*, all you had to do was get rid of the body. Make sure the body of the troublemaker is removed after running a spear through his side, then secure it in a big tomb with a big rock and big guards standing watch all night—or, heaven forbid, some other *body* will steal the *body* and then we'll have a cult of the risen *body* on our hands.

By the time the church got around to writing this story, Jesus had been dead for a long time, but apparently not to his followers.

In other words, the leaven of resurrection hidden in the hearts of his closest friends had begun to rise at once. The movement was small and irrepressible, and it began to swell first in the loaf of the forgotten. Rome had tried to clean every last bit of leaven out of the Judean house, but it was too late. It was nothing short of a scandal, these unclean people worshiping an unclean God. Women had kept the movement alive of course. After all, don't women live most of their lives in defiance of the odds? The men thought it was an "idle tale," but that's because they don't do the baking.

What was flat and dead had begun to rise, yet this seemed so improbable and counterintuitive that they wisely kept it hidden, sharing the news of the corruption with only a few. In the original ending to Mark's gospel, the women have it exactly right—fleeing from the tomb, "for terror and amazement had seized them; and they said nothing to anyone, for they were afraid" (16:8).

At Pentecost, the corrupted loaf of the body of Christ fairly exploded right under their noses, packing enough spiritual leaven to get "devout Jews from every nation under heaven living in Jerusalem" involved in a kind of multilingual sing-along. The fermentation was so dramatic that some of the unleavened people around them accused them of acting under the influence of fermented grapes—at nine o'clock in the morning no less!

Let's face it. Nobody accuses us Christians of being drunk on joy these days. Today we have taken all the danger out of Easter. We speak of the tomb as if it were a tunnel and Jesus were a "slider"—to put it in the lingo of the fast food business. He wasn't really dead, just passing through. Easter is a foregone conclusion. Just drive around any town during Holy Week and you'll see that the wayside pulpits and electronic sign boards are all announcing the resurrection at the beginning of the week. In other words, in the scheme of things, he is raised before he has even been crucified. Because everyone knows how the story ends, we end up pretending to be joyful about what we pretended to be sad about in the first place.

In fact, we have so literalized the narratives of the passion that we just assume that all three measures of the Easter meal were leavened in seventy-two hours. On the third day, the corruption was complete, and by that evening, Jesus had appeared to his closest followers, and all was leavened. Or to put it in John Dominic Crossan's words, "Friday was hard, Saturday was long, but by Sunday all was resolved."[5]

Perhaps in the Underground Church, instead of just placing an exclamation mark at the end of every sentence in the Easter bulletin, we should begin by considering that the resurrection exposes all who take it seriously to a form of moral corruption. It is a claim that we cannot make without being claimed ourselves. Because we have heard it so many times in church, "He is Risen!" may not be the most audacious thing to say these days. Perhaps in the Underground Church we should put it differently. For if we are only an observer of the Easter spectacle, we can safely shout Hallelujah! But if we are Easter People, corrupted by the leaven of the resurrection, then we really ought to say, *We are Rising!*

No More Company Clergy

The great Presbyterian preacher Ernest Campbell said once, "Nothing is sadder in the eyes of God than a minister who started out with a calling and ended up with a career." For all their talk of faith, ministers are often a nervously cautious lot. They are often more versed in bylaws and ecclesiastical disciplines than in the use of scripture for corruption. Someone is always upset about something in every church, of course, but we have often neglected to tell the clergy (who have a strong need to be loved and admired) that their job is not to make everyone happy. Once this becomes the object of ministry, one has effectively ceased doing ministry.

Fred Craddock tells the story of a young minister who had been called to a new parish and was thrilled. He was on fire to save the world and couldn't wait to get started. He arrived with his family at the parsonage, unloaded the furniture, and was welcomed by members of the search committee, who hosted a cookout to welcome him.

Everyone stood around eating hamburgers; men moved in the furniture, and women stocked the pantry. It was a new beginning. That is, until the minister got into a conversation with one of the members of the committee. The young pastor said, "You can't imagine what a delight it is to come to a church and know that you've been elected and chosen to come by unanimous vote."

The fellow flipping the hamburgers said, "Well, it was practically unanimous."

"Well, what do you mean, 'practically unanimous'?"

"Well, it was practically unanimous."

"Well, what do you mean *practically* unanimous?"

"Well, let's just say that it was unanimous."

"Well, but it wasn't—is that what you are saying?"

"I'm saying it was *almost* unanimous."

"Almost? Almost? What was the vote?"

"Well, if you insist, it was 234 to 2."

To two, thinks the minister to himself. *To two. I wonder who are the two?* Suddenly the minister becomes a detective, determined to uncover the identity of "the two." He spends six months at the task and feels certain that he has identified them. Then he spends the next six months trying to please those two. At the end of the year, the congregation had to let him go. The vote was 234 to 2.

One of the most important things that we can teach men and women who are seeking ordination is to take themselves less seriously and learn to ignore certain kinds of behavior in the church. As symbols of the holy, ministers soon discover that they are the object of what psychologists call "transference." All kinds of baggage (and not all of it healthy or even rational) gets brought to church to be unloaded on the designated scapegoat. No one will survive in the pastorate who doesn't know how to let a lot of it roll right off. Some quarrels are merely attention-getting strategies, and to feed them is to encourage them. Besides, if everyone agrees with the minister, something strange and dangerous is going on.

Recently I received an invitation from my alma mater, Phillips Theological Seminary, to preach at commencement. Using the parable of the leaven as my text, I reminded those who were about to begin the strangest and most ill defined of all professions (parish ministry) that they are among the last people on earth who do not work for the Empire. Like the woman making bread (the one who took action against the odds), as ministers of the gospel our first responsibility is to make a solid commitment to do the improbable, if not the impossible. It is our sacred duty. We are responsible by virtue of our ordination to take action against the odds, believing that we stand in a long line of those who hide leaven in the loaf of the Empire.

Standing in the pulpit of a downtown Tulsa church, I looked out on the faces of the latest graduating class and thought about how strange it is to spend three or four years studying to become a misfit. I thought about myself all those years ago, unsure whether I even wanted to add "Reverend" in front my name, but quite certain that the road ahead would somehow grow wider and smoother as time went by. I thought about how little I knew when I graduated and how much undeserved trust would be placed in me to tell people the secrets of their own hearts—especially when it could be argued that I did not yet know my own. So this is part of what I said to them, because this is what I wish someone had said to me:

> Dear Graduates,
> Not only do we live in the Empire. The Empire lives in us. . . . But in the name of Jesus of Nazareth, our Teacher and Lord, we do not have to obey the Empire. We do not have to cower before it, or subsidize it, or

be its compliant acolyte. We can be like leaven in the imperial loaf, working on behalf of an unclean God until there is enough bread corrupted by love to feed everyone at the messianic banquet. It will be a messy affair, with open seating and no head table.

Instead of passing one more resolution about the importance of feeding the hungry, we can simply resolve to actually *feed* them—and then resolutely go about doing so. We can refuse to give up on the lost; we can forgive those who have wronged us; we can reject violence in all of its guises. We can refuse to participate in the glamorizing of war and tell the gospel truth: war is sin. It is the greatest failure of the human species. Baptism once meant a rejection of all violence. What would happen today if we raised more conscientious objectors in our churches than soldiers?

We can boycott products that hurt workers or children or this earthly garden that has been given to us. Those of us who have more than we need will share out of our excess with those who have less than they need. We will not participate in making a scapegoat of our Hispanic sisters and brothers, and we will make arrangements ahead of time to hide an innocent Muslim family should another major terrorist attack occur. We promise God and one another that we will find ways to withdraw our cooperation from all systems that deal death and diminish dignity. We will begin by admitting that the most powerful way to get the attention of the Empire is not to fund it. Every time we buy something, we make a statement about what we truly value.

Every communion table should be open, and all human beings should be welcomed as children of God. Loyalty to a new ethic, The Way of Jesus, will be our only creed. And worship will be as diverse as the human family. We will stop fighting over music in the church long enough to remember that without it, in all its magnificent variety, many of us would not believe in God. Instead of pretending to know everything, we will admit that the older we get the less we know, so that we will not confuse faith with certainty or knowledge with redemption.

We will seek to live comfortably inside our own skins and in harmony with a beleaguered planet. We will regard the final act of grace to be that which makes a person gracious. Love of God and neighbor will be more important than arguments over the virgin birth or endless enterprising calculations about the end times. We will build communities in which no one can be denied access to an experience of the divine. The final act of love will be to love even the unlovable. We will do strange and wonderful things that make no sense to anyone and then we will smile when someone wonders why improbably wonderful things keep happening to us.

Can we do this? Yes we can. We can do it because it has already been done for us. We don't have to make it up. We just have to turn it loose. Heaven's imperial rule is like leaven that a woman took and concealed in three measures of flour until it was all leavened.

Let the corruption begin.

No More Crumbs at a Closed Table

Many of us in the American Protestant tradition grew up with a very similar experience of Holy Communion. The table wasn't really a table, but a piece of furniture with three closed sides for standing around. And the "elements" (the bread and wine or grape juice) were served from silver or gold-plated trays that stacked neatly one on top of another. The bread was often cut into tiny cubes without any crust, making it resemble a pile of spongy dice. The wine or grape juice was predispensed into tiny shot glasses that the ladies of the church (and it was always the ladies) complained were very time-consuming to wash. In truth nothing on the communion table resembled real food, and nobody would come to this table in search of enough calories to make it through the day.

It is all "symbolic," of course, but what exactly does it symbol-ize? We have argued for centuries over the meaning of the Eucharist, but one thing is certain: we are not really sharing a meal. We are engaged in a ritual that imitates a shared meal and that is almost always served to people who are not really hungry. What's more, it comes in the middle or at the end of the service. So it is served to those already present, rather than to anyone who might have actually come to church looking for food. And because it is served only to those present in worship, it is almost entirely an "insider" ritual, a sacrament served by the choir to the choir (metaphorically speaking).

No homeless person, for example, would advise hitting up churches on Sunday morning for a hot communion meal, unless the church has a soup kitchen. How odd that those churches that actually do have a soup kitchen, or find regular ways to feed the poor outside the church, are actually engaged in the most authentic kind of communion. This is because the Eucharistic meal among the first followers of The Way was actually a meal—provided for by disciples who served it to all comers from an open table heaped high with the gifts of the faithful.

Early Christian art makes it clear that the Eucharist was the "bread of heaven" come down to earth to eternally satisfy hunger and thirst in the mystical metaphors of John's gospel. The first followers of Jesus took the story of the loaves and the fishes much more seriously than we take it in the church today. It is the most oft told story in the New Testament (appearing no fewer than five times in the gospels).[6] The great divine cleanup of the world begins with a meal to which all are invited. It is freely offered, and no one is turned away. It is the essential sacrament of sharing the abundance of God's creation. This beautiful feast of life, modeled on the story of the loaves and fishes, is the consummate example of ethical grace. In God's household, no one goes hungry.

Unfortunately, liberals and conservatives in the church have mostly argued over whether the story of the loaves and fishes is a true miracle or just a metaphor. The answer is yes. One does not have to believe that those five loaves and two fish magically multiplied like popcorn in a microwave to know that this is a miracle. Suspension of natural law is not the only working definition of a miracle. Neither is it the case that a metaphor is a demotion of the miraculous—sometimes it is the only way to explain it.

Watching Jesus take bread, give thanks, bless it, break it, and share it with his disciples must have provided a model for everyone in the crowd. His example was the leaven in the loaf. When the others took what little they had and shared it, following the same formula (take and give thanks, bless, break, and share) there is enough for everyone. The stated miracle of the story is that *all are fed*. There is even some left over, but nobody says in amazement, "How did he do that?"

When artists sought to depict the heart of early Christian worship, the image that shows up again and again is of the loaves and fishes. But there is nothing meager or merely symbolic about the art that has been discovered in the Christian catacombs. As Brock and Parker tell us, "Large baskets of bread and platters of fish are set around a table with seven people enjoying the food. One delightful image in the Priscilla catacombs shows a table of women. In another, an inscription says the women call 'Bring it warm!' The early church framed its most important ritual meal as this act of feeding."[7]

This was at the heart of what it meant to be the beloved community—*food first*, provided by the community for the community as one continuous messianic banquet. This is the how the great thanksgiving meal "multiplied." This is how everyone has enough even though we have always been told that there is not enough for everyone. Starvation in the world is not the result of lack of food, but of a failure to share. There is enough for everyone, with some left over, but not if the gifts of the earth are reduced to a commodity that is sold to the highest bidder. "Whatever the market will bear" becomes unbearable if you are poor.

Now, this Great Thanksgiving meal, once the centerpiece of the first gatherings of the Jesus People, has devolved into a somber ritual often using leftover wine and breadcrumbs that have lost any resemblance to real bread. Bread without crust is like life without pain (unreal and unsustainable). In many communion "meals," the bread is a flat wafer, dry and tasteless, often placed into the mouth of a passive recipient by the priest. But no one eats this way—or we haven't since we were babies.

In a time when fewer children gather even once a day at the table to eat with their families, collective meals are more important than ever. This is the basic human sacrament. This is where one learns the most basic forms of etiquette. This is where one learns not to take more than one's share, to hold a fork, to put the napkin in one's lap, to chew slowly, and to speak when spoken to (without a mouthful of food). Eating together is the primary socializing ritual, but communion in most churches is a mostly silent and individual transaction. Whatever it is we are doing, we are not feasting. Yet we follow a *feasting* Jesus, not a *fasting* John the Baptist.[8]

Granted, there are real theological, not to mention logistical, objections that might be raised here. Because in our ritualized meal we say the words of institution (this is my body, this is my blood), we know *what* these elements stand for. But if our communion is a real meal, served to both members and guests (some of them poor or strangers), then what *exactly* are they eating? Given that Jesus described the bread as his body, then what is someone off the street to think of the symbolic significance of his dinner roll? Can we sanctify iced tea the same way we make a sacrament of the wine or grape juice? In the Underground Church, the answer is yes.

We can only speculate on the various rituals that preceded the sharing of the communion meal in the early church. But we know that they were actual meals serving the poor and not just the inner circle. This begs the question about the very meaning of communion in today's dying church. Why not try, as much as possible, to recover the spirit of actually feeding people without giving up on the sacramental power of the Eucharist? Can we not take a sweet potato and say, "This is my body"? Can't a pitcher of tea, lemonade, apple juice, or water be poured at each table after the minister has lifted it, given thanks, and pronounced it the blood of Christ?

Granted, this is easier to consider for a radical Protestant like myself, but I would invite all of us in the church to imagine the Eucharist more broadly defined and less legalistically implemented. It seems to me that much of the ministry of Jesus made the sacred and the profane indistinguishable, yet we are always trying to cobble that partition back together again. Episcopal priest and author Barbara Brown Taylor has put her remarkable eloquence in service to helping us recognize the holy in everything. We think of an altar as something only to be found in a church, but Taylor finds altars everywhere in the world, especially in what we blindly call the "mundane." She sees God in walking, paying attention, and saying no to work on the Sabbath; even hanging laundry on the line can be seen as setting up a prayer flag, for God's sake.[9]

It was Gerard Manley Hopkins who said, "The world is charged with the grandeur of God. It will flame out, like shining from shook foil."[10] In the Underground Church, we must recover the idea of the *sacramental* less narrowly (even idolatrously) defined. The physical world is designed to help us experience the spiritual one in what Taylor calls the "luminous web." Perhaps that is why it is good for all of us to remember that most of the ministry of Jesus took place outdoors. The gospel even *sounds* different when it is read outdoors. How odd, then, that we have bottled up in our temples what he so freely poured out on the ground.

Let us also never forget that communion is a subversive act. When Jesus prayed to heaven to bless the food he offered, he stood against the Roman Empire, whose rulers maintained their power by controlling the distribution of bread to the poor. In the Underground Church, the Eucharist needs to recapture these same anti-imperial roots. All who have something to contribute should bring their gifts to place on the table, and then all should be welcomed to the kind of feast that only sharing makes possible. What is important is that food comes first (broken, blessed, and shared), and then those who are fed should be invited to worship following the meal—to give thanks for the abundance that has been leavened by the generosity of the community.

This may seem impractical if not impossible in many churches, but some congregations might want to try it once a month, with familiar communion rituals offered as well. Remember that in the church, we have always known how to do one thing better than anyone else: the potluck. It is the closest thing we have to loaves and fishes, and anyone who hangs around a church long enough knows that there is a mysterious equilibrium to such randomly constructed meals. Even if no one divides up the responsibilities by last names (A-G bring meat, H-P bring vegetables, Q-Z bring dessert), it not only seems to work (with some left over), but people often bring their favorite (and best) dishes. The effect is that the potluck whole is much more than the sum of its parts. Grace hangs over the potluck because when we share, our best is made even better.

In the Underground Church, we might want to consider having the potluck holy meal *before* church, instead of after it—and then call it communion. We should avoid food that is purchased and processed, bringing as much as possible out of our gardens and ovens. Members who have more will understand that they are expected to bring more. The Underground Church will advertise the time and date of such "open feasts" or "communion meals." Instead of one communion table, we will have as many tables as we need to feed the crowd. The liturgy will be as simple as it is timeless: take and give thanks, bless, break, and serve. When strangers arrive, they should be seated immediately, even if this means that regular members must stand. In the Underground Church, the most important person in any room will always be the stranger.

We will feed each other in order that we might live, of course. But we will also be showing the most elemental form of compassion. What we will not do in the Underground Church is use food to recruit members or save souls. The communion meal will be the centerpiece of our approach to love of God and neighbor: grace freely offered just as it has been freely received. We did not make ourselves, and we did not bring the food up out of the soil. It is all a gift: "A good measure, pressed down, shaken together, running over, will be put into your lap; for the measure you give will be the measure you get back" (Luke 6:38).

In the Underground Church, we recognize the beauty that is inherent in the earth from which we arose. We are a community of real faces, not electronic postings, and we speak and embrace one another in real time with all our real problems and real possibilities. The Underground Church must model an alternative community in which all the divisions of human contrivance, all our prejudices, all our self-serving and self-destructive tendencies are mitigated by a higher loyalty to the body of Christ. We are called to role-play a glimpse of the kingdom before it has yet arrived, and in so doing we hide the leaven of love in the loaf of a world that is desperate for transformation.

So often people think that becoming a Christian is a sudden, convulsive affair, where repentance is immediately and dramatically on display in the form of a new creature. But mostly we have to get there one step at a time, and we have to act the part before it becomes second nature to us. When people ask me what they should do to begin the process of becoming a Christian, I think they often expect me to provide them with a list of beliefs. But what I suggest that they do first is to say to the young black man who sacks their groceries, "Thank you sir."

The first thing we must do as a community, however, is eat! First we bring the gifts of the earth, the garden, the cupboard, and the cellar. We place them on the altar to share, and no one is turned away. We have created nothing in the world, including ourselves, and yet the feeling we get when we share these gifts is joy. In the Underground Church, nothing is for sale, and no one can be purchased. We step out of the madness of the world of buying and selling on the Sabbath. What has been freely given is freely offered. "The church has been planted as *paradises* [paradise] in the world," said Irenaeus, bishop of Lyon. That paradise begins with food and remains only when everyone has enough.

After we have eaten, however, our work is just beginning. We do not get a belly full in order to rub it and fall asleep. If the church is to model paradise, then it must also corrupt whatever destroys paradise. The American church in particular must awaken from its long, deadly slumber, move out of the king's quarters, and stretch its wings. We can't speak truth to power as long as we are locked inside a cage. The gospel is a scandal that we have turned into a decent devotional.

Whether we are liberal or conservative or something in between, the time has come for all of us to study together again—as if we were reading the Bible again for the first time. The church of Jesus Christ is a sleeping giant in a world of screaming pain and desperate loneliness. At precisely the moment when the message of grace and peace is desperately needed, the last place some people think they will find it is in church.

Once, when I was sitting in a class taught by Fred Craddock, he suddenly veered off course from his lecture and confused us all. At first we thought he was babbling or had a screw loose or just wanted to see if anyone was paying attention. This is what he said:

> The other day I saw a nine-pound sparrow in front of my house, walking down the street. So I asked the sparrow, "Aren't you a little heavy?"

The sparrow said, "Yeah, that's why I'm out walking, trying to get some of this weight off."

And I said, "Why don't you fly?"

The sparrow looked at me like I was stupid and said, "Fly? I've never flown. I could get hurt!"

I said, "What's your name?"

And he said, "Church."

CHAPTER EIGHT

Jesus Followers on the No-Fly List

Jesus and his followers . . . were hippies in a world of Augustan yuppies. . . . The historical Jesus was a *peasant Jewish Cynic*. . . . His strategy, implicitly for himself and explicitly for his followers, was the combination of *free healing and common eating*, a religious and economic egalitarianism that negated alike and at once the hierarchical and patronal normalcies of Jewish religion and Roman power.
—JOHN DOMINIC CROSSAN

By now it should be obvious that the purpose of this book is not to cast one more stone against the glass house of the church from the outside, lest any of its dingy windows remain unbroken. My hope is to renew it from the inside. My life has been given to the church, but my gathering conviction after three decades of parish ministry is that Christians now blend in so well with the dominant culture that we have effectively disappeared. The community that used to give the Empire fits now fits right in with the Empire.

The church has indeed become like that nine-pound sparrow that Dr. Craddock alluded to, walking for exercise instead of flying, even though flying is what it was born to do. Ironically, our government maintains a list of people considered too dangerous to fly (suspected terrorists or other "persons of interest"). It's called the "no-fly list." But chances are there aren't many respectable, middle-class, patriotic American Christians on that list. We are too busy safely walking and trying to "keep the peace" in our congregations by avoiding all controversy that might be what nervous pastors call "divisive."

Dietrich Bonhoeffer's voice from the 1940s is prophetic, arguing as he did that Christianity would become increasingly irrelevant, a path to social respectability rather than a commitment to justice. Love of God and neighbor, he said, constituted "costly grace." "It is grace because it calls us to follow Jesus Christ. It is costly because it costs a man his life."[1] The question for us is what constitutes costly grace in the church today. Our culture regards the church as a mostly quaint, stabilizing force that teaches moral lessons and builds character, not unlike the Boy Scouts. Bonhoeffer saw the gathering clouds of fascism in his native Germany. He could have escaped it all by staying in New York and not leaving his post at Union Theological Seminary. But he chose to go back and confront the acquiescence of the church to the new National Socialist state as part of the confessing church movement. It was an underground movement that trained pastors to resist. It was a decision that cost Bonhoeffer his life. After the Gestapo forbade him to lecture, write, or make speeches, they arrested and imprisoned him on April 5, 1943. Two years later, after he led fellow prisoners in worship, Nazi authorities took him away to be hanged. Costly grace indeed.

While in prison, Bonhoeffer wondered what Christianity had become. Countless German Christians had capitulated to Hitler's vision of an Aryan utopia and thus helped sanctify mass murder. Before his death, Bonhoeffer questioned whether Christianity was "over" as a religion and wondered if it made any sense now or was merely a "garment." Then he asked about what he called a "religionless Christianity," where faith was not about salvation or escaping the suffering of the world, but required ultimate allegiance to a God who is the "beyond" in the midst of our lives. Theologians have argued ever since about what he meant by "religionless Christianity," but one thing is certain. He could not imagine a follower of Jesus who did not resist the ways of death, even if it meant paying the ultimate price.

When someone says the word "pastor" these days, what image comes to mind? We still occupy a respected profession, but we tend not to be thought of as "resisters." We are not sent off to seminary to learn the arts of noncompliance. We learn how to run churches, how to be present in love, how to preach sermons that won't get us fired—all good things. But who teaches us how to be subversive?

This is not Nazi Germany, of course, but totalitarianism comes in many guises. As multinational corporations control more of our lives, as the gap between rich and poor explodes, as the middle class disappears and one in four American children cannot be certain where the next meal is coming from, pastors today seem overwhelmingly aligned with the status quo, not with the poor. When they try to push back—by opening a food pantry, for example—they are often forced to resign by people complaining about the unsavory characters who actually show up to be fed. Real ministry has a strong odor. Following Jesus quite literally stinks.

When pastors dare to speak out against unjust wars based on lies, unjust wages that trap people in poverty, or hateful rhetoric or behavior toward those who are not white, straight, or Christian—they are called "unpatriotic" or "ungrateful." What then are we supposed to be—chaplains for the Empire?

Religion has become more of a curiosity than a respected force in American life. The media comes calling at Christmas and Easter (as do many members of the church alumni association) to secure a sound bite for the evening news about the latest religious controversy or to peddle nostalgia about Jesus "meek and mild, gentle as a child." But none of it has anything to do with real wisdom, only with marketing the culture wars. In the culture at large, Jesus has become another seasonal product, a story to fill the blank spaces between the ads for cars and clothes and diets. In a celebrity culture, he is one more celebrity. Ministers are expected to give safe, spiritually neutral commentary at times of great importance. The church is expected to offer up expert witnesses about matters spiritual, as long as we don't say anything un-American or, as we call it in Oklahoma, "peculiar." During the heady days following the assassination of the world's most famous terrorist, a local news personality, coiffed and impatient in her red lipstick, asked me, "So, Robin, is it OK for a Christian to be happy about the killing of Osama Bin Laden?"

It is in this context that we do the ministry of a very peculiar Jesus. In Crossan's words quoted in the epigraph, we glimpse the radical nature of a scandalous and subversive gospel. First, when Crossan refers to Jesus and his followers as "hippies in a world of Augustan yuppies." Second, when he defines the heart of the ministry of Jesus as "free healing and common eating." Would that more preachers could recast core biblical principles in such contemporary language; yet this is more than just an attempt by Crossan at being hip.

Contented simplicity and a refusal to practice conspicuous consumption have long been denigrated in our culture by the use of the word "hippie." Many progressive Christians today are referred to as "old hippies," and it is not meant to be a compliment. Many of my students at the university find my stories of collective action again social injustice ("back in the day") to be quaint, but not nearly as exciting as private ambition. "Tree huggers" and "feminists" are now so commonly associated with lack of masculinity that a whole movement has arisen in the church to recapture a more muscular Jesus.

Yet there is no getting around the fact that the rhetoric of Jesus is the antithesis of what might be heard in the locker room. What's more, anyone who participates today in an itinerant ministry of "free healing and common eating" is going to become a "person of interest." Who really wants to eat with the riffraff? We love private dining, skyboxes, and VIP rooms. Anyone who wanders around in comfortable shoes sharing everything he owns, while asking others to do the same, will do more than just stand out in such a world. He will be suspected of being mentally ill—perhaps the victim of "melancholy madness."

If Jesus is the model for our ministry, then our real answers to what ails this weary world must come in the form of Christlike behaviors. Subversive talk is cheap (and very satisfying), but subversive action is expensive. It puts everything we value at risk. When a fiery preacher named John the Baptist inquired about Jesus from prison, "Are you he who is to come, or shall we look for another?" the answer was a litany of the signs of the new age: the blind will receive their sight, the lame will walk, the lepers will be cleansed, the deaf will hear, the dead will be raised up, and the poor will have good news preached to them. "And blessed is he who takes no offense at me" (Matt. 11:4–6).

At the time, all these afflictions were thought to be punishments for sin. So the first people to receive the good news were those who had nothing in their life but bad news. Then Jesus pronounces a blessing on anyone who hears such an extraordinary claim but does not take offense. The most well known version of the Beatitudes is found in Matthew's version of the Sermon on the Mount. They may be strange, upside-down ideas, but at least they are positive. Often they are crocheted and hung in the church parlor. Blessed are the meek, the pure in heart, the peacemakers, and so on. Lovely. But there is a downright scary version in Luke (6:24–26) that would be hard to ignore in most American churches:

But woe to you who are rich,
for you have received your
consolation.
Woe to you who are full now,
for you will be hungry.

Woe to you who are laughing now,
for you will mourn and weep.
Woe to you when all speak well of you,
for that is what their ancestors did to the false prophets.

Someone once referred to these as the "Woebetudes," and they
are often passed over by preachers in favor of something a little
more upbeat. The message, however, is not hard to miss, which is
exactly what makes it hard to preach. Those who have it all now
will not always have it. Those who have nothing now are being
given *hope*, and hope is a powerful thing. The question for our time
is not whether liberals and conservatives would hear a completely
different message in this text, but whether or not the "politics
of the gospel" has been preached faithfully enough to offend
everyone.

Honesty demands that we all admit how much we have invested
in the status quo. What then are we to make of the fact that the
announcement of the coming of the kingdom is presented not as
a critique of the status quo but as its *destruction?* How many ministers
could honestly be described as threats to the status quo? How
many of us are on anyone's no-fly list? We're too busy walking,
like the nine-pound sparrow. And besides, we have our own kids
to feed.

If the gospel was called the Great Offense, then why are
Christians considered offensive only when they practice fearful
condemnation and self-righteous hatred? Everyone has heard of
Fred Phelps, the pastor from Topeka, Kansas, who sends a small
contingent of his church (mostly his children) to picket at the
funerals of dead soldiers. His obsession is homosexuality, but his
tactics are beyond belief. Thus he becomes the subject of a national
conversation that includes the Florida pastor who burned the Koran
and the New Orleans pastor who blamed Hurricane Katrina on
abortion. No wonder religion has such a bad reputation.

Sometimes I think we focus on the culture wars because the cast of characters is so outrageous. But nobody wants to talk about the real threat to health and happiness in our time. Nobody wants to touch the issue of *economic justice*. In the Bible, the words "righteousness" and "justice" are used interchangeably, and the Lord's Prayer, which liberals and conservatives alike intone every Sunday in worship, is grounded in the need for daily bread (from God, not from Rome), and the forgiveness of debt (which was and remains a form of slavery). We are so busy arguing over abortion and gay marriage that we forget how much the payday loan and check-cashing industry feeds on the despair of the poor and deepens it.

In the Underground Church, we need to shift our attention from the culture wars to the war being waged against the poor. Indeed, Christians should all become economists. We should know the difference between supply-side and Keynesian economic theory, because there are real consequences in terms of how the pie gets sliced. Our concern about the ever-widening gap between rich and poor and the dramatic rise of the power of corporations in our time should not be based solely on our religious or political views. This is the world we all live in. The fortunes of our neighbors and their children are at stake. The ones we say we love. People are starving to death. Children without dental insurance are dying from an infected tooth.

As we debate who is going to heaven, there is more and more hell on earth. Is it really such a radical idea to suggest that everyone have enough? Perhaps our real problem is that the gospel of grace and peace has been largely replaced by various impostor gospels of greed and judgment. The prosperity gospel, for example, which claims that the more wealth one has, the more God loves you. Or the gospel of "whatever the market will bear," which claims that Adam Smith's invisible hand is indistinguishable from the hand of God. If you are poor, you must be lazy. If you are wealthy, you must be ambitious and righteous. Can it really be that simple?

And if these perversions of the gospel are offensive, then pastors need to say so. "Get behind me, Satan!" does not sound like Jesus meek and mild, gentle as a child. Let us not forget that at the end of his first sermon, people tried to kill Jesus, and then at the end of his brief public ministry, they succeeded!

The late, great Peter Gomes tells us of a famous *New Yorker* cartoon that shows plutocrats leaving a church after having said sweet nothings to the preacher at the door. In the caption, the wife, swathed in furs and jewels, says to her top-hatted husband, "It can't be easy for him not to offend us."[2]

Again, our problem is one of theological emphasis. We focus on the death of Jesus, but that is not what is radical. It is the content of his preaching and its manifestation in his living that offend. As Gomes put it,

> If the focus is nearly always on the man for others who in the short term loses but who one of these days will return in triumph to win, then it is no wonder that so much of Christian faith is either obsessed by the past or seduced by the prospects of a glorious future. In the meantime, things continue in their bad old way, and we live as realists in a world in which reality is nearly always the worst-case scenario. The last thing the faithful wish for is to be disturbed. Thus it is easy to favor the Bible over the gospel, because the gospel can somehow be seen as those nice, even compelling, stories about Jesus that have nothing to do with us "until he comes." . . . It is not that we are ignorant. We know what gives offense, which is probably why we spend so much time talking about sex and Jesus spent so much time talking about money.[3]

Perhaps in the spirit of this book, we should talk about both. But make no mistake, the more taboo of the two subjects is money. The great Presbyterian preacher Ernest Campbell said that it is possible to talk about anything in the church today *except* money. That's because we are all "economically located," and our assumption is that everyone is located exactly where God wants him or her to be.

Some are reaping the rewards of their creativity and entrepreneurial spirit; others are suffering from their laziness or immorality.

The cruelest of American myths is that everyone has exactly the same opportunity to succeed. In the Underground Church, we know that the truth can set us free, but only if we speak it and then live it. Not only does the marketplace not solve all the problems of life, but it also creates some of the worst ones. If the church is to have a future, followers of Jesus will have to consider creating an alternative economy in the church—and that's something we haven't thought about, or wanted to talk about, for a long, long time.

Meet the Real Whore of Babylon

To my way of thinking, everyone deserves to take a shot at identifying who is really the whore of Babylon, the allegorical symbol of the Antichrist in Revelation whose downfall is prophesied to take place at the hands of the beast with seven heads and ten horns. She has served conveniently as the all-purpose symbol of evil for centuries. When John first penned his bizarre vision of a world ruled by a slain lamb, she was surely a symbol of the antithesis of the New Jerusalem.

In my own lifetime, however, she has been identified as the Roman Catholic Church, the Soviet Union, secular humanism, and now radical Islam. She is, in truth, whatever anyone finds abominable or threatening. But in the context of the big bad dream of Revelation, she represents, as two biblical scholars have said, God's judgment on "all human attempts to displace God from the center of reality in favor of human power arrangements."[4]

Yet in the long list of her ever-changing identities, I have yet to hear the whore of Babylon identified as one of the seven deadly sins. The true whore of Babylon is *greed*. She is not merely someone's chosen enemy of the moment, but the eternal enemy of the human race in this and every age. Greed is the destroyer of worlds. Why then are there so few sermons about greed?

Even after thirty years of economic policies tilted toward the rich brought us the Great Recession, and even though the corruption by bankers and Wall Street bandits that pushed us over the edge was breathtaking, preachers still seem very nervous about the subject of economic justice. Could it be that a whole society based on private ambition and the myth of rational markets has made hypocrites of us all? Is capitalism not by nature an immoral system that must be constantly restrained and regulated lest we destroy the neighbor we are commanded to love? History has proved repeatedly that human beings will do terrible things to one another just to make a buck. Perhaps in the end the most dangerous idea out there is that *enough is never enough.*

So if we are going to use this offensive (and politically incorrect) word "whore" (from the Greek *porne*) to signify what is implied by it ("whoring" as infidelity to one's covenant partner, originally YAHWEH), then we should all admit to how easily we are seduced by what has been called the "business of business." Because idolatry is the mother and father of all sins, we should begin with a confession. Our most sacred shrine in America is not the Statue of Liberty, but Arturo di Modica's bronze sculpture that marks the entrance to Wall Street: the so-called charging bull. This is America's Golden Calf.

We talk a lot in the church about the importance of the family, as well we should. But immoral sexual behavior is not the only threat to the family. Greed steals fathers from their children. Greed makes women betray their highest virtues. Greed fuels a culture of entitlement thinking, where I can break the law, pollute the environment, cut corners, and use my wealth as a weapon against those who are desperate—so long as it enriches me. That tired truism that perverts the Golden Rule into "Those with the gold rule" may be a cliché, but that doesn't make it untrue. In the Underground Church, Greed is the whore of Babylon.

So what shall we do, besides rail against it? Here is an opportunity for the Underground Church to do something more than just pretend to be subversive. *We should return to the ancient practice of running our own underground economy in the church, including the redistribution of wealth and the loaning of money at no interest to other members of the community.*

Something tells me that at this moment I have many skeptical readers. Surely this cannot be a serious suggestion? Give money to those in need with no strings attached? Loan money at no interest to members of the community who do not have enough to make a down payment on even a modest house? Pool the resources of the Beloved Community to help bail out someone who is being crushed by medical bills? Pay someone's educational expenses in pursuit of a new job and then ask that person to repay the loan at no interest after she starts working—so that we can loan that money out to others in need? In other words, *use money to help people, not to make money?* Where on earth would anyone get such a radical idea? Surely not from the Bible?

Now the whole group of those who believed were of one heart and soul, and no one claimed private ownership of any possessions, but everything they owned was held in common. . . . There was not a needy person among them, for as many as owned lands or houses sold them and brought the proceeds of what was sold. They laid it at the apostle's feet, and it was distributed to each as any had need (Acts 4:32–35).

America has long been obsessed with using the term "socialism" to discredit anything that resembles collective social responsibility for the common good. Yet we often claim to be a "Christian nation." Obviously we have no idea what was really going on in the early church. It was the antithesis of "every man and woman for himself and herself." Jesus followers pushed back against the idea that money was a sign of God's favor by the simple act of sharing—because nothing enslaves a person like debt, and nothing crushes the human spirit like economic hopelessness.

Among the many ways in which the whore of Babylon symbolized accommodation to (and corruption by) the Roman Empire, one in particular was poignant and powerful: Babylon was an economic *exploiter*. She stood for the seductions of wealth and affluence, "clothed in purple and scarlet, and having been gilded with gold and precious stones and pearls, having in her hand a gold cup" (Rev. 17:4). These items were available only to the elite of Roman society. As imports from Babylon, they are destroyed in the fall of the city. All who have come to love them are lost.

Babylon "crashes" if you will (not unlike 1929 and 2009 Wall Street), and the result is the weeping and wailing of those who are undone by the collapse of any global trading system on which their prosperity depends. Reminiscent of the words of Jesus, "Woe to you who are full now, for you will be hungry," John reminds us that all imperial economic systems collapse and their "merchant princes" fall. But for those who are not part of Babylon, there are no tears, because their riches are not of this earth.

It would be difficult to imagine anything more countercultural in the church today than to see members of the Beloved Community practice a new economy that serves people instead of creating wealth. Who is not weary to the bone with the idea that everything in the world is for sale? That everything is a *commodity*, including people? Granted, the landscape of such utopian attempts at communitarian economic systems is littered with failures, especially in the nineteenth century. Even my ancestors, the pilgrims of the Massachusetts Bay colonies, tried and failed to achieve what John Winthrop called in his famous sermon, "A New Modell of Christian Charity." As governor of what he called "a city on a hill" (from the Sermon on the Mount), he hoped for a new community defined by its nonconformity to the ways of the Old World. Although the practice of holding all things in common for the well-being of all was attempted on the Plimoth Plantation, it felt victim to what Bradford called "the conceit of Plato." The colony reverted in time to a more realistic policy of "no work, no eat."

What is being suggested here is not, however, a form of church-enforced socialism. Everyone in the Underground Church still lives and works in the world of free enterprise and capitalism. The church, however, mitigates the hard edges of such a system when dealing with people in need. This means that in the Underground Church, we maintain benevolence funds that are not used to operate the church, but are available for emergency assistance. Such funds are provided by members who contribute voluntarily, who recognize that sometimes a person needs a gift, not a loan.

A more radical idea, and one that would set the Underground Church apart from more conventional communities, is the idea of a revolving fund of money available to lend to members who apply and who repay at no interest to maintain the fund for use by others. In other words, the church becomes an underground bank, restoring the ancient Christian practice of not charging interest.

There would still need to be safeguards in place, of course— such as collateral, and recourse for failure to make payments. This would not be "free money" available to anyone off the street, but would be funds loaned only to members who have a covenant with the community. What's more, pledging to the church that has loaned you money at no interest is not optional, no matter how modest the contribution. Nor is it acceptable to receive such a loan from a church in which you are not an active participant. If handled correctly and treated as a ministry of the church, lending by the Beloved Community at no interest to other members of the Beloved Community might just turn out to be the greatest incentive to church membership since Paul told adult male Gentiles that in order to become Christian they did not have to cut off the end of their penis!

If all we do is complain about the usury Empire, the imperial economy, but do nothing to subvert it, then what good have we done? Often overlooked in the vivid imagery of Revelation is the distinction between slaves whose bodies were owned by others and what John called "human souls" whose accommodation to the Empire was more subtle but also oppressive. It is exactly what a modern recasting of Descartes would mean: "I shop, therefore I am."

When John critiques the imperial economy, he moves from the image of Babylon to that of the "Beast," claiming that "it causes all, both small and great, both rich and poor, both free and slave, to be marked on the right hand or the forehead, so that no one can buy or sell who does not have the mark, that is, the name of the beast or the number of its name" (Rev. 13:16–17).

Whatever appears on the forehead was believed to be present to the mind of the wearer, whether as a citizen of the New Jerusalem or of Babylon. But whereas the citizens of Babylon have the mark of the Beast on their forehead, the citizens of New Jerusalem are "sealed" with the name of God. But only the citizens of Babylon have a sign on their right hand.

The long-lost significance here is that what is held in the hand enables buying and selling—the imperial stamp and coin, the medium of imperial commerce. It bore the image, name, year, and titles of the emperor and was thus an affront to those who claimed that Jesus, not Caesar, was Lord. At least one of the messages hidden in the coded language of Revelation should be of particular interest to the Underground Church, namely that, as Wes Howard Brook and Anthony Gwyther say, "it is not possible to denounce Rome as satanic and simultaneously to use the Empire's medium of exchange—its currency."[5]

John is clearly making way for an alternative economy that will compete with Rome. I have heard my share of sermons on Revelation, but never this one. Not once have I heard a preacher decode this message: *that followers of the Lamb cannot both choose Christ and do business with Rome.*

Talk about subversive.

The Noneconomic Uses of Money

The late William Sloane Coffin Jr. used to say that it is the "noneconomic" uses of money that make it so dangerous, so seductive, and at times so demonic. "Jesus saw the demonic side when he saw money as a rival god capable of inspiring great devotion. 'You cannot serve God and mammon.' Note that only money is put on a par with God, not knowledge, not family nobility, not reputation, not talent: only money is elevated to divine status. No wonder Jesus talked more about money than any other subject except the kingdom of God."[6]

Money used for noneconomic reasons gives the wealthy enormous influence. They can use it to buy favors, to intimidate and control those who depend on their generosity, to gain status and power by rewarding friends and punishing enemies. In churches, the wealthiest members who contribute the most money are often coddled and feared. Their opinions are considered more important. Ministers recruit the wealthy with more vigor than they pursue those of more modest means because every church has to make its budget. But this only duplicates the ethics of the imperial economy.

Every pastor knows that a wealthy patron can make him or her into a subservient client, just as Rome maintained its power through the patron-client pyramid. In the Underground Church, however, we must make every attempt to "flatten" such hierarchies, at least in the way we treat one another. Both the rich and the poor "you shall have with you always," but in God's economy there must be a different way of responding to wealth (and to the lack of it) that is palpable.

Despite all the apocalyptic interpretations, the real message of Revelation may have mostly to do with social order: "God no longer resides above the people but in their midst. The (vertical) pyramid is replaced by a (horizontal) egalitarian communion between God and humanity. Because the heavenly order mirrored the social order, this necessarily repudiated the social pyramid sustained by the patron-client network. As a consequence of God living among the people, social hierarchy disappears."[7]

One of the defining marks of membership in the Beloved Community of the Underground Church is a return to the ancient practice of calling everyone, not by exalted titles, but by the simple designation of "brother" or "sister." In this way we practice radical egalitarianism while declaring everyone to be family. We govern ourselves as an assembly (ekklesia), a coming together of people to pursue a consensus in the body about what constitutes the best expression of our commitment to serve God and neighbor through nonviolence, hospitality, generosity, and encouragement. All have equal status, unlike the pervasive hierarchies of the Empire. This makes us look, act, and sound strange. We genuflect to nothing and to no one. The kissing of rings is strictly forbidden. Either everyone counts for something or no one counts for anything. There will be no dress code in the Underground Church, even though everyone will want to look his or her best.

What the world is constantly arranging vertically, we will rearrange horizontally. Instead of whatever the market will bear, our orientation will be gratitude for abundance as the obvious prerequuisite to sharing. Again, it is important to remember that we did not make ourselves or anything else in the garden. We therefore do not seek to possess but rather to enjoy. Striving is replaced by thankfulness, and the concern of the community should be for everyone to have enough. Those with more than they need will give to those with less than they need.

What's more, decisions in the Underground Church will be made about whether and under what circumstances we should withdraw support for commercial transactions that destroy community, degrade human integrity, or cause death and disease. The most powerful weapon that consumers have in the Empire is the *boycott*—a word that strikes fear into the hearts of corporations everywhere. Righteous indignation is not enough. When we support companies that are unethical, we subsidize unethical behavior. When we fail to support local farmers or to become producers of food that we share from our own gardens, we perpetuate unsustainable forms of agriculture that are destroying the environment. To put it in the ancient and often confusing language of Revelation, when we trade with each other rather than with those who bear the mark of the Beast, we give birth to a new economic order. When enough people withdraw from the Empire and begin to practice God's alternative economy, the Empire loses some of its power, and that power is reclaimed by The Way.

Our problem now is that most people feel powerless to exist outside the Empire. Many of us know that we go along to get along, but we feel that we are giving up a part of our souls. The object becomes to get through one more day, earn a paycheck, and perhaps buy a lottery ticket before watching something on television to which we have attached unnatural significance—such as who wins a game or gets voted off the island.

In Orwell's classic, 1984, it is the "proles," the mindless proletariat whose job it is to work and breed, drink beer and watch football, who hold the real power. A central theme of the novel is that the world will change only when the proles revolt, but the Party knows that will never happen because the proles are too busy just existing. Big Brother has a slogan to describe the proles: "Proles and animals are free." The Party even provides them with porn, just in case the lottery does not provide enough false and fantastic hope.

Sometimes I think the Empire looks at the church as a vast collection of pious proles—doing the decent thing on Sunday morning, focused only on getting right with God before we die. We are endlessly distracted by theological arguments and incensed over the chosen enemy of the moment. But in the end, the Empire knows we will not resist, much less revolt, because we do not even know that we are oppressed. If the economy falls, then alcohol and drug use simply rises, but nobody thinks to ask questions of those who run the economy. What fools we are, even today, to think that supply and demand has anything to do with the price of gas.

In the Underground Church, however, we will train and empower *activists*. We will be not just a community of nonconformity but a community of *resistance*. We will name the principalities and powers and give people the means of creative noncooperation. This is the only way to get the Empire's attention. Money will be a means to an end, not an end unto itself. We will regard it not as the ultimate arbiter of value but simply as a portable form of power. It can be used (or misused) for good or for evil. Money can bring life, or it can bring death. It can build a school, or it can silence the voice of a whistleblower. It can guarantee that an unqualified candidate gets elected to office, or it can make certain that an unknown candidate gets heard. Money can buy a spouse, but it cannot buy love. It can build a house, but it cannot purchase a home. It can rent space in a five-star hotel, but it cannot guarantee a blissful vacation.

If a member of the Underground Church has accumulated significant wealth, he or she should not expect to have a different status in the church, only more opportunities and obligations. The words of Luke come to mind: *From everyone to whom much has been given, much will be required; and from the one to whom much has been entrusted, even more will be demanded.*

Those who become part of the Underground Church movement will be committed to counterimperial praxis more than to doctrinal uniformity. The Empire couldn't care less about our debates, as long as we continue to be mindless consumers. Remember, one of the first things that the Jesus People did was refrain from eating meat that had been offered to idols. But there was a market for such meat, because all meat was scarce in those days. When the "little Christs" stopped worshiping in the temples and buying meat offered to idols, the Empire took notice. Listen to the words of a letter written by Pliny, governor of the province of Bithynia-Pontus, to the emperor Trajan (110 CE). It gives us a hint about how effectively The Way was disrupting commerce:

> At any rate it is certain enough that the almost deserted temples begin to be resorted to, that long disused ceremonies of religion are almost restored, and the flesh of sacrificial victims finds a market, whereas buyers until now were very few (Pliny, *Letter to Trajan* 10.96).[8]

The Jesus People were involved in a de facto boycott, and it had real economic consequences. More than anything the Jesus People believed, this disruption of commerce on which the Empire depended led Pliny to call followers of The Way a "wretched cult." What happened on a small scale might happen on a larger scale. If people are being encouraged to conceive of and create alternatives to the Empire, then this threatens the most important component of the status quo: *the business of business.*

Many churches, for example, are now participating in what is called the fair trade movement. They agree to purchase and sell items like coffee, chocolate, and crafts made by artisans in the developing world who are paid more by eliminating the middleman. Mayflower has become a fair trade church by agreeing not to serve coffee or tea after church or at meetings that has not been certified as a fair trade product. On average, fair trade coffee purchasers pay the local producer $1.35 a pound, instead of the $.70 a pound paid by commercial coffee companies.

In the Underground Church, we simply will not participate in business as usual. We will create our own internal economy. If a credit card company is involved in unethical practices, we will invite members to cut up those cards and return them with a note explaining why they cannot participate in what they believe are unethical and, in some cases, criminal enterprises. This very course of action was recommended from the Mayflower pulpit. The payday loan industry that makes money off the misery and desperation of the poor should be shut down, and the church should take the lead in pressing for legislation to outlaw these companies. "Those who oppress the poor insult their Maker," says one of the proverbs. What then should we call it when we punish them for *being* poor?

Just as the Sabbath "belongs to man," so the economy belongs to human beings. The world has come to accept such policy truisms as the impossibility of full employment and the premise that social welfare programs are inflationary. We may not have lost the "war on poverty" so much as we surrendered. In the meantime, the Underground Church must align itself with the gospel's own "preferential option on the poor," to quote the social gospel teachings of the Roman Catholic Church. After all, what right do we have to *reverse* the priorities of Mary's *Magnificat*, filling the rich with good things and sending the poor away empty?

America's deepening poverty is not confined to one religious class or ideology. We are all on this sinking ship together. If a Baptist is starving, why shouldn't an Episcopalian feed him? If an atheist has become homeless, why shouldn't a Baptist give him shelter? If the house of two gay men burns to the ground, why should anyone's view of homosexuality keep him from offering aid and comfort? All it takes to become a member of the Underground Church movement is the simple conviction that it is more important to be loving than to be right.

After Hurricane Katrina devastated New Orleans, Mayflower adopted and relocated two families from the Ninth Ward who lost their homes when the levies broke. We found shelter, moved furniture, paid the first six months of rent, and arranged to get the children into the best possible public schools. Both families recovered fully; one returned to New Orleans, and one stayed in Oklahoma. If every church in the country had adopted just one family after Katrina, there would have been no need for the infamous FEMA trailers. Everyone who wanted help could have found it. Do you think it matters to a homeless person whether his or her rent in paid by a Pentecostal or a Unitarian?

Someone asked Dorothy Day to comment on Jesus' saying, "Render unto Caesar the things which are Caesar's and unto God the things which are God's." She took a moment to think about it and then replied, "If we were to render unto God all the things which are God's, there would be nothing left for Caesar."

How to Become a "Person of Interest"

Surely the most dangerous verse in the Bible is Romans 12:2. There Paul endorses Christian nonconformity: *Do not be conformed to this world, but be transformed by the renewing of your minds, so that you may discern what is the will of God—what is good and acceptable and perfect.* This is an invitation to submit to the process of personal transformation that is unavoidable if one takes the gospel seriously. All change is risky and difficult, but we are called to nothing less in a broken world. We must become radicals.

Granted, the word *radical* has suffered from abuse. It has the same root as the radius of a circle, and simply means to get at the center of things. Getting at the center of things, however, means being mindful of how far away from the center most of us live. How shallow is our commitment to the painful truth; how inane are the words we use to communicate with one another; how thoroughly self-absorbed are most of our waking moments. The great irony of the church in the Western world is that nobody considers Christians or Christianity to be dangerous; nobody regards us as anything other than dependably decent; certainly nobody refers to us as "persons of interest." The charge against Jesus was that he "stirred up the people," and the fate of the apostles was persecution and even death. Our movement was born as *contra mundum* (against the world). How then did we become so at home in the world?

Whenever the church gains worldly power, it almost always loses its capacity to critique the very power that it now enjoys. We have to live in the world, of course, but then how do we live against it? This tension is as old as the church itself and never goes away. Lately, however, it has become hard to name anything that the church does that is countercultural. Indeed, many church communities are among the most homogeneous gatherings to be found in any town or city.

Far from being models of nonconformity, many churches today have adopted the trappings of commercial secular culture in order to be "successful." The church "campus" is popular, with multiple buildings designed to duplicate the attractions and services that appeal most to families. The attraction comes from occupying spaces that mirror the world, not unlike the mall, with bookstores and cafeterias and play spaces for the children. The feeling is one of sequestered security, with birds of a feather flocking together. The last thing anyone would think to call it is subversive.

Although the church has often worked on behalf of social change in America (temperance, women's rights, public education, the abolition of slavery), it is difficult to name the unpopular causes that the church today is pressing at any real risk to itself. With the exception of the pacifist traditions like the Quakers and Mennonites, the church can hardly claim to be antiwar. As a group, many of us are often louder and more militant in our support of American wars than is the general population. For all the talk of "pro-life" in many quarters, there is a preoccupation with redemptive violence in the church that is deeply disturbing. Among liberals, there is less support for war but hardly a willingness to sacrifice anything of value to stop one. How then can the church be truly countercultural today?

To put it simply: What would make church people into something other than a cartoon or a stereotype? What would make us "persons of interest"? To begin, any group of Christians today that stubbornly clings to the pacifist traditions of the early church will not only receive lots of attention but also find more than its share of disturbing phone messages left on the church answering machine. The selling of war occupies our brightest minds, and the glorification of war is a national pastime assisted by fawning celebrities. Now that most wars are wars of choice rather than necessity, the last thing we need is a church that acts as a chaplain to the Pentagon, forfeiting its own rich tradition of resistance.

Very few things could distinguish the church of the future more than for it to become again the last place one would expect to find support for war. What if, during the run-up to the next war, the talking heads on cable said something like this: "As our brave men and women prepare to deploy to fight [fill in the blank] in order to protect our freedom, opposition is coming for the usual places, especially the church." Of course we will support them, caring for them as individuals, praying for them, providing counseling if requested and help for their families while they are deployed. But our support for the soldier is never to be confused with support for the war.

Another way to become a person of interest is to embrace doubt as a healthy and necessary ingredient to a mature spirituality. Many people expect pastors to be super-Christians whose faith is stronger than the doubts that "normal" people experience. When a pastor admits that he "does not know" the answer to some question or experiences honest doubt about some long-accepted doctrine, many church leaders will begin to suspect that he is unfit to lead. But the opposite is true: if he lied about his doubt, he would be unfit to lead. Faith, as we have discussed, is not about absolute certainty. It is about a resilient trust.

Any group of Christians today that professes to love the poor and pledges to help them but does not challenge the economic systems that keep them poor confuses charity (which is necessary in the short run), with justice (which is biblical and takes the long view). Those who run for public office as Bible-believing Christians and then fight every effort to raise the minimum wage reveal just how serious they are about helping the poor. One of the attributes of power is that it gives those who have it the ability to define reality and to make others believe in their definition. The church needs to maintain its independence from the Empire so that sanctuaries can be "safe spaces" for asking painful but necessary questions. What if someone admires President Obama but hates his decision to expand the war in Afghanistan? What if a follower of Jesus objects to the assassination of notorious terrorists without trial by jury? What if one no longer believes in hell but is afraid to say so in church?

One of the hallmarks of the modern church is its intellectual dishonesty and its partisan blindness. Once, when Peter Gomes suggested that people at Harvard should pray for Richard Nixon, there was hissing in the audience. But when Billy Graham announced that he would not preach to segregated audiences, many white Christians in the South were hissing as well. How dare the church be a place where our sacred cows are skewered?

Any group of Christians today that advocates for the return of the ancient practice of tithing will almost certainly draw the ire of those who want to have church on the cheap and who confuse privacy and confidentiality with lack of commitment. It is as countercultural today to preach in favor of tithing in liberal churches as it is radical to preach acceptance of gays and lesbians in conservative churches. Methinks both groups doth protest too much.

Any group of Christians today that seriously engages followers of Islam and seeks to learn more about the faith of the second-largest (and fastest-growing) religion in the world will almost certainly find itself on somebody's no-fly list. Islamophobia is a scourge in American society, and we are on the verge of witnessing widespread violence against our Muslim sisters and brothers should there be another terrorist attack on U.S. soil. If the church wants to be genuinely subversive and radically inclusive, it will find regular ways to work for stronger and more peaceful relations with the local mosque. We should also make plans to hide innocent Muslims if necessary, even if it means defying the law.

Any group of Christians today that insists on having frank conversations about sex in the church will almost certainly be accused of breaking one of the church's last tenacious taboos. After centuries of sexual dualism (the soul is good, but the body is bad), our troubled society gets no help from the church at all. Conservatives are often fixated on sins of the flesh; liberals are fixated on sins of society. But the truth is that both are sins and cannot be separated without doing harm to the full meaning of discipleship.

At Mayflower, we offer classes in sex education for fifth and sixth graders, using a frank but dignified curriculum called "Straight Talk." Some people (mostly the ones who are not parents) think that fifth and sixth graders are too young to deal with these issues. Others think that information about sex is an incentive to have sex. Believe me, after an hour spent discussing in detail the causes and consequences of sexually transmitted diseases, the idea of casual sex never seemed less casual.

Any group of Christians today that intentionally sets out to welcome and protect the stranger in our midst will stand out in a world of fear and isolation. In particular, who is going to defend undocumented workers in America and insist that immigration reform be just, instead of just mean? And the Bible is perfectly clear about our obligation to welcome the stranger and treat him or her with respect. "The alien who resides with you shall be to you as the citizens among you; you shall love the alien as yourself, for you were aliens in the land of Egypt: I am the LORD your God" (Lev. 19:34).

In the Underground Church, it is a moral imperative to identify the stranger in our midst who is most at risk and then make plans to be her advocate and defender. We will not use English-only laws as a weapon. We will learn to speak Spanish so that we can teach English to our immigrant brothers and sisters. In the Underground Church, bilingual is beautiful. God, after all, ordains no one language, just as no one country is best loved by God. Remember that at Pentecost, the language issue was resolved without shame.

Perhaps the real issue here is again our old nemesis—fear. Perhaps deep down, we are afraid that "illegals" will take bread meant for us or will crowd our children out of schools or services because there won't be enough to go around. In other words, despite the clear mandates in the gospel to welcome the stranger, the stranger is a threat to us. This fear is often exploited by incendiary rhetoric that pits us against the other in a zero-sum game. Again, we are expected to understand the economy in human terms, where scarcity and competition make us enemies.

Any group of Christians today that self-consciously pushes back against fear as the enemy of the moral life will draw fire from the fearful. The poet Robert Frost once said, "There's nothing I'm afraid of like scared people." Listening to much religious language these days is a depressing exercise in fear mongering. Everything is a conspiracy, and all differences are really deficiencies. Whether it is the right warning us against secular humanists or the left warning us against Bible-thumping lunatics, the message is the same: "Be afraid, be very afraid!" Yet the heart of the gospel is "fear not." Our story does not end on Good Friday, but begins on Easter morning.

In the Underground Church, no one will expect special exemptions from pain and suffering, because it should be obvious that people of faith are granted no such exemptions. But in the collective care of a Beloved Community there is enormous power. Eating alone, after all, is one of the saddest of all human experiences. If the church wants to stand out as leaven in the loaf of the Empire, all it has to do is live as if there is no task to which God calls us that God cannot equip us to accomplish.

In short, any group of Christians today that practices nonviolence, radical hospitality, and reckless generosity—creating a community of compassion and encouragement—will seem strange to the world indeed. In the Underground Church, not every action needs to be newsworthy to be radical. Visiting a nursing home is one of the most countercultural things a human being can do. All it takes is mindful noncompliance with the forces of death and division. All it takes is a refusal to accept the status quo when the status quo is immoral. If our good news is not bad news to those who steal the future, then what right do we have to sing our hymns about the "sweet by and by"? We should not make promises about things that we refuse to help deliver.

Gandhi once provided a list of seven social sins, which ought to animate the Underground Church, uniting both liberals and conservatives around principles worth fighting for. He said we must resist politics without principle, wealth without work, commerce without morality, pleasure without conscience, education without character, science without humanity, and worship without sacrifice.

Instead of offering up more tired arguments about theological and doctrinal "purity," let us claim a future that we are simultaneously involved in creating. Christian eschatology is not escapism, not fear mongering, not the anticipation of the ultimate cosmic revenge. It is, as the great New Testament scholar and poet Amos Niven Wilder points out, the basis for Christian ethics. We behave justly in anticipation of a just future.

What could be more radical than that?

CHAPTER NINE

The Underground Church on War, Sex, Money, Family, and the Environment

*The gospel gives us different priorities from those of
the popular culture, and offers us a different agenda
from that of the political economy.*
—JIM WALLIS

When people ask me for ideas about how to renew the church in our time, I am almost embarrassed by how coarse and simple my answer sounds. "Just *do* something." Find a need in your congregation or in your community and make a plan to meet it. Identify a way to love God and neighbor here and now, and then just *show up*. Don't spend too many hours planning it or talking it to death, because nothing takes the place of *doing*. Grace is a by-product not of good intentions but of good deeds performed by imperfect people for the right reasons. Most of the moments of joy and clarity in my ministry have come in the midst of the *performance* of ministry, not in the contemplation of the performance of ministry.

It would be difficult to overstate how mired the mainline church is in hyperintellectualism. We are factories of good ideas; we form committees to study problems and then appoint task forces to propose possible solutions to the problems that we already knew existed. A report is issued, voted on, and filed—confirming all the evils of the age and what should be done to address them. Often the energy expended to identify and articulate the mess that the world is in steals most of the energy needed to actually do something about it! We create mission categories like a quarterly emphasis on peace, but alas, after ninety days, war appears unfazed by our resolutions against it.

There is something very seductive and satisfying about naming sin and recommending repentance—as if what we have encouraged we have accomplished. Preachers are the ones most at risk, because they are public speakers of the gospel. They are constantly condemning evil and recommending love—are they also expected to actually resist evil and practice love? *Surely it is clear that I am a loving person,* thinks the pastor; *I just preached a six-part sermon series on love, and lots of people asked me for a copy.* This confusion, between thinking about doing something and actually doing it, causes little pieces of the soul to break off and fall on the shower floor. It is why more members of the clergy end up in psychotherapy than do those of any other profession.

It also lulls the church into the complacency that results from assuming that a discussion of *what* is Christian is more important than a demonstration of *how* one is Christian. Again the words of Fred Craddock post a warning here:

> It is one thing to talk about a concept such as love, and quite another to have the capacity to love. And the one does not lead directly to the other. Knowledge about ethical concepts does not make one ethical. Burghardt [W.E.B.] DuBois, the great black educator, sociologist, and historian, upon completion of studies at Fisk, Harvard, and University of Berlin, was convinced that change in the condition of the American black could be effected by careful scientific investigations into the truth about the black in America. So he proceeded. His research was flawless and his graphs and charts impeccable. After waiting several years and hearing not the slightest stir of reform, Dr. DuBois had to accept the

truth about the Truth: its being available does not mean it will be appropriated.[1]

This is why the renewal of the church will come only when right practice replaces right belief, when our desire to do the work of real compassion in the world is stronger than our impulse to convert others to our way of thinking; when we become *doers* of the Word and not just *hearers* only, to use the language of James.

Don't get me wrong. I am not opposed to thinking in the church. I like thinking. I think we should do more of it! I am also not suggesting that theology is unimportant or that our traditions do not matter. Indeed, the essential task of biblical interpretation is not just to tell people what a text *said*, but what it *says*. Yet even when this is done well, it's not enough. Take the parable of the Good Samaritan, for example. If I should happen to be beaten and left half dead by the side of the road, I would prefer to be bandaged and delivered into the care of an innkeeper, rather than to grant an interview to a Christian reporter doing research to publish an article about how dangerous that particular road has become.

For twenty years, my congregation has participated in an annual spring ritual called "Christmas in April" (now called "Rebuilding Together" lest we offend non-Christian sensibilities). We select a house that is in need of substantial repair. Over one weekend, a mob of pilgrims descends on that house in what might best be described as the ecclesiastical version of *Extreme Makeover*. All the furniture gets moved out, plumbing is repaired, walls are painted, and new carpet is installed. The youth group landscapes the yard and plants flowers; skilled laborers install new windows and doors; the older women of the Guild who can't work prepare lunch, deliver it, and urge us to use sunscreen. To say there is a good vibe that permeates the morning would be an understatement. All are volunteers, and some work long into the night. It is blissfully exhausting.

The person who lives in that house, usually an elderly Oklahoman, spends the workday day elsewhere (lest he or she find the gutting of the home unbearable) and then returns to find it gloriously restored. It would difficult to describe how this feels if you have never experienced it. Nobody worries about whether the home belongs to a Baptist or a Catholic or an agnostic. We do not use the project as a recruiting tool, and the last thing on anyone's mind is the virgin birth. What happens is that we are *reconnected* to one another, reminded that the world is full of people whose lives we will never know, and sobered by the deep divisions of race, class, and culture. Yet we know that everyone needs to live in dignity and that everyone has a name. Rebuilding Together is one of Mayflower's High Holy Days.

It should go without saying, however, that seldom are our motives "pure." Many of us wake on that morning thinking, "Haven't I got something better to do? Tend my own garden perhaps? Play with my own kids? Paint my own house? Watch the game?" Of course. But it is in the *doing* of a good deed for the stranger (who then becomes the neighbor) that we experience something transcendent. The experience of collective compassion trumps the satisfactions of private ambition every time. Yet the world and all its cleverness is mostly devoted to private ambition.

In the Underground Church, *we should talk less and do more.* We should appreciate how powerful it is when people go about quietly doing good works. If you want to attract a gaggle of the neighborhood kids, just start digging a hole in your front yard. They will gather, stare into the hole, and wonder why you are not engaged in a running commentary about the project. Just dig in silence and the questions will begin: "What are you looking for? Is that a grave? Are you going all the way to China?"

Likewise with the Underground Church, we resist explaining everything we are doing lest we push people away. It's not the *reasons* that people are interested in anyway; it is our strange behavior. Take the announcements in the worship service, for example. When visitors come to the service and we report the marriage of Joe and Sarah, we will not pause to explain who they are, how they met, where they work, or why this is such a joyful moment. If you are a visitor and want to know more about Joe and Sarah, join the church!

What moves people is that we are trying to create a community that can exist outside the frantic and impersonal world of buying and selling, of scheming and lying, of manufactured sentiment and shallow conversation. What people are looking for, and desperately, is something *real*. When a beloved member of the church is dying, then that's what we say: "Mr. Morgan is dying." In the Underground Church, we shun euphemisms when the subject matter matters. No "passing away," no "going to be with Jesus," and please, no "transitions." It makes a dying person sound like someone at a graduation ceremony.

In the Underground Church, we do not avoid what is unpleasant lest we miss the hidden blessings inherent in the authentic life. That means we don't always do what we *feel* like doing. I don't know how many times I've forced myself to make a hospital call (who likes to go to hospitals?) and then come out feeling as if nothing I have done recently, or will do in the near future, is as important as the time I spent sitting in silence beside the bed of a dying person. The Beloved Community needs to preach and teach constantly this lesson: *to hell with how you feel about it! Is it right?*

Likewise the purpose of a church that functions subversively is not simply to confirm or to inspire but to *undo* people. The ultimate objective of preaching is not to score performance points or create a fan club but to create in everyone present the feeling that the more one trusts in the basic equation of the gospel (we lose our lives in order to find them), the more *obligated* we feel to let go of the sickness that is self-sufficiency. *Me, Myself, and I* is the unholy trinity.

Looking out for number one is the anti-gospel. *Enough is never enough* will ultimately be enough to do us all in.

What then shall we *do* to awaken the slumbering giant that is the church in the Western world? Many churches are just barely hanging on, and none of us are getting any younger. Those of the next generation, dubbed the Millennials, are not wild about our solemn assemblies. But they seem endlessly fascinated by Jesus and the ways of nonviolence, hospitality, generosity, and encouragement. Not all of them buy into the myth of a partisan God who votes a straight party ticket and teaches us to hate. What's more, too many of them have seen what religion does to church people, and they don't like it. Not only do many Christians strike them as frightened and judgmental, but they also continue to act as if there were something endearing about ignorance.

So what can the Underground Church offer them? How about the path of *most* resistance? How about an alternative to the madness of the age? How about the chance to be leaven, corrupting the corruption of the Empire? Let's be bold, shall we?

On War

War is a coward's escape from the problems of peace.
—THOMAS MANN

Let the Underground Church clear its throat and shout this from the mountaintop. We hate war. We despise it. We are committed to doing everything possible to avoid it. This is not a conservative or liberal position. This is the deepest of all human laments. War is hell. It is monstrous and demonic. To use a biblical metaphor, it stinks to high heaven in the nostrils of God.

When it is chosen as an instrument of foreign policy or economic advantage, it is the gravest of sins. When it is called "holy" (as if God rides into battle wearing a particular uniform), it is blasphemy. When it is an act of vengeance, it spits in the eye of the gospel. "War," said Plato, "is humanity's most chronic and incurable disease. . . . Only the dead have seen an end to war." But to give up on peace is to give up on God.

My generation learned this lesson the hard way, in that monstrous futility known as the Vietnam War. More than fifty-eight thousand men died for a cruel deception, sent to the rice paddies of southeast Asia to fight communism on a borrowed battlefield. Our generals and our politicians lied about it (truth, as the saying goes, is the first casualty of war), then failed to end it for fear of the political cost, only to abandon the country to a political system soon to collapse under the weight of its own ineptness. But first we killed more than two million Vietnamese and divided our own nation. There are sons my age who have never again spoken to their fathers.

When I say the word "Vietnam" in my classroom, I see nothing on the faces of my students. It's all ancient history to them, and besides, they have their own wars to worry about. The big difference is that they don't receive a draft notice on their eighteenth birthday. War is now outsourced like everything else; people volunteer to do the job, and we train, equip, and cheer them as they do it. Many of these young people sign up in need of money for college or because there are no other options. Others continue a military tradition in their families.

So to help my students understand war in a less abstract way, I tell them a story, a true story about one night in 1970 when I was a freshman in college and all my friends carried a draft card in their wallet. We didn't burn them (it was Kansas, after all), but they were a constant reminder that we might not be able to buy our way out of conscription. Most of us had no famous relatives to make sure we could hide out in the National Guard.

In those days we had something called the draft lottery—in which birth dates were arbitrarily drawn to determine who would next ship out to "Nam" (as we called it in those days). It was nothing if not surreal. The lottery was a televised event during which a lovely young woman who worked for the Defense Department would stand next to a lottery machine and draw out numbers. They were printed on little Ping-Pong balls that danced on jets of air and floated up into a tube to be retrieved one by one and then arranged in a sequence before the camera.

But the nice lady was not spelling out a winning lottery ticket. She was drawing out numbers that were arranged to create the numerical sequence of birth dates. If you were born in the chosen year, your birthday number had to be in there somewhere, so you prayed that it did not come up. It was like a lottery of life and death.

It was not uncommon for young men in those days to have lottery draft watch parties. I went to one once, and this is how it worked. Twenty or thirty of us would gather in someone's dorm room, order pizza, and then write our birth dates on a blackboard with our names beside them and hang it on the wall. Then we would watch nervously, hoping that our number would not be drawn.

One night, at one of these strange parties, the first number drawn was the birthday of one of my friends. Everyone in the room turned at once to look at him, and he was white as a sheet. Then he moved silently toward the bathroom. After he closed the door behind him, the room fell silent. The next sound we heard was the sound of him vomiting. To say the least, the party was over.

When I tell this story, my students also fall silent. That's because one of the reasons that war never ends is that there is no end to our illusions about it. Every generation of young soldiers hits the reset button on invincibility. Killing those who wish to kill you first is said to be the ultimate rush. Being killed first, however, is not even in the playbook. The advertisers who must recruit new soldiers make war seem like a grand, romantic, self-fulfilling adventure. It's how you become a "real man."

Meanwhile the citizens who must give their consent are constantly told the Big Lie, which is that our brave young men and women are fighting somewhere to "keep us free." But our wars of late, dressed in beautiful names like "Desert Storm" and "Operation Enduring Freedom," are not responses to threats to our freedom, but rather to threats to the privileges that freedom has brought to us. A bumper sticker seen recently on a Hummer says it all: *Powered by Iraqi Blood.*

Now we are fighting a worldwide war against terrorism, often using high-tech unmanned weapons that minimize American deaths but kill innocent civilians. Images of body bags on nightly TV turned public opinion against Vietnam, so in many ways we have found ways to sanitize war and hide its cost from public view. But with each drone strike, with each cruise missile, with each midnight raid to assassinate our enemies, we make more enemies than we subdue. More and more we are becoming the authors of the terrorism of which we are also the target.

The role of the Underground Church to resist war must take as its premise Augustine's insight: *never fight evil as if it were something that arose totally outside of yourself.* If the sanctuary is to be a place that is truly set aside from the world, then we must be able to ask any question there, including questions that no one else dares to ask: Do we have the truth about this war? Have all other options besides war been exhausted? Is it really unavoidable to prevent an even greater loss of life? Are we pushing back an invader or stopping genocide—or is this just a war for economic or geopolitical advantage? The reasons for going to war are often complex, but one thing is not: it should always be the last resort. If any politician advocates war to get reelected, he should be defeated instead.

What other institution in our society can ask these questions if not the church? Our marching orders are not the nation's marching orders. In the rush to each new war, if the church does not throw itself across the tracks, then who will? Because war is big

business and corporations are now more powerful than govern-
ments, what other nonprofit but the church (with millions of
members meeting every week) can possibly make a dent in the
business of war? Just as the black church protected the civil rights
movement as a last refuge, the church should be the last refuge of
the antiwar movement. On Mother's Day, when we are passing
out the carnations, we should at least tell people the truth: Julia
Ward Howe established Mother's Day to try to stop war.

Yet our call is not just to protest war or condemn war or
commit acts of civil disobedience. We must also identify all forms
of violence in our society and withdraw our cooperation. While
railing against gratuitous sex, many parents look the other way
when their children play violent video games. Indeed, our culture
(as confirmed by recent Supreme Court decisions) seems to believe
that no image is too violent for a child at any age and that sexual
images constitute the real threat. A woman's breast may not be
exposed if the viewer is too young, but the First Amendment protects video games in which that woman can be bound, gagged,
dismembered, or beheaded—so long as she is not topless.

The culture of professional sports celebrates violence, and in
countless homes, domestic violence is a way of life. In a larger sense,
when people starve to death or even go hungry, a kind of violence
is taking place. This "structural violence" may not make the head-
lines, but it is to be resisted in the Underground Church. *We will do
no harm where harm can be avoided.*

Finally, in the Underground Church, we shall not let people
forget what they would rather not remember—that there is no final
peace and security until the world is completely free of nuclear
weapons. Members of the "nuclear club" of nations, who insist that
other nations not be allowed to join, are guilty of rank hypocrisy.
Either we all lay down our nuclear arms or someday every nation
will possess them. Among the most prominent voices to call for a
world free of nuclear weapons are George Shultz, William Perry,

Henry Kissinger, and Sam Nunn—hardly a group of liberal peace-niks.[2] Surely if their dream can be published in the *Wall Street Journal*, it can sound forth from the pulpits of the land.

The Underground Church must live and work under the banner of nonviolence. We must constantly remind the world that vengeance is not justice. We must raise our children to be gentle. We must not permit the term *pro-life* to be the exclusive property of those who oppose abortion; rather we must also discern its meaning with regard to capital punishment, poverty, and health care. We must withdraw our consent from the machinery of war, the funding of war, and the glorification of war—including the insidious assumption that our wars are just and that our God rejoices in the slaughter. Whether one is liberal or conservative, membership in the Underground Church means a commitment to nonviolence and an abhorrence of war. Period.

On Sex

Discipline is a vehicle for joy.
—ROBERT FRIPP (KING CRIMSON)

I remember well the awkwardness of it all. My father intended to have "the talk" with me, and came home armed with some brochures produced by the church. Because actual body parts could not be mentioned, Sammie Sperm was to meet Olivia Ovum and then wonderful things would happen. My father did his best, but it is not easy to turn *Eros*, the universal energy of desire at the heart of the universe, into an object lesson minus the objects. He spoke of attraction and desire as natural, yet there was something dreadfully unnatural about it. Without saying so, I knew that we were talking about a subject as mysterious as it was dangerous, something sacred—but also a destroyer of worlds. Unable to handle the cosmic questions, my young mind turned to more practical matters. I asked my father, "So how *exactly* do Sammie and Olivia meet?"

In case you haven't noticed, the church does not have a great reputation for bringing together body and soul. In fact, when it comes to the mystery and power of human sexuality, the church has mostly told us that the soul is good and the body is bad. It was, after all, when Adam and Eve discovered that they were naked that they covered themselves, and shame was born. We have been much better in the church at warning people against the deadly sin of lust than in recommending the erotic joy of *The Song of Songs*.

Now we live in a world that is saturated with porn, that objectifies desire to sell every conceivable product, and that peddles the myth that when you lie down with someone, your bodies are not really making a promise to each other. Sex as recreation or as ego gratification or as a form of power and control over another human being has brought so much pain and suffering as to be impossible to calculate. But what have we done to educate our children about sex in a way that makes it sacred? And if the church can't mediate the sacred, then what business are we in?

In the sixteenth century, Protestant reformers "simplified the prevailing sacramental system by reducing the number of sacraments from seven to two (baptism and communion). But if there was ever a 'baby out with the bathwater' scenario in Christian theological history, this is it."[3] In the Underground Church, sex should be one of the sacraments, just not one that we celebrate in church!

We must be able to speak openly and honestly about sex as a part of our vision of God's love in everyday life. This is, after all, what a sacrament is.

Besides, let's face it. This is one of the great divides between liberals and conservatives in the church, at least in theory. Because we all know that most people have sex before they are married, and half of those marriages fail (most often because of infidelity), conservatives have pushed abstinence only and the notion of purity, chastity, and "saving oneself." Liberals have mostly talked about how to be "smart" and avoid pregnancy, fearing that anything resembling moral instruction would be hypocritical. Hence the myth is perpetuated that conservatives are obsessed with the sex other people are having while liberals are obsessed with finding a way to excuse the sex they are having!

Meanwhile, into this sacramental vacuum flow all manner of destructive and dysfunctional sexual attitudes and behaviors. Men are not challenged to stop treating women as objects; women are not challenged to avoid using sex as a weapon. When it comes to talking about sex, most human beings are inept. As a result, we take our cue about what is "normal" and "fulfilling" from the media or friends or the Internet. There is an industry out there devoted to making us feel unsatisfied, while in the church, all we hear is awkward silence.

The early church showed us how to regard sex as both an earthly pleasure and a heavenly treasure. Thus one should no more violate the marriage bed than one should use an altar candle to light a cigarette. Because the best things in life are the easiest to corrupt, the church needs to approach sex as a feast, a gift, a delight that, because it is so sublime, requires a breathtaking level of responsibility. It seems that at one time we were not so shy about this:

Let him kiss me with the kisses of his mouth!
For your love is better than wine,
Your anointing oils are fragrant, your name is perfume poured
    out;
Therefore the maidens love you.
Draw me after you, let us make haste. (Song of Songs 1:1–3)

This poem is a feast for the senses, and over time it seems that the smile of the church turned into an awkward grimace. "Don't read too literally," some commentators seem to say. "This song isn't actually about sex or carnal appetite. That bag of myrrh lying between the woman's breasts—it isn't what it appears to be. In fact, the song is an allegory, a figurative portrait of the love between God and God's people, between Christ and his bride, the church."[4]

OK, I get the metaphor, but that doesn't change the fact that what we have embraced to illuminate God's love is erotic poetry. When poets turn to the tender depths and madness of love, they do so because these things are intensely *real*. Much of the language of the church, however, does not seem real, even though our whole gospel is about incarnation—about the word becoming *flesh*. The desire to touch a lover, to be playful and surprised and delighted, is what points us toward the ultimate mystery of communion with God. Everything can go wrong, of course. But everything can also go right.

The language of the church is the language of covenant for a reason. Partnership produces the reciprocity that makes joy possible. Otherwise we are just *using* each other. In the Underground Church, we will try to strike a balance between the prudish and the cavalier. We will also respect those who choose not to have sex and not to get married, for there is a place for everyone at the table. Most of all, however, we will resolve not to fall victim to the age-old dualities of spirit and flesh, as our fullest expression of God's spirit came to us "en-fleshed."

Because the issue of homosexuality has so divided the church, there is an opportunity here for churches to focus on the *integrity of relationships*, rather than simply arguing over the morality of sexual acts. Conservatives often speak of churches that welcome gays and lesbians as being guilty of "approving a lifestyle." But choosing to welcome our GLBT sisters and brothers is not the endorsement of any "lifestyle" if that means the condoning of promiscuity and broken promises. We condemn these behaviors regardless of sexual orientation. In the Underground Church, we will stress the making and keeping of promises, not the certain knowledge that we can identify a sinner based on whom the sinner loves.

In the meantime, our children deserve both candor and tenderness when it comes to learning about the mysteries of human sexuality. Information about sex at an appropriate age is not an inducement to sexual behavior. If anything, exactly the opposite seems to be true. It is out of ignorance and peer pressure that young people often make mistakes. The very least we owe our children is honesty about their bodies and the challenges of being sexual creatures.

Years ago I wrote about parenting using the metaphor "Big gods and Little gods." The parents are the Big gods, and the children are the Little gods, and worship is twenty-four hours a day in the temple of the home. "When the Big gods are happy, all is well with the Little gods. But when there's trouble above, there's trouble below."

This came to me when my children were young, and I realized that whenever I was having an argument with my wife, we could hear the children begin to have their own argument in another part of the house. It is frightening to realize how much good and bad karma is being soaked up by your children, but "no amount of *Ozzie and Harriet* incense waved over a temple of constant discord can make the Little gods feel like singing."[5]

The same is true of human sexuality. The home is the temple of Eros, and parents are the ones who model a healthy and sacramental view of sex. In the Underground Church, we will teach parents how important it is to make holy the space between them, so that children will one day find it harder to separate love and sex when it's their turn to run the temple.

The theory once was: never fight in front of your children, and never kiss in front of them either. The result? A whole generation which assumed that passion in all its forms was a thing to be feared and

hidden and that romance always precedes marriage but never sustains
it. . . . Let your children see you kiss. Let them see you embrace. Let
them overhear your teasing, your gentle rebukes, even your well-
intentioned jealousy. Domestic courtship reinforces the notion that
people are together because they *want* to be together, not because it's
the decent, practical thing to do.[6]

On Money

It was not with a check drawn on Caesar's bank that Jesus sent
his apostles out into the world.
—LAMENAIS

The *Onion*, a satirical magazine, ran an article once titled "Majority
of Money Donated at Church Doesn't Make It to God."

> Washington—A shocking report released Monday by the Internal
> Revenue Service revealed that more than 65 percent of the money
> donated at churches across the world never reaches God.
>   "Unfortunately, almost half of all collections go toward
> administrative expenses such as management, utilities, and clerical
> costs," said Virginia Raeburn, a spokesperson for the Lord Almighty,
> adding that another 25 percent of heavenly funding is needed just to
> cover payroll for the angelic hierarchy. "People always assume God is
> filthy rich, but they'd be surprised to learn His net worth is only
> around $8 million—and most of that is tied up in real estate."
> According to Raeburn, God currently has enough money saved to live
> comfortably through all eternity, but He may be forced to shutter a
> number of under-performing religions.[7]

Although the *Onion* is always good for a laugh, the subject
matter here is serious. Most of the money given at church does not
in fact make it to God. It doesn't even make it out the door!
Churches are, after all, religious businesses, and business is not
good these days. There is so much anxiety about "making the

budget" and paying the bills that mission spending is an after-thought, if anyone thinks of it at all.

The process by which most congregations set their annual budget is to anticipate their income (usually by having members make pledges of financial support) and then stretch those dollars as far as they will go to pay salaries, debt, utilities, supplies, upkeep, and miscellaneous expenses. Then, after all those "fixed" expenses are met, the trustees will see if there is anything "left over" for mission. Usually there isn't, or the amount is pathetic. There has to be a better way.

First of all, when people see how little of their money goes to mission projects, they tend to be as stingy with their contributions as the church is with its benevolence. Giving to pay the utilities is important, but hardly inspirational. More and more, members see their pledge going to "keep the doors open," and then a darker and more insidious question forms in the mind: for what purpose?

In the Underground Church, there will be only two kinds of giving—that is, of the monetary kind. First, everyone who belongs to the church must make a pledge if he or she wishes to be considered a member of the church. That pledge, which represents the most basic responsibility of the covenant of membership, goes into the church's operating account and is used to pay the church's fixed obligations. Tithing is recommended, but at the very least a modern tithe (5 percent) should be the goal. If someone cannot afford to do this, however, then that person gives whatever he or she can faithfully provide to support the church—but pledging is not optional unless one considers membership optional. In our society, people pay for what they value, and no one should expect to receive the services of any organization that he or she does not support.

This means, of course, that the church will have to get its priorities straight. Before it can require an operating pledge from its members, it must demonstrate that the purpose is not just to survive but also to exist in order to do mission. In this way, mainline churches can join evangelicals in what has come to be known as the "missional church," a movement that holds great promise in bringing together Christians of different theological persuasions around the essential work of following Jesus.

Unfortunately, many people who attend church today give whatever change happens to be in their pockets left over from the night before. Or they are like many listeners to National Public Radio, who assume that if they turn on the radio and NPR is broadcasting, they don't need to contribute. Because giving to a church is not required to enter the church, many enter without any feeling that financial support is part of the covenant. This only makes the idea of covenant a sham.

The trustees of the Underground Church tally the pledges and construct the church's *operating* budget around available funds, including all forms of income to the church. The number of ministers and administrative personnel in any local congregation thus reflects the amount pledged to operate that church. The church should not run a deficit. Then, after the operating obligations are met, the real giving opportunities begin.

In the Underground Church, mission projects are primarily the result of the initiative of members of the church, rather than the clergy. The clergy's responsibility is to interpret the text, to live a life of theological reflection and demonstrable wisdom, to create and offer the most meaningful possible worship experiences, and to perform the duties that fall to an ordained minister (teaching; preaching; counseling; presiding at weddings, funerals, and baptisms; sharing in administrative duties; and so on). Mission work, however, *is the responsibility of the people.* Ministers are also people, of course, so some mission projects may be their idea, and they may participate—but mission in the Underground Church is a people's movement, and the people fund it. This they do *in addition to*, not *in lieu of*, their basic operating pledge.

Welcome to the most ecumenical idea in the world—the "Missional Renaissance," as Reggie McNeal, an evangelical leader, put it in his book by the same title. This is the "single biggest development in Christianity since the Reformation," he writes. It will undo Christianity as a religion and "go way beyond denominational affiliations, party labels (liberal, conservative, mainline, evangelical), corporate worship styles (contemporary, traditional), program methodological approaches (purpose-driven, seeker-friendly), or even cultural stances (postmodern, emergent, emerging). . . . These differences are so huge as to make missional and nonmissional expressions of Christianity practically unrecognizable to each other."[8]

Instead of following conventional models for the "successful" church (internally focused on programs and numbers rather than externally focused on the redemptive work of God), the missional church movement sees the development of people as its core activity and shifts the emphasis from leadership and church programs to community transformation. A goal like making certain that no child goes hungry in the county where a missional church is located is not something only conservatives or liberals can agree on. It's something we can all work together on. As for giving, people in this so-called altruism economy contribute to the projects that bring results, not merely to institutions that have no higher goal than self-preservation.

Mainline progressive Christians need to get over theological differences long enough to become acquainted with the missional church movement. Chances are, if they read the following definition of a missional church, they would assume that it was written by a social gospel liberal, not by evangelical authors Michael Frost and Alan Hirsch:

> The missional church . . . will be an anticlone of the existing traditional model. [First], rather than being attractional, it will be incarnational. It will leave its own religious zones and live comfortably with non-church goers, seeping into the host culture like salt and light. It will be an infiltrating, transformational community. Second, rather than being

dualistic, it will embrace a messianic spirituality, . . . a spirituality of engagement with culture and the world in the same mode as the Messiah himself. And third, the missional church will develop an apostolic form of leadership rather than the traditional hierarchical model.[9]

Conventional wisdom—in mainline Protestantism—says this will not work. But then, honestly speaking, conventional wisdom doesn't have much to brag about in church these days. Our theological differences need not stop us from working together on mission priorities that transcend doctrine, especially those that return us to the most basic expression of discipleship: love of God and neighbor. This means we have to think about church finances in new ways, because our building-centered approach to church (the edifice complex) drains money like a vampire from the real work of following Jesus.

Some argue that allowing people more freedom to fund the projects they believe in or are most passionate about will "rob Peter to pay Paul." But like so much that is unexamined or untried in the church, the truth often turns out to be exactly the opposite. When people are given an opportunity to fund their mission of choice (after they have met their basic obligation to ensure the continued operation of the church), they give more money than if their pledge was used primarily (or entirely) to keep the doors open.

The idea is simple enough. Without a church, there is no umbrella under which to do mission, and no common meeting space to worship, learn, and be inspired. Everyone's primary pledge makes certain that the church exists as a meeting place for our common mission. It's where we go to eat, worship, and then decide how to serve. But that is only the first step in a two-step stewardship model. The second step is to find the mission you wish to support, commit yourself to it, and then sustain it along with other members with your time and with money out of your pocket.

At Mayflower, we established a benevolence board that receives funds designated for charity and promised not to spend that money for any other purpose. When we saw that fund growing as the church grew, we decided to open up the possibility of other "self-funded" mission projects—so long as the primary pledge was not compromised. Now our medical mission and boarding school in Nicaragua is funded entirely by the people who run it and serve it ($100,000 a year). Our 363 program, which feeds the homeless, is also an out-of-pocket mission ($40,000) a year. People give themselves and their money to their particular mission project, and to their church they pay rent.

Our goal at Mayflower is to give $1 beyond the walls of the church in mission for every $1 we spend to keep house. We are moving steadily toward that goal and expect to reach it soon. It should be the goal of everyone in the Underground Church movement to spend as much money on others as we spend to keep our house. It may seem unrealistic, and it may take a long time to achieve, but once this system of self-funded missions is in place, it becomes a real possibility. If you add up the total funds spent to operate all the churches in America and then consider what that amount spent on mission would mean to our sisters and brothers in need, it staggers the mind. In an age of government cutbacks, such voluntary charity should be a moral imperative that transcends all our differences. As for church growth, when the money starts flowing out and the community realizes that the church is not just a social club but a force for love and compassion, the people will start flowing in.

On Family

Then his mother and his brothers came to him, but they could not reach him because of the crowd. And he was told, "Your mother and your brothers are standing outside, wanting to see you." But he said to

> them, "My mother and my brothers are those who hear the word
> of God and do it."
> —LUKE 8:19–21

It is hard to imagine a more radical or countercultural text in the Bible than this. In a time when the family (which was patriarchal) was the primary social unit, the center of both personal identity and material security, this teaching turns the idea of family and "family values" on its head. A "good" family was considered to be one of the primary blessings from God, yet Jesus spoke of leaving family and even of "hating" family. Marcus Borg tells us, "Indeed, his words, 'Call no man on earth your father, for you have one Father, who is in heaven' may very well be directed against the patriarchal family, which as the primary social unit in that world was a microcosm of a hierarchical system. If so, this is a fascinating instance of Jesus using the image of God as Father in a way that subverted patriarchy."[10]

Clearly Jesus was in favor of loving one's family—after all, he asked us to love our enemies—but his attitude toward family is not blindly affirmative. Family could actually be the problem, as his strained relations with his own family reveal. They came looking for him because they thought he had lost his mind, and it was only after Easter that some of his own family became part of the movement. What Jesus calls us to do as followers is to create a world in which family is not a matter of blood, but of spirit. This more expansive view of family sounds lovely in theory, but is absolutely radical in practice.

Among the distinctive traits of the Underground Church should be the sound of people calling one another "brother" or "sister" before adding their first names. In so doing, we demonstrate that we have in fact created a new family that has nothing to do with last names (where patriarchy is maintained). As for titles, they may be appropriate to designate leadership qualifications and show respect, but on an interpersonal level, why not diminish our use of "Reverend Doctor," "Your Honor," "Counselor," "Professor"? Instead of "Mr.," "Miss," or "Ms.," why not just say "sister so-and-so, brother so-and-so"? Try it at church and see what happens. Those who need their titles may not like it. Those without the status conferred by titles will be lifted up. "I truly understand that God shows no partiality" (Acts 10:34).

In many churches, certain key families dominate the congregation. They have power, wealth, status, and perhaps a deep need to control others. But in the Underground Church, our aim is to flatten the social pyramids just as the first followers of The Way flattened the Roman pyramid. This includes finding ways for everyone to serve and be served, and that can be time-consuming, exhausting, and at times maddening. It's much easier to let the people with the good graces and the good china run the world.

At Mayflower, we have an autistic man in his forties who is a fixture at the church. His mother and father have both died, and part of his routine is to worship at Mayflower and drive us all crazy. Because of his autism, he asks everyone the same questions week after week after week. His favorite actress is Julie Andrews, who reminds him of his second-grade teacher, Mrs. Crepps. Lately he has asked me every week for forty-seven consecutive weeks if I think that children in East St. Louis ought to be required by law to sing Christmas carols. He usually asks me this just as I am lining up to enter the sanctuary and preach. I have told him no forty-seven times, and this coming Sunday he will ask me again.

He roams the hall before and after church, looking disheveled and wearing part of his last meal on his shirt, often blissfully unaware that his pants are half unzipped. In particular, he enjoys talking to the most attractive women in the congregation (whom he approaches with deliberate and unself-conscious admiration). He asks these refined and beautiful women the same questions again and again, and they do not turn away. They answer him patiently, again and again and again—believing him to be more valuable as a human being than he is frightening in his mental illness.

In fact, the sight of these people I have known for a quarter of a century, many of whom are accomplished and successful human beings, patiently engaging him one more time when they could not be blamed for turning and walking away, has become one of my favorite moments in church. He has been adopted into the Beloved Community. He is part of the family. In fact, we are the only family he's got. Not long ago, I saw him engaging one of the members of the Supreme Court of Oklahoma—no doubt asking him about mandatory Christmas carols. It was a beautiful sight.

On the Environment

The certified Christian seems just as likely as anyone else
to join the military-industrial conspiracy to murder Creation.
—WENDELL BERRY

It is no accident that we speak of the fate of creation last. In the poetry of Genesis, the first word out of God's mouth is *Everything*. It rolled off the divine tongue in the form of spiral nebulae. In the beginning there was an endless, breathless *Nothing*. Now there is a pulsing, fantastic, and incomprehensible *Something*. Our question as human beings is as simple as it is urgent: *Why is there anything? Why is there matter, and does it matter?*

Obviously this is a somewhat larger question than what one thinks of Al Gore, for example, or his movie, *An Inconvenient Truth*. Those debates are in keeping with the whose-side-are-you-on spirit of the age, but they keep us from having the real debate, which ought to be taking place first in the church. Why have we assumed that the gift of creation is to be plundered rather than treasured? Why do some people look at a mountain and see something divine, a place from whence help comes (Ps. 121), while others see a mountaintop that needs to be blown off, sifted, and sold, and then the remains dumped into the river? Could there be anything more irreligious sounding than "mountaintop removal"?

The survival of both Christianity and creation cannot be separated because we have been operating for centuries as if we own the world, or at least certain parts of it. But this is not biblical, in case you want to have the argument based on scripture: "The earth is the LORD'S and all that is in it, the world, and those who live in it" (Ps. 24:1). What we continue to confuse (and our survival depends on making amends) is the difference between "land ownership" as a practical matter and the idea that we *possess* the earth, which is idolatry.

It has become something of an idle sport for the rich to acquire larger and larger tracts of land, so that individual kingdoms may stretch as far as the eye can see, but such things are expressly forbidden in Leviticus 25, where landowners are temporary stewards of what they do not possess: "The land shall not be sold in perpetuity, for the land is mine; with me you are but aliens and tenants" (25:23).

If this is our song, then we must be singing it without paying attention to the words. People of faith consider creation to be not only an intentional act but also something that carries value. This Something is "very good," better than the Nothing that came before. Heaven and earth are not different destination points, but part of the same magnificent mystery. Berry points out, "People who quote John 3:16 as an easy formula for getting to Heaven neglect to see the great difficulty implied in the statement that the advent of Christ was made possible by God's love for the world—not God's love for Heaven or for the world as it might be but for the world as it was and is."[11]

Therefore, regardless of one's political or theological identity, there is overwhelming evidence that we are in the midst of destroying the gift of creation that is planet earth. This is not just stupid economics or bad stewardship. It is blasphemy. As Berry says, "It is flinging God's gifts into His face, as if they were of no worth beyond that assigned to them by our destruction of them. . . . We have no entitlement from the Bible to exterminate or permanently destroy or hold in contempt anything on the earth or in the heavens above it or in the waters beneath it. We have the right to use the gifts of nature but not to ruin or waste them. . . . How can modern Christianity have so solemnly folded its hands while so much of the work of God was and is being destroyed?"[12]

In the year this book was written, the earth experienced the most extreme weather events since humans began keeping reliable records. It was also the hottest year on record. Polar ice caps are melting, permafrost is buckling, and droughts and floods are not just our old nemeses—they are now our constant and lethal companions. The oceans out of which all life came have a fever, water levels are rising, and coral reefs are bleaching. These facts are not part of a liberal plot, nor should they be grist for the mill of conspiracy theorists or antigovernment zealots. They are the signs that we are expected to read. They are warnings about what we are doing to the earth because we are *using* it instead of *loving* it.

In the Underground Church, concern for the environment should be the ultimate bipartisan issue, considering that liberals and conservatives alike are guaranteed to perish in a nonpartisan way. All our grand rhetoric about children and the future and those "purple mountains' majesty" will crumble in our mouth like dust. What could be more sinful than to live unsustainably with that which sustains us?

To join the Underground Church movement is to become an environmentalist and then never to apologize for being one. For conservatives, it will be a chance to recover the essence of the word itself—to conserve. For liberals, it will be a chance to do more than be politically correct about recycling while leaving a giant carbon footprint. For the church universal, it will be a test and one we dare not fail. Our worship spaces must exist in harmony with the land. We must practice sustainable methods of eating, of consuming, and, yes, even of lawn care. What do those chemical trucks with the long hoses and the men in protective gear who come to spray something called "the perfect lawn" say about our priorities? Have we gone mad?

And if intellectual honesty is to be a hallmark of the Underground Church, then it must be a safe place to tell the truth about the connection between the destruction of the environment and that whore of Babylon—greed. We don't want to talk about global climate change in the church because it would require sacrifice from all of us, and real changes in the lifestyles to which we are not only accustomed but also, we believe, divinely entitled. Few things could be more subversive, or more critical to the survival of the human race, than for the church to speak with one voice in condemnation of those who profit from environmental destruction. Wouldn't it be amazing if Christians *really* spoke up about caring for creation?

In the Underground Church, the church itself is not the location of the holy; rather it is the meeting place where we gather to remind ourselves that our homes and farms and shops, even our backyards, are holy. It matters what we put in the landfill, and it matters what we dump into the river. The separation of the sacred and the profane has been a disaster for creation, and in the Underground Church, we will regard every square inch of it as the Cosmic Christ.

While we are at it, more religion needs to happen *outdoors*, if we really want to be biblical about it. Berry tells us, "From Abraham to Jesus, the most important people are not priests but shepherds, soldiers, property owners, workers, housewives, queens and kings, manservants and maidservants, fishermen, prisoners, whores, even bureaucrats. The great visionary encounters did not take place in temples but in sheep pastures, in the desert, in the wilderness, on mountains, on the shores of rivers and the seas, in the middle of the sea, in prisons."[13]

Let us not deny the spirit and worthiness in all life forms (yes, even the non-Christian and nonhuman forms), and let us never use anything in creation without respect. Let us make with our hands only that which is useful and beautiful, while wasting nothing. If our pleasures are at the expense of the next generation, then how can we truly enjoy them? If body and soul cannot be separated, then neither can the creature be separated from creation. Neither can work be separated from art, for all of us work with "found objects." Strangely enough, the fact that we are "dust, and to dust we shall return" should make us have more reverence for dust.

In the Underground Church, let us be careful about how we work the garden that has been given to us. Let us leaven bread and bake it and serve it to a hungry world. Let us swear to do no harm where harm can be avoided, to pull up a chair for the stranger, to be generous out of our abundance, and to encourage someone who is lost and looking for home. Whatever labels we carry around inside our heads, the ones we use to keep ourselves at a safe distance from one another, should be brought to the altar and laid down. Calling each other sister and brother, we should sing and pray and laugh at the foolish, magnificent creatures that we are. All our sermons should find new ways to say the same thing every Sunday: *that love is all there is in this beautiful, terrible, wonderful world.*

After all of us have given thanks, blessed, broken, and shared what we did not create but cannot live without, the world will begin to understand what it means to belong to the Underground Church. When you walk by the window, you will hear more singing from us than arguing. If you come inside and look around, you may notice that we are nobody special. Yet at the same time, in some mysterious way, you will also see that we are a collection of saints—

mysterious, magnificent, infinitely precious human beings who are busy getting over ourselves long enough to help others.

The humming sound you hear will be the messy, chaotic, subversive energy of the beloved community finding ways to love God and neighbor in this time and place. We will come together from many different places and traditions to tell our story in a place where people consider listening to be one of the sacraments. The only thing we'll have in common is the desire to follow Jesus and then trust in the power of grace to save us. Wherever his spirit leads us we will go, and if that means doing subversive things for the cause of love, then so be it. If it means taking risks for the sake of peace and justice, then so be it. If it means throwing a stone, like David, against the Goliath that is fear and hatred, then so be it. We have never been asked to calculate the chances of success and then make a decision. We have only been asked to do what is right, what is merciful, what is just.

Will you join us? Will you take the first step? Will you agree to stand up some Sunday morning in your local church or in a coffee shop among friends or in the home of those you love to ask for a moment of silence—so that you can read the following poem by Wendell Berry? It's called "Manifesto: The Mad Farmer Liberation Front."[14]

Read it well. Read it aloud with feeling. Trust the words. Trust yourself. Trust in the power of the spirit to mediate the melancholy madness of Jesus. Trust that these words will not come back empty, because the revolution is here. The Underground Church movement has already begun and cannot be stopped. Listen carefully now . . .

Love the quick profit, the annual raise,
vacation with pay. Want more
of everything ready-made. Be afraid
to know your neighbors and to die.
And you will have a window in your head.

Not even your future will be a mystery
any more. Your mind will be punched in a card
and shut away in a little drawer.
When they want you to buy something
they will call you. When they want you
to die for profit they will let you know.

So friends, every day do something
that won't compute. Love the Lord.
Love the world. Work for nothing.
Take all that you have and be poor.
Love someone who does not deserve it.
Denounce the government and embrace
the flag. Hope to live in that free
republic for which it stands.
Give your approval to all you cannot
understand. Praise ignorance, for what man
has not encountered he has not destroyed.

Ask the questions that have no answers.
Invest in the millennium. Plant sequoias.
Say that your main crop is the forest
that you did not plant,
that you will not live to harvest.
Say that the leaves are harvested
when they have rotted into the mold.
Call that profit. Prophesy such returns.

Put your faith in two inches of humus
that will build under the trees
every thousand years.
Listen to carrion—put your ear
close, and hear the faint chattering
of the songs that are to come.

Expect the end of the world. Laugh.
Laughter is immeasurable. Be joyful
though you have considered all the facts.
So long as women do not go cheap
for power, please women more than men.
Ask yourself: Will this satisfy
a woman satisfied to bear a child?
Will this disturb the sleep
of a woman near to giving birth?

Go with your love to the fields.
Lie down in the shade. Rest your head
in her lap. Swear allegiance
to what is nighest your thoughts.
As soon as the generals and the politicos
can predict the motions of your mind,
lose it. Leave it as a sign
to mark the false trail, the way
you didn't go. Be like the fox
who makes more tracks than necessary,
some in the wrong direction.
Practice resurrection.

Beyond Belief
The Manifesto of the Underground Church

The Underground Church is a movement of the *spirit*, not an
organization that seeks to perpetuate itself, convert disciples to
a certain belief system, or make cosmic promises based on human
calculations. In this sense it is not a church at all. It is a *covenant*. It
is entered into freely by a diverse group of Christians, former
Christians, and spiritual seekers who understand that the winds of
change are blowing down the church as we have known it and
raising up something new in its place, something best called the
Beloved Community.

It is not a movement for those who resist change or cling to
traditions as inviolate. It is not for theological or liturgical purists.
It is not for those who wish to focus entirely on personal piety,
individual morality, or the salvation of the soul—but is offered as
a second chance on faith as a way of life, not as a set of creeds and
doctrines demanding total agreement.

For this reason, it will be difficult to recognize an Underground
Church community without first understanding what those who
are committed to the movement actually *do in the world*. You won't
know it by the architecture of the building; you won't recognize it
based on whether worship is traditional or contemporary, formal

or emergent, Pentecostal or Catholic. You will, however, be able to identify members of the Underground Church by their obvious commitment to being *subversive* for the cause of love.

Compared to many contemporary churchgoing Christians, they will appear downright peculiar. They will truly live "in the world," but not be "of the world," choosing instead to create an alternative set of values and priorities to those of the Empire. They will of course be misunderstood and will face persecution, as all noncooperation with Empire is a threat to the future of the Empire. But all social change will be grounded in nonviolence. It will be communitarian rather than individualistic. It will be characterized by consideration, empathy, and self-sacrifice in a world that so often encourages just the opposite.

When the Underground Church gathers, it may be in a traditional church building or in a retreat center. It may be in people's homes or in coffee shops. It may march under the banner of classical Christian liturgy and music, or it may march to the beat of a completely different drummer. It may employ ordained ministers or be led by devoted laypersons with a vision of what it means to love God and neighbor. But it will stand out in a world of hyperpolemics and partisan rancor by quietly demonstrating that what is *born of love and acts in love can always unite what is divided by human conceptions of purity.* Conservatives and liberals alike will find their religious and political identities taking a backseat to their desire to love this world, to heal this world, to live as gracious members of *one* human family.

The Underground Church is not a building, but meets as a joyful collection of grateful souls, knowing how much we do not know—but knowing enough about the redemptive power of love to invite everyone into the conversation. We may not pray the same way, sing the same songs, or agree on what constitutes a "great" sermon. But this much we know: God requires justice for all creation, and hospitality is an open table, with enough for everyone and no reserved seating.

Those who wish to accept the invitation to join the Underground Church movement can figure out ways to build the Beloved Community in their own time and place, but in particular they will be urged to consider making some or all of the following seven changes in what it means to be truly radical.

1. As often as possible, the Underground Church will celebrate communion by serving an *actual meal*, before or after the service. It will be provided and served by the members of the community, who bring food and share with all those who come, especially the poor.

2. Membership in the Underground Church is not by "profession of faith" but by the *profession of trust* in the redemptive power of unconditional love, revealed to the community through the mystery of the incarnation and sustained by that love, not by creeds and doctrines demanding total agreement.

3. Worship styles and music in the Underground Church are to be *intentionally diverse*, joyful, and meant to bring worshipers into an experience of the divine. Individual communities will decide what music and liturgical forms are most meaningful to them, and the creation of services that reflect both more traditional and less traditional approaches to worship is encouraged. No musical snobs, please.

4. Members of the Underground Church will be committed to mission projects that mark the community off as *countercultural and anti-imperial*. We will be committed to nonviolence, radical hospitality, collective generosity, and the ministry of encouragement.

5. The Underground Church will give special attention to the *stranger*, the forgotten, the weak, and the dispossessed. When the Empire marks off certain groups of people as scapegoats or as "enemies," we will make certain that there is room for them at the table and, if necessary, protect them from persecution.

6. The Underground Church will *create its own economic system* in the community by requiring a pledge of financial support from all members to support the operation of the church, while encouraging individuals to contribute additional funds to mission projects that they are particularly passionate about. We will not rob Peter to pay Paul; we will pay Peter first so that in the work that truly matters, we can fully fund Paul. We will loan money at no interest and bear one another's burdens.

7. The Underground Church will seek to work together with all others who share the conviction that *it is more important to be loving than to be right*. We will not insist that others agree with us on all matters theological—only that we offer each other the benefit of the doubt, mutual respect, and the chance to become the rarest and most precious of all things: a community that declares its loyalty only to love incarnate, not to Caesar.

So Just Imagine . . .

—A church where Baptists and Catholics, Pentecostals and Unitarians, Presbyterians and Quakers, [fill in your group and some other group here], all show up at the food pantry with something to feed the hungry and then do not get into an argument—at least until everyone is fed.

—A church where women are truly equal to men, and never patronized.

—A church where straights and gays worship together as children of God.

—A church where the mission budget is as large as the operating budget.

—A church where children are cherished in practice, not just in theory.

—A church where conscientious objectors are considered as heroic as soldiers.

—A church where following Jesus is just as important as worshiping Christ.

—A church where trying to discern what Jesus taught us about God is more important than arguing over what the church has taught us about Jesus.

—A church where the clergy are on neither a pedestal nor a chopping block.

—A church where the music is as diverse as the humans who make it and the creation it celebrates.

—A church where we earn our tax-exempt status by giving space back to the communities we serve in ways that create community and bring people into true fellowship with one another.

—A church where learning is not subversive and science is not the enemy of faith.

—A church where fear is never an instrument of religious conversion or conversation.

—A church where the enemy is not death but rather our failure to truly live.

—A church where the waters of baptism, no matter how they are administered, trap us all in the irreversible claim of God upon our lives.

—A church where the best possible education for every child is a moral imperative, requiring that we join forces to adopt and assist our most troubled schools, lest we fail our mandate toward "the least of these."

—A church where we tend the small garden we have been given and do not participate in the murder of creation.

—A church where everyone encourages one another, never assuming that when someone says she is "just fine," she means it.

—A church where beauty is the effortless manifestation of
inner peace.

—A church where being rich means having everything you need
instead of everything you want.

—A church where there is no acceptable alternative to hope, no
substitute for joy, and no excuse not to offer the same
unconditional love to others that has been so freely lavished
on us.

This is the Underground Church.
Are you ready to join?
How about this Sunday?
Come as you are.

NOTES

Prologue: Empty Sermons, Empty Pews

1. William Butler Yeats, "The Second Coming," first printed in *The Dial* in November 1920, and later in numerous collections, including *The Classic Hundred Poems*, ed. William Harmon (New York: Columbia University Press, 1998).

Chapter 1: Sweet Jesus

1. John Dominic Crossan, *The Greatest Prayer: Rediscovering the Revolutionary Message of the Lord's Prayer* (New York: HarperOne, 2010), 33.

2. "W. S. Merwin Interview," *Academy of Achievement*, July 3, 2008, http://www.achievement.org/autodoc/page/mer0int-1.

3. Albert Schweitzer, *The Quest of the Historical Jesus*, trans. W. Montgomery (New York: Macmillan, 1968), 403.

4. Mary Oliver, "Maybe," *New and Selected Poems* (Boston: Beacon Press, 1993), 1:97–98.

5. The Gospel of Thomas is the best known of the documents discovered in a cave near Nag Hammadi in 1946, and contains 118 "sayings" of Jesus, without any narrative elements. The Q gospel is a hypothetical sayings source believed to have provided the common material in Matthew and Luke that is not found in their primary source, Mark.

6. Albert Schweitzer, *The Psychiatric Study of Jesus* (Boston: Beacon Press, 1913), 35.

7. Emil Rasmussen, author of *Jesus: A Comparative Study in Psychopathology*, cited in Don Havis, "An Inquiry into the Mental Health of Jesus: Was He Crazy?" San Francisco Atheists [blog] (July 1, 2003) http://sfatheists.blogspot.com/2003/07/inquiry-into-mental-health-of-jesus.html.

8. Thomas Merton, "A Devout Meditation in Memory of Adolf Eichmann," from *Raids on the Unspeakable*, copyright 1966 by the Abbey of Gethsemani, Inc. Reprinted by permission of New Directions Publishing Corp. in

Approaches to Peace: A Reader in Peace Studies, 2nd ed., ed. David P. Barash (New York: Oxford University Press, 2010), 240–241.

9. Ibid.
10. Ibid.
11. Ibid.

Chapter 2: The Early Church That Never Was

1. Laurie Goodstein, "Basic Religion Test Stumps Many Americans," *New York Times*, September 28, 2010, http://www.nytimes.com/2010/09/28/us/28religion.html.

2. Harvey Cox, *The Future of Faith* (San Francisco: HarperOne, 2009), 56.

3. Ibid., 59.

4. John Dominic Crossan, *God and Empire* (San Francisco: HarperSanFrancisco, 2007), 218.

5. See Rodney Stark, *The Rise of Christianity* (San Francisco: HarperSanFrancisco, 1997), especially "The Class Basis of Early Christianity" and "The Role of Women in Christian Growth."

6. Cox, *Future of Faith*, 82.

7. Diana Butler Bass, *A People's History of Christianity: The Other Side of the Story* (San Francisco: HarperOne, 2009), 15.

8. Cox, *Future of Faith*, 64.

9. Robert J. Miller, ed., *The Complete Gospels: Annotated Scholars Version* (Sonoma, CA: Polebridge Press, 1992), 301.

10. Cox, *Future of Faith*, 66.

11. See Robert L. Wilken, *The Christians as the Romans Saw Them* (New Haven, CT: Yale University Press, 1984).

12. Justin Martyr, 1 Apol. 14, quoted in Butler Bass, *People's History of Christianity*, 27–28.

13. Cox, *Future of Faith*, 68.

14. Ibid.

15. Ibid., 69.

16. Ibid., 73.

17. "Didache," Roberts-Donaldson translation, *Early Christian Writings*, http://www.earlychristianwritings.com/text/didache-roberts.html.

18. Rita Nakashima Brock and Rebecca Ann Parker, *Saving Paradise: How Christianity Traded Love of This World for Crucifixion and Empire* (Boston: Beacon Press, 2008), ix.

Chapter 3: Waking Up in Bed with Constantine

1. Roland Bainton, *The Church of Our Fathers* (Philadelphia: Westminster, 1950), 43.
2. Diana Butler Bass, *A People's History of Christianity: The Other Side of the Story* (San Francisco: HarperOne, 2009), 67.
3. Verna Dozier, *The Dream of God: A Call to Return* (Cambridge, MA: Cowley, 1991), 55.
4. Barbara Tuchman, *A Distant Mirror* (New York: Knopf, 1984), 6.
5. Butler Bass, *A People's History of Christianity*, 78.
6. Harvey Cox, *The Future of Faith* (San Francisco: HarperOne, 2009), 87.
7. Ibid., 94.
8. Quoted in Hans von Campenhousen, *Ecclesiastical Authority and Spiritual Power in the Church of the First Three Centuries* (Stanford, CA: Stanford University Press, 1969), 242.
9. Cox, *Future of Faith*, 97.
10. Paul Johnson, *A History of Christianity* (New York: Athenaeum, 1976), 88.
11. Philip Jenkins, *Jesus Wars: How Four Patriarchs, Three Queens, and Two Emperors Decided What Christians Would Believe for the Next 1,500 Years* (San Francisco: HarperOne, 2010), 1.
12. Peter Gomes, *The Scandalous Gospel of Jesus: What's So Good About the Good News?* (San Francisco: HarperOne, 2007), 18.
13. Cox, *Future of Faith*, 6.
14. Dozier, *Dream of God*, 57.
15. Ibid., 59.
16. Ibid., 60.
17. David Kinnaman, with Gabe Lyons, *UnChristian: What a New Generation Really Thinks About Christianity . . . and Why It Matters* (Grand Rapids, MI: Baker Books, 2007), 21–40, quoted in Butler Bass, *People's History of Christianity*, 31.

Chapter 4: Onward Christian Soldiers?

1. Rev. Jerry Falwell, "God Is Pro-War," *WorldNetDaily*, January 31, 2004, http://www.wnd.com/news/article.asp?ARTICLE_ID=36859.

2. Martin Luther King Jr., quoted by David P. Barash in *Approaches to Peace: A Reader in Peace Studies*, ed. David P. Barash (Oxford University Press, 2010), 190.

3. Chalmers Johnson, *The Sorrows of Empire: Militarism, Secrecy, and the End of the Republic* (New York: Metropolitan Books, 2004), 3.

4. Hannah Arendt, *On Violence* (New York: Harcourt Brace and World, 1969).

5. Martin Luther King Jr. used this phrase in many speeches, and it is believed to be a paraphrase from a line in the sermon "Of Justice and the Conscience," by Theodore Parker, 1853.

6. John Dominic Crossan, *God and Empire: Jesus Against Rome, Then and Now* (San Francisco: HarperSanFrancisco, 2007), 3–4.

7. Ibid., 4–5.

8. Written as a promotional piece for the magazine *Free Inquiry* in 2009, and used with the kind permission of Mr. Dawkins.

9. John Shelby Spong, *The Sins of Scripture* (San Francisco: HarperSanFrancisco, 2005), 3–4.

10. Ibid., 272.

11. This abbreviated version is drawn from the complete text of the story in Diana Butler Bass's *A People's History of Christianity: The Other Side of the Story* (HarperOne, 2009), 70–71.

12. Ibid., 71.

13. Tertullian, *Of the Crown* (ca. 201), quoted in Butler Bass, *People's History of Christianity*, 72. (Text of *Of the Crown* is available at http://www.tertullian.org/lfc/LFC10-11_de_corona.htm.)

Chapter 5: Faith as Radically Embodied Trust

1. Richard Dawkins, writing in *The Guardian*, September 12, 2001, quoted in Douglas John Hall, "Against Religion," *Christian Century* 128, no. 1 (2011): 30, http://www.christiancentury.org/article/2010-12/against-religion.

2. Ludwig Feuerbach, *The Essence of Christianity* (Buffalo, NY: Prometheus Books, 1989), 253.

3. Karl Barth, *Church Dogmatics*, vol. 1, quoted in Hall, "Against Religion," 30.

4. Ibid.

5. Ibid., 33.

6. See Robert Rosenthal and Lenore Jacobson, *Pygmalion in the Classroom: Teacher Expectation and Pupils' Intellectual Development* (New York: Irvington, 1992).

7. Explanations for the mass bird kill at Beebe run the gamut from poisoning to hail to fireworks. Even after considerable investigation, the final cause remains a mystery. http://www.usatoday.com/news/nation/2011–01–03-dead-birds_N.htm.

Chapter 6: Renewing the Church Through Shared Mission

1. Phil Snider and Emily Bowen, *Toward a Hopeful Future: Why the Emergent Church Is Good News for Mainline Congregations* (Cleveland, OH: Pilgrim Press, 2010), 2.

2. Phillip Gulley, *If the Church Were Christian: Rediscovering the Values of Jesus* (San Francisco: HarperOne, 2010).

3. Fred B. Craddock, *Overhearing the Gospel* (Nashville, TN: Abingdon, 1978), 12.

4. Quoted in Rodney Stark, *The Rise of Christianity: A Sociologist Reconsiders History* (Princeton, NJ: Princeton University Press, 1996), 211.

5. William Sloane Coffin Jr., *Credo* (Louisville, KY: Westminster John Knox Press, 2004), 168.

6. Ibid., 171.

7. Diana Butler Bass, *A People's History of Christianity: The Other Side of the Story* (San Francisco: HarperOne, 2009), 62.

8. Wendell Berry, *Sex, Economy, Freedom & Community* (New York: Pantheon Books, 1993), xi.

9. Tertullian, *Apology* 39, quoted in Stark, *Rise of Christianity*, 87.

10. A. J. Muste, "Holy Disobedience" (New York: Harper, 1952), in *Approaches to Peace: A Reader in Peace Studies*, 2nd ed., ed. David P. Barash (New York: Oxford University Press, 2010), 238.

11. Excepts from "Letter from a Birmingham Jail" reprinted with permission in Barash, *Approaches to Peace*, 174, by arrangement with The Heirs to the Estate of Martin Luther King Jr., c/o Writers House as agent for the proprietor, New York, NY. Copyright © Dr. Martin Luther King Jr.; copyright renewed 1991 Coretta Scott King.

Chapter 7: Leavening the Imperial Loaf

1. See Brandon Scott, Re-Imagine the World: An Introduction to the Parables of Jesus (Sonoma, CA: Polebridge Press, 2001), 29.

2. Ibid., 30.

3. John Dominic Crossan uses this wonderful phrase frequently to describe what God as a Householder would implement as a model of distributive justice.

4. Diana Butler Bass, Christianity for the Rest of Us: How the Neighborhood Church Is Transforming the Faith (San Francisco: HarperOne, 2006), 24.

5. John Dominic Crossan, Jesus: A Revolutionary Biography (San Francisco: HarperSanFrancisco, 1995), 160.

6. Matt. 14:13–21, 15:32–39; Mark 8:1–9; Luke 9:10–17; and John 6:1–13.

7. Rita Nakashima Brock and Rebecca Ann Parker, Saving Paradise: How Christianity Traded Love of This World for Crucifixion and Empire (Boston: Beacon Press, 2008), 30.

8. Crossan, Jesus, 48.

9. See Barbara Brown Taylor, An Altar in the World (San Francisco: Harper One, 2010).

10. Gerard Manley Hopkins, from the poem "God's Grandeur," in Poems of Gerard Manley Hopkins, ed. Robert Bridges (London: Humphrey Milford, 1918).

Chapter 8: Jesus Followers on the No-Fly List

1. Dietrich Bonhoeffer, The Cost of Discipleship (New York: Macmillan, 1963), 40, 47.

2. Peter Gomes, The Scandalous Gospel of Jesus: What's So Good About the Good News? (San Francisco: HarperOne, 2007), 18–19.

3. Ibid., 19.

4. Wes Howard Brook and Anthony Gwyther, Unveiling: Reading Revelation Then and Now (Maryknoll, NY: Orbis Books, 1999), 158.

5. Ibid., 175.

6. William Sloane Coffin Jr., Credo (Lexington, KY: Westminster John Knox Press, 2004), 59.

7. Brook and Gwyther, Unveiling, 193.

8. Ibid., 195.

Chapter 9: The Underground Church on War, Sex, Money, Family, and the Environment

1. Fred B. Craddock, *Overhearing the Gospel* (Nashville, TN: Abingdon, 1978), 15.

2. George Shultz, William Perry, Henry Kissinger, and Sam Nunn, "How to Protect Our Nuclear Deterrent," *Wall Street Journal*, January 19, 2010, http://online.wsj.com/article/SB1000142405274870415280457462 8344282735008.html.

3. Elizabeth Myer Boulton and Matthew Myer Boulton, "Sacramental Sex," *Christian Century*, March 22, 2011, 28.

4. Ibid., 29.

5. Robin R. Meyers, *Morning Sun on a White Piano: Simple Pleasures and the Sacramental Life* (New York: Doubleday, 1998), 40.

6. Ibid., 81.

7. "Report: Majority of Money Donated at Church Doesn't Make It to God," *Onion*, January 10, 2011, http://www.theonion.com/articles/ report-majority-of-money-donated-at-church-doesnt,18765/. Used with permission.

8. Reggie McNeal, *Missional Renaissance* (San Francisco: Jossey-Bass, 2009), xiii, xiv.

9. Michael Frost and Alan Hirsch, *The Shaping of Things to Come* (Peabody, Mass.: Hendrickson, 2003), 30.

10. Marcus Borg, *Meeting Jesus Again for the First Time* (San Francisco: HarperSanFrancisco, 1994), 81–82.

11. Wendell Berry, *Sex, Economy, Freedom & Community* (New York: Pantheon Books, 1992), 97.

12. Ibid., 98–99.

13. Ibid., 102.

14. Wendell Berry, "Manifesto: The Mad Farmer Liberation Front," in *The Country of Marriage* (New York: Harcourt Brace Jovanovich, 1973). Used with the kind permission of Mr. Berry.

THE AUTHOR

Robin Meyers is an ordained minister in the United Church of Christ (UCC), and Distinguished Professor Emeritus in the philosophy department at Oklahoma City University. He has led Mayflower Congregational UCC church in Oklahoma City for 35 years, one of the largest and most progressive UCC churches in the country. Born in Oklahoma City and raised in Wichita, Kansas, he graduated from Phillips Theology Seminary (M.Div. 1979), earned a Doctor of Ministry degree from the Theological School of Drew University (1981), and was awarded a PhD in Rhetoric from the Communication Department at the University of Oklahoma (1991) based on his work applying modern persuasion theory to preaching.

He is the author of eight books on religion and culture, including, *With Ears to Hear: Preaching as Self-Persuasion* (Pilgrim Press, 1993), *Morning Sun on a White Piano: Simple Pleasures and the Sacramental Life* (Doubleday, 1998), *The Virtue in the Vice: Finding Seven Lively Virtues in the Seven Deadly Sins* (HCI, 2004), *Why the Christian Right is Wrong: A Minister's Manifesto for Taking Back Your Faith, Your Flag, and Your Future* (Jossey-Bass, 2006), *Saving Jesus from the Church: How to Stop Worshiping Christ and Start Following Jesus* (HarperOne, 2009), *The Underground Church: Reclaiming the Subversive Way of Jesus* (Jossey-Bass, 2012 / Fortress Press, 2020), *Spiritual Defiance: Building a Beloved Community of Resistance* (Yale University Press, 2015), and *Saving God from Religion: A Minister's Search for Faith in a Skeptical Age* (Convergent, Penguin/Random House, forthcoming).

Meyers delivered the Earl Lectures at Berkeley and gave the Lyman Beecher Lectures at Yale Divinity School. His efforts to save the first woman executed in Oklahoma is chronicled in an HBO documentary, *The Execution of Wanda Jean*. He is currently a member of the God Seminar of the Westar Institute (home of the Jesus Seminar), and was twice a finalist for the pulpit of the Riverside Church in New York City. He is married to Shawn Meyers, an artist and professor, and they have three children and three granddaughters.